THE DAWN OF
HUMAN CULTURE

♛   ♛   ♛

THE DAWN OF HUMAN CULTURE

Richard G. Klein with Blake Edgar

A Peter N. Nevraumont Book

John Wiley & Sons, Inc.

Published by John Wiley & Sons, Inc., New York
Published simultaneously in Canada

This publication is designed to provide accurate and authoritative information in regard
to the subject matter covered. It is sold with the understanding that the publisher is not
engaged in rendering professional services. If professional advice or other expert assistance is required, the services of a competent professional person should be sought.

ISBN 0-471-25252-2

CREATED AND PRODUCED BY
NEVRAUMONT PUBLISHING COMPANY
NEW YORK, NEW YORK

Ann J. Perrini, President
Book design: Frances White

Printed in the United States of America

10 9 8 7 6 5 4 3 2

CONTENTS

✻ ✻ ✻

PREFACE

Human beings are naturally interested in their origins, and every culture has devised its own account. Most such explanations center on supernatural creators, and their acceptance is entirely a matter of faith. Science, however, has produced a different kind of narrative that can be tested, even rejected, with testimony from the ground, or, increasingly, from within the human genome.

The scientific evidence for human evolution has been accumulating for more than 150 years, and much has been added in just the past decade. The sum now allows a broad outline that is likely to stand the test of time. Thus, we can say with reasonable certainty that humans, defined by their habit of walking bipedally, evolved about 6 million years ago from an African ape; that multiple bipedal species appeared between 6 million and 2.5 million years ago; that all these early bipeds remained remarkably ape-like in brain size and upper body form; that some human species, perhaps the first whose brain exceeded that of an ape in size, invented stone flaking about 2.5 million years ago; that the earliest stone tool makers used their tools to add animal flesh and marrow to a mainly vegetarian diet; that people first spread from Africa to Eurasia sometime after 2 million years ago; that humans had begun to diverge into different physical types on different continents by 1 million years ago; that the modern human type evolved exclusively in Africa; and finally, that modern Africans expanded to Eurasia about 50,000 years ago where they swamped or replaced the Neanderthals and other non-modern Eurasians. We show here how fossils, artifacts, and genes underpin these conclusions and especially how they document the African origin of modern humanity.

Archeology links the expansion of modern humans to their highly evolved ability to invent tools, social forms, and ideas, in short, to their fully modern capacity for culture. We suggest that this capacity stemmed from a genetic change that promoted the fully modern brain in Africa around 50,000 years ago. However, the evidence for a genetic change is circumstantial, and our more fundamental point is that the spread of modern humanity is tied to the dawn of culture as we know it. Arguably, the "dawn" was the most significant prehistoric event that archeologists will ever detect. Before it, human anatomical and behavioral change proceeded very slowly, more or less hand-in-hand. Afterwards, the human form remained remarkably stable, while behavioral change accelerated dramatically. In the space of less than 40,000 years, ever more closely packed cultural "revolutions" have taken humanity from the status of a relatively rare large mammal to something more like a geologic force.

Fossils and artifacts provide the hard evidence for human evolution, but they would be of little use if they could not be ordered in time. Recent advances in our understanding of human evolution owe as much to methods of dating as they do to new fossil and archeological discoveries. We have therefore described the principal dating methods in the text. Since the descriptions are scattered, we have summarized them in an appendix that refers back to the more detailed descriptions in previous chapters.

Peter N. Nevraumont conceived this book, based on Richard G. Klein's more technical writing on human evolution. Blake Edgar produced an initial draft, which Klein rewrote to provide the present version. Jim Bischoff, Frank Brown, David deGusta, Jim O'Connell, Kathryn Cruz-Uribe, Don Grayson, Teresa Steele, and Tim Weaver kindly commented on portions of the text. We owe a special debt to Kathryn Cruz-Uribe, who carefully edited the final manuscript to enhance consistency and clarity and who skillfully produced many wonderful illustrations to support textual descriptions of fossils and artifacts. Blake Edgar would like to thank the following individuals for their ideas, information, and time during discussions and interviews about the topics in this book: Stanley Ambrose, Susan Antón, Ofer Bar-Yosef, Alison Brooks, Michael Chazan, Steve Churchill, Margaret Conkey, Iain Davidson, Bruce Dickson, Nina Jablonski, Anthony Marks, April Nowell, John Shea, Fred Smith, Ian Tattersall, Nick Toth, Alan Walker, Tim White, Bernard Wood, and Tom Wynn. Finally, we are deeply indebted to the numerous paleoanthropologists whose data and ideas underlie our synthesis. We have cited many of these scientists in the text and in a bibliography ("Selected Further Reading") that lists our principal published sources.

RICHARD G. KLEIN
STANFORD, CALIFORNIA

♛ ♛ ♛

1
DAWN AT TWILIGHT CAVE

igh above the western shore of Lake Naivasha, a blue pool on the parched floor of East Africa's Great Rift Valley, sits a small rock-shelter carved into the Mau Escarpment. Maasai pastoralists who once occupied this region in central Kenya called the place Enkapune Ya Muto, or "Twilight Cave." People have long sought shelter there. The cave's sediments record important cultural changes during the past few thousand years, including the first local experiments with agriculture and with sheep and goat domestication. Buried more than 3 meters (10 feet) deep in the sand, silt, and loam at Enkapune Ya Muto, however, lie the traces of an earlier and far more significant event in human pre-history. Tens of thousands of pieces of obsidian, a jet-black volcanic glass, were long ago fashioned into finger-length knives with scalpel-sharp edges, thumbnail-sized scrapers, and other stone tools, made on the spot at an ancient workshop. But what most impressed archeologist Stanley Ambrose were nearly six hundred fragments of ostrich eggshell, including thirteen that had been fashioned into disk-shaped beads, about 6 millimeters (0.25 inches) in diameter (Figure 1.1). Forty thousand years ago, a person or persons crouched near the mouth of Enkapune Ya Muto to drill holes through angular fragments of ostrich eggshell and to grind the edges of each piece until only a delicate ring remained. Many shell fragments snapped in half under pressure from the stone drill or from the edge-grinding that followed. The crafts-people discarded each broken piece and began again with a fresh frag-ment of shell.

Why did the occupants of Enkapune Ya Muto take so many hours from more essential activities like foraging just to make a hand-ful of beads? The question is particularly appropriate, since they were not the only ones to pursue this seemingly esoteric activity. More than 30,000 years ago, the stone age people who occupied Mumba and Kisese II Rockshelters in Tanzania and Border and Boomplaas Caves in South Africa also produced carefully shaped ostrich eggshell beads.

Ambrose believes that these ancient beads played a key role in the survival strategy of the craftspeople and their families. In the Kalahari Desert of Botswana, !Kung San hunter-gatherers practice a system of gift exchange known as *hxaro*. Certain items, such as food, are readily shared among the !Kung but never exchanged as gifts. The most appropriate gifts for all occasions just happen to be strands of ostrich eggshell beads. The generic word for gift is synonymous with the !Kung word for sewn beadwork. Although the nomadic !Kung carry the barest minimum of personal possessions, they invest considerable time and energy in creating eggshell beads.

The beads serve as symbols. They represent reciprocity between neighboring or distant bands of people. Should a drought or other

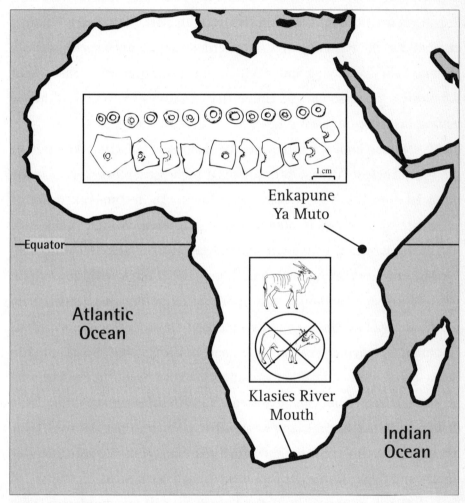

Figure 1.1

The locations of Enkapune Ya Muto and Klasies River Mouth. Enkapune Ya Muto has provided ostrich eggshell beads and bead blanks or preforms dated to about 40,000 years ago. Klasies River Mouth shows that between about 120,000 and 60,000 years ago human hunters preferred the docile eland to the more dangerous buffalo.

sudden climatic or environmental change leave food in scarce supply, a group can move to another group's territory, where they rely on aid and support from those with whom they have established *hxaro* ties. For the !Kung, beads provide a lightweight, portable token of mutual obligations—the currency of a long-term, long-distance social security system. "They're paying into their health insurance, in a sense," says Ambrose, a professor at the University of Illinois in Urbana. "They're paying insurance to each other."

No one knows whether the toolmakers at Enkapune Ya Muto or the other ancient African sites intended their ostrich eggshell beads to be social gifts. But if these beads were invested with symbolic meaning similar to that of beads among the !Kung, then Twilight Cave may record the dawning of modern human behavior. Communicating with symbols provides an unambiguous signature of our modernity. Within the grand scope of human evolution, symbolic behavior was a very recent innovation. Once symbols appear in the archeological record, as enigmatic geometric designs, as human or animal figurines carved in ivory, or as beads and other ornaments, we know we're dealing with people like us: people with advanced cognitive skills who could not only invent sophisticated tools and weapons and develop complex social networks for mutual security, but could also marvel at the intricacies of nature and their place in it; people who were self-aware.

The deep antiquity of the Enkapune Ya Muto beads is almost certain. Ambrose discovered that ostrich eggshell beads and beads-in-the-making (preforms) were ten times more numerous per cubic meter in the deepest part of the deposit than they were higher up. That could attest to the importance the early inhabitants placed on bead manufacture, but it also reduces the likelihood that the beads are simply younger artifacts that filtered down into deeper and older sediments with the passage of time and the burrowing of animals. Ambrose argues that the social value attached to eggshell beads by contemporary Kalahari people likewise attests to a deep-rooted symbolic meaning, carried across millennia from a time when far more ancient hunter-gatherer bands were scattered across southern and eastern Africa.

If, as Ambrose conjectures, the Enkapune Ya Muto beads helped to ensure survival during hard times, they may have emboldened early modern people to strike out into riskier environments—perhaps even some beyond Africa itself. "With this social safety net they could do better than people without symbolic means of establishing future permanent ties of reciprocity," he surmises. "You could say it's like weaving lifelines between people, and the lifelines are strings of beads."

The other artifacts from Enkapune Ya Muto represent an initial form of the stone technology associated only with fully modern humans in Africa, after 50,000 years ago. More than any sophisticated stone tool, however, the simple beads, laboriously crafted from ostrich eggshell, suggest that people in eastern Africa at this time had achieved cognitive capacities beyond those of any preceding human population, in Africa or anywhere else. Thus, our evolutionary success and the rich array of cultures from later times may have depended not so much on physical qualities or intimidating weapons as on the intellectual capacity to conceive, create, and communicate in symbols. To understand why evidence from sites such as Enkapune Ya Muto bespeaks a significant departure from all previous human behavior, we must move a bit further back into our African past and travel to the southern tip of the continent.

♛ ♛ ♛

Four thousand kilometers (2400 miles) southwest of Enkapune Ya Muto, the Indian Ocean relentlessly pounds the southern coast of Africa. Where the waves meet steep coastal cliffs, they have scoured out caves in which ancient stone age people could shelter. The most famous caves are clustered about 40 kilometers (24 miles) west of Cape St. Francis and 700 kilometers (420 miles) east of Cape Town, on a 1-kilometer (0.6-mile) strip of coast where the small perennial Klasies River enters the sea (Figure 1.1). The caves are thus known collectively as the Klasies River Mouth site. These cave deposits have produced fossils of early modern or near-modern humans, along with their stone tools and fireplaces, and the remains of the mammals, birds, and mollusks that they ate.

The roughly two dozen human fossils from the caves are admittedly few and fragmentary. Yet, they include key parts of the skull that reveal how anatomically modern these people were. A nearly complete lower jaw, for example, shows that the owner had an essentially modern, short, broad, flat face quite unlike the long, narrow, forwardly projecting faces of the Neanderthals who occupied Europe at the same time, about 100,000 years ago. And a fragment of bone from above one eye socket (orbit) lacks the brow ridge that marks the skulls of primitive members of the human genus. (This piece of bone also exhibits stone tool cutmarks suggesting that the skull was defleshed, perhaps for food. Other human fragments were slashed, bashed, and burned, implying that human parts were sometimes processed like those of antelopes and seals. This suggests to scientists that like some historic people, the Klasies people occasionally practiced cannibalism.)

While the Klasies fossils do vary widely in size, in their basic form they are undeniably modern. The people are plausible ancestors for historic Africans, or for historic people everywhere, and their bones date from as much as 120,000 years ago. With brief interruptions, they lived at Klasies River Mouth from 120,000 years ago until about 60,000 years ago, when the onset of extreme aridity perhaps forced people to abandon the region for tens of thousands of years.

Excavated first by Ronald Singer and John Wymer from the University of Chicago and more recently by Hilary Deacon from the University of Stellenbosch, the Klasies caves preserve abundant kitchen debris of the occupants. These include the shells of mussels, limpets, and other mollusks that can still be collected at low tide nearby. They place the Klasies people among humanity's oldest known shellfish gourmets. The caves are equally rich in fragmentary animal bones and in stone tools that were often flaked from cobbles collected on the beach. Burnt shells and bones show that the people engaged in cooking, and their fireplaces are so common that it seems certain they could make fire at will. Deacon suggests that each fireplace marks the domestic hearth of an individual family and that the people therefore resembled modern hunter-gatherers in nuclear family structure. Yet none of the Klasies Caves has provided ostrich eggshell beads like those from Enkapune Ya Muto, nor have they provided any other object that is unambiguously symbolic.

The animal bones exhibit numerous cutmarks, and they were often broken for the extraction of marrow. The implication is that the Klasies people consumed a wide range of game, from small, greyhound-size antelope like the Cape grysbok to more imposing quarry like buffalo and eland, as well as seals and penguins. The number and location of stone tool cutmarks and the rarity of carnivore tooth marks indicate that the people were not restricted to scavenging from lions or hyenas, and they often gained first access to the intact carcasses of even large mammals like buffalo and eland.

But the bones also show that the people tended to avoid confrontations with the more common—and more dangerous—buffalo to pursue a more docile but less common antelope, the eland. Both buffalo and eland are very large animals, but buffalo stand and resist potential predators, while eland panic and flee at signs of danger. The Klasies people did hunt buffalo, and a broken tip from a stone point is still imbedded in a neck vertebra of an extinct "giant" long-horned buffalo. The people focused, however, on the less threatening young or old members in buffalo herds. The stone points found at Klasies could have been used to arm thrusting spears, but there is nothing to suggest that the people had projectiles that could be launched from a distance, and they may thus have limited their personal risk by concentrating on eland herds that could be chased to exhaustion or driven into traps. The numerous eland bones in the Klasies layers represent roughly the same proportion of prime-age adults that would occur in a living herd. This pattern suggests the animals were not victims of accidents or endemic diseases which tend to selectively remove the very young and the old, but rather that they suffered a catastrophe that affected individuals of all ages equally. The deposits preserve no evidence of a great flood, volcanic eruption, or epidemic disease, and from an eland perspective, the catastrophe was probably the human ability to drive whole herds over nearby cliffs.

In contrast to Klasies River Mouth, other much younger archeological sites nearby such as Nelson Bay Cave contain many more bones of dangerous prey like buffalo and wild pigs and many fewer of eland. The reason is probably that by this time, around 20,000 years ago, people had developed projectile weapons like the bow and arrow that allowed them to attack dangerous prey from a distance and therefore to limit their personal risk. The advantage was considerable, because the ancient environment probably broadly resembled the historic one, in which buffalo and pigs greatly outnumbered eland nearby.

The Klasies people not only avoided the most dangerous game, they also failed to take full advantage of other widely available resources. The ages of seals in the Klasies deposits show that the people remained at the coast more or less throughout the year, including times when resources were probably more abundant in the interior. In contrast, much later people like those at Nelson Bay Cave timed their coastal visits to the late winter/early fall interval when they could literally harvest 9- to 11-month-old seals on the beach, and they moved inland when resources became more plentiful there. The ability of these later people to pursue an efficient seasonal strategy probably depended in part on their use of ostrich eggshells as canteens. Fragments of such canteens, with carefully positioned openings to allow water out and air in, have been found in their sites but not at Klasies River Mouth or other sites that are older than 50,000 years. The inability of the Klasies people to transport water may have forced them to remain near the river throughout the year.

Fish have always been common in the offshore waters near Klasies River Mouth, and roosting cormorants, which sheltered in the caves when people were absent, sometimes carried in tiny fish. However, in layers where artifacts and fireplaces indicate intense human occupation, fish bones are all but absent. Fish bones are likewise rare or missing at other comparably ancient sites on the South

African coast, even though the sites were often only a stone's throw from the sea. At much more recent archeological sites like Nelson Bay Cave, fish bones often dominate the food debris, and the difference probably reflects a difference in technology. Only the more recent sites contain probable fishing gear like grooved stones for weighting nets or lines and carefully shaped toothpick-size bone splinters that could have been baited and tied to lines like hooks. In short, only the more recent people undeniably possessed the technology for fishing.

The ancient Klasies people also largely ignored birds, except for the flightless jackass penguins that they could have caught or scavenged on the beach. Gulls, cormorants, and other airborne birds were surely common nearby, but their bones are scarce at human sites until much more recent times. When they finally do appear in large numbers, they are accompanied by bone rods that were probably parts of arrow shafts and by small stone bits (microliths) like those that historic people used to tip arrows. Historic hunters have often demonstrated the utility of the bow and arrow for fowling. The bottom line is that the archeological and faunal evidence together show that South African hunter-gatherers who lived before 50,000 years ago were much less efficient hunter-gatherers than their successors. Archeology demonstrates that more efficient, fully modern hunting-gathering appeared only after 50,000 years ago, among the kinds of people who made the ostrich eggshell beads at Enkapune Ya Muto.

ﾑ ﾑ ﾑ

These two sites of Enkapune Ya Muto and Klasies River Mouth, separated by four thousand kilometers in space and up to 70,000 years in time, illustrate a critical conundrum for understanding how, when, and where modern humans evolved. Human fossils from Klasies River Mouth and other African sites and from sites in Israel immediately adjacent to Africa show that people who were anatomically like us had appeared in Africa by 100,000 years ago. Despite their modern appearance, however, these people left artifacts and animal remains which show that they were not fully modern in behavior. It is only after 50,000 years ago that behavioral evolution caught up and it is only afterwards that people were both anatomically and behaviorally modern.

Before 50,000 years ago, human anatomy and human behavior appear to have evolved relatively slowly, more or less in concert. After 50,000 years ago, anatomical evolution all but ceased, while behavioral evolution accelerated dramatically. Now, for the first time, humans possessed the full-blown capacity for culture, based on an almost infinite ability to innovate. They had evolved a unique capacity to adapt to environment not through their anatomy or physiology but through culture. Cultural evolution began to follow its own trajectory, and it took the fast track. Even as our bodies have changed little in the past 50,000 years, culture has evolved at an astonishing and ever-accelerating rate.

Our aims in this book are to outline the evidence for human anatomical and behavioral evolution before 50,000 years ago and to explore the circumstances surrounding the behavioral revolution that occurred afterwards. One obvious question we must confront at the outset is: what sparked the revolution? Unfortunately, there is no conclusive answer. To attempt one, we must look back at other important biological and behavioral changes that occurred along evolution's meandering path from our remotest ape-like ancestor to the curious, creative reader of this book. Human evolution has followed twists and turns and encountered occasional dead ends. The earliest part of our story still remains rather obscure. This is when some ape-like creature began to walk habitually on two legs. From the time of that pivotal innovation, human evolution can be viewed as a series of at least three and perhaps four sudden and profound events spaced between lengthy stretches of time when little happened.

From Darwin's day onward, most scientists have perceived evolution as a gradual and cumulative process, a slow, stately unfolding of life's history. In 1972, however, evolutionary biologists Niles Eldredge of the American Museum of Natural History and Stephen Jay Gould, now at Harvard University, challenged this perspective. They proposed that conspicuous and long-recognized gaps in the fossil record of past life actually provided vital information about the pace and pulse of evolution. As they wrote in a 1972 article, "Many breaks in the fossil record are real; they express the way in which evolution occurs, not the fragments of an imperfect record." Eldredge and Gould called their hypothesis punctuated equilibrium. Its key idea was that true evolutionary innovations appear suddenly and infrequently. It is at these points of abrupt change, often sparked by major climatic or environmental shifts, that new species tend to arise. Major climatic shifts not only open up fresh ecological opportunities, they also extinguish existing species, clearing the ecological playing field for new ones. Viewed from the present, the fossil record appears to show a sudden inflection after a period of constancy, a species-spawning event captured in a flash of geologic time, which punctuates an otherwise prolonged period of evolutionary equilibrium. In other words, stability is the norm, while speciation (the formation of new species) is the rarer but essential exception.

Evolution, in Eldredge and Gould's view, resembles a roller coaster ride: slow and steady ascents interrupted by breakneck plunges and curves. Just as the ascents occupy most of the brief roller coaster ride, gradual change comprises most of evolutionary time. But punctuations hold all the action and excitement.

New species probably most often arise in small, isolated populations where genetic changes (mutations) are particularly likely to take hold and become dominant. In large populations or in small populations that are in regular contact with others, genetic changes, even advantageous ones, are more likely to be swamped and to disappear strictly by chance. Each of the three or four punctuation events that we propose led up to the dawn of modern human culture occurred when human populations were small and geographically limited by modern standards. Each apparently occurred in Africa, and on present evidence, each appears to mark a coincidence of major biological and behavioral change. The first event occurred around 2.5 million years ago, when flaked stone tools made their initial appearance. These comprise the earliest enduring evidence for human culture, and their emergence probably coincided closely with the evolution of the first people whose brains were significantly larger than those of apes. The second event took place around 1.7 million years ago. The people this time were the first to possess fully human as opposed to ape-like body proportions, and they invented the more sophisticated stone artifacts that archeologists call hand axes. They may also have been the first to venture out of Africa. The third and most weakly documented event occurred around 600,000 years ago, and it involved a rapid spurt in brain size, together with significant changes in the quality of hand axes and other stone tools. The fourth and most recent event occurred about 50,000 years ago and it was arguably the most important of all, for it produced the fully modern ability to invent and manipulate culture. In its wake, humanity was transformed from a relatively rare and insignificant large mammal to something more like a geologic force.

Archeology demonstrates the radical nature and consequences of the last event, but it says nothing about what prompted it, and it is here that we face a conundrum. Arguably, the most plausible cause was a genetic mutation that promoted the fully modern brain. This mutation could have originated in a small east African population, and the evolutionary advantage it conferred would have enabled the population to grow and expand. This is because it permitted its possessors to extract far more energy from nature and to invest it in society. It also allowed human populations to colonize new and challenging environments. Possibly the most critical aspect of the neural change was that it allowed the kind of rapidly spoken phonemic language that is inseparable from culture as we know it today. This ability not only facilitates communication, but at least equally important, it allows people to conceive and model complex natural and social circumstances entirely within their minds.

Some might object that a neurological explanation for the explosion of culture after 50,000 years ago is simplistic biological determinism, a just-so story or a *deus ex machina* explanation for a paleontological paradox. The idea admittedly fails one important measure of a proper scientific hypothesis: it cannot be tested or falsified by experiment or by examination of relevant human fossils. Human brains had reached fully modern size many hundreds of thousands of years earlier, and skulls reveal little about the functioning of the brain underneath. There is nothing in the skulls of people from shortly before and after 50,000 years ago to show that a significant neurological change had occurred. The neurological hypothesis does, however, measure up to one important scientific standard: it is the simplest, most parsimonious explanation for the available archeological evidence. And that evidence, as incomplete and imperfect as it is, is what we must rely upon to reconstruct our evolutionary past.

Other explanations for the origin of modern human behavior hypothesize that some radical social or demographic event sparked a behavioral revolution about 50,000 years ago. These explanations, however, are at least as circular as the neurological hypothesis, because the evidence for the social or demographic change is simply the behavioral revolution they are meant to explain. And they offer no reason for why the momentous social or demographic change failed to occur tens of thousands of years earlier. Nominating a genetic mutation as the cause answers the "why" question. Mutations arise all the time in individuals and populations. Some are harmful, even lethal; most are neutral, conferring neither benefit nor burden. But a few give their possessors an advantage that, however slight, improves their odds in the game of evolution. If this advantage aids in the ability to obtain or process food, to acquire a mate, and to raise offspring to reproductive age, it is likely to spread within a population. The greater the advantage the mutation confers, the more rapidly it will spread, and no one could question the advantage of a mutation that promoted the fully modern brain. By enhancing the brain's cognitive and communicative capacity, it would have allowed humanity's external and internal journeys of discovery that continue to this day.

Fossil, archeological, genetic, and linguistic evidence all point to Africa as the place where the 50,000-year-old behavioral breakthrough occurred. And based on what we know at the moment, only eastern Africa harbored substantial human populations in the interval surrounding 50,000 years ago. Elsewhere in Africa, severe aridity appears to have sharply reduced human populations from 60,000 years ago or before until 30,000 years ago or later. Thus, only east African sites like Enkapune Ya Muto may record the dawn of human culture. The more certain point, however, is that the dawn did not occur in Europe. Although our concept of early symbolism is inevitably skewed by resplendent European examples like the charcoal rhinoceroses and bears on the walls of Grotte Chauvet or the multicolored bulls and horses of Lascaux, these all postdate the emergence of modern behavior and the arrival in Europe of fully modern humans. Had the crucial mutation occurred first in Europe, the earliest evidence for modern behavior would be there, and students of human evolution today would be Neanderthals marveling at the peculiar people who used to live in Africa and then abruptly disappeared.

Culture provides a uniquely advantageous means for adapting to environmental change. Cultural innovations can accumulate far more rapidly than genetic mutations, and good ideas can spread horizontally across populations as well as vertically between generations. This strategy of cultural adaptation, more than anything else, has enabled our species to transform itself from a relatively insignificant large African mammal to the dominant life form on Earth. We have developed an unprecedented ability to adapt to a wide variety of environments and, sometimes unfortunately, to alter them irrevocably. Having acquired this seminal cultural advantage, the earliest fully modern humans were able to disperse from Africa, northwards through the Near East to Europe and eastwards across Asia to China and beyond. Because people could now obtain more resources to produce and feed yet more people, population numbers began their long, steep climb to the levels that we now enjoy. Humans colonized new and increasingly challenging environments and began to develop the forms of complex social organization that are both a blessing and a curse today. And the rest, as they say, is history.

♛ ♛ ♛

2
BIPEDAL APES

Human evolution is still unfolding, and we don't know if or how it may end. The beginning of the story is easier to construct, but it is still not entirely in focus. We know the setting—somewhere in equatorial Africa—and the time interval—sometime between 7 and 5 million years ago. It was then that the evolutionary line leading to humans separated from the line leading to the chimpanzees, our closest living relatives. The earliest representatives of the human line still looked and acted much like apes, and a casual observer might have mistaken them for a kind of chimpanzee. There was one essential difference, however: on the ground, they preferred to walk upright, on two legs. We know them today technically as the australopithecines, but in appearance and behavior, they could as well be called bipedal apes. They are important to the dawn of human culture because they demonstrate humanity's humble roots, and they show just how much we have changed in a remarkably short time. Measured against an individual human life span, the 5 to 7 million years of human history may seem unimaginably long, but it is very brief compared to the 3.5-billion-year history of life on Earth or even to the 25-million-year history of the monkeys and apes.

♛ ♛ ♛

The discovery of the bipedal apes was important not just to anthropology, but to all of science. The year was 1924, the place was South Africa, and the discoverer was a young professor of anatomy at the University of the Witwatersrand in Johannesburg. His name was Raymond Dart, and he had only recently arrived from Britain to teach anatomy to medical students. He had a deep and abiding interest in evolution, and he encouraged his students to bring him fossils for a museum in his department. In 1924, a student showed him a fossil baboon skull from a cave exposed in a lime quarry at Taung, about 320 kilometers (190 miles) southwest of Johannesburg (Figure 2.1). Dart later obtained two crates of fossil-bearing deposit from the same cave or one nearby. The deposit was a mix of sand and bone, cemented by limy glue into a rock type known as "breccia." When Dart opened the crates, he saw breccia blocks from which numerous baboon fossils peeked out. But to his amazement and delight, one block also contained a natural cast from inside the skull of a more advanced primate. The cast was made of lime precipitated from water that once filled the skull. The lime replicated the skull's interior, and the replica matched a depression in a second breccia block. When Dart looked inside the depression, he could see traces of bone.

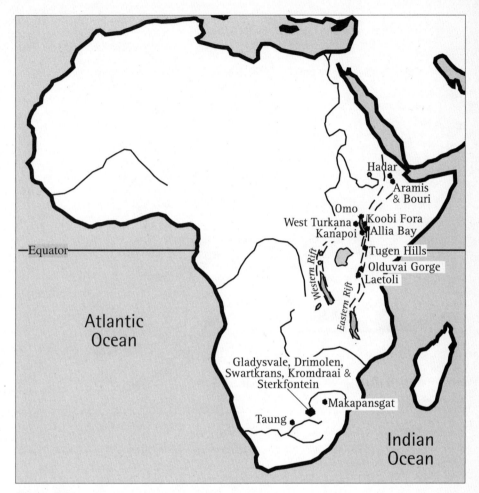

FIGURE 2.1
Locations of the australopith sites mentioned in the text.

Working with a hammer, chisels, and sharpened knitting needles, Dart set out to free the bone from its breccia prison. After a few weeks, he exposed the face and adjacent parts of the skull of a young ape-like creature (Figure 2.2). Its first molars were just erupting when it died, and the best current estimate is that it never reached its fourth birthday. The individual was thus a child, but Dart estimated that if it had reached adulthood, its brain would have been only slightly bigger than

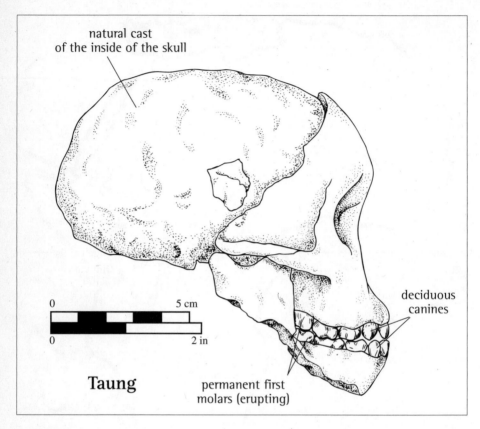

natural cast
of the inside of the skull

0   5 cm

0   2 in

Taung

deciduous
canines

permanent first
molars (erupting)

FIGURE 2.2
The child's skull from Taung, South Africa (drawn by Kathryn Cruz-Uribe from photographs and
casts) (Copyright Kathryn Cruz-Uribe).

a chimpanzee's and only a third the size of living person's. At the same
time, he saw that its milk (deciduous) canines were much smaller than
those of a chimpanzee, and even more striking, that the foramen magnum or "large hole" on the base of the skull was in the human position.
The foramen magnum allows connections to pass between the spinal
column and the brain, and in humans it is further forward and more
downward facing than in apes. This is because in normal posture, only
humans balance their heads directly on top of their spinal columns. On
February 7, 1925, Dart described the child's skull in the prestigious jour-

nal *Nature,* and he assigned it to a previously unknown species that was "intermediate between living anthropoids [apes] and man." He called the new species *Australopithecus africanus,* or "African southern ape," but he regarded it as a human ancestor. Much later, others coined the name australopithecine for *africanus* and related species. The idea was to separate them formally from more advanced human species, but the separation has become blurred with time. Hence, we prefer the shortened, less formal term "australopith."

Critics thought that Dart had been too hasty, and some suggested that the child might have become more ape-like if it had reached adulthood. Some also criticized Dart for inferring bipedalism from the skull and not from bones of the leg or foot, whose shapes are the best indication of how a creature walked or ran. Another objection stemmed partly from the Piltdown Hoax, a skull and lower jaw that had been deliberately altered to look ancient and then planted with genuinely ancient animal fossils at Piltdown, England in 1911–12. The hoax was finally exposed only in 1953, and in 1925, Piltdown implied that humans evolved their large brain early on, while *Australopithecus africanus* suggested that the brain came late, after bipedalism had developed. In addition, some scientists discounted *africanus,* because they thought that fossils found in Java in 1891–92 proclaimed Asia, not Africa, as the cradle of humanity. The Javan fossils were genuine, but we now know that they are geologically much younger than *africanus,* and they are commonly assigned to the more advanced species, *Homo erectus.* Finally, there was the problem that Dart could not estimate the geologic age of the Taung skull. Its antiquity remains uncertain to this day, but well-established dates for australopith fossils at other sites indicate that the Taung site formed at least 2 million years ago.

Controversy over the Taung skull boiled on for more than a decade, and Dart was vindicated only through the efforts of his colleague and supporter, Robert Broom. Broom was a Scottish-born physician and authority on fossil reptiles, who had settled in Pretoria, about 90 kilometers (55 miles) north of Johannesburg. He was among the first scientists to examine the original Taung specimen, and he quickly accepted Dart's diagnosis. Much more critically, however, he began a search for additional fossils, and in 1936 he was rewarded with a partial adult skull from breccia filling a cave on Sterkfontein farm, near the town of Krugersdorp, about 25 kilometers (15 miles) northwest of Johannesburg. He subsequently recovered the knee end of a thigh bone (femur) at Sterkfontein and a second adult skull and a heel bone (talus or astragalus) from cave breccia on the nearby farm of Kromdraai. By 1939, he had skulls which showed that adult australopiths were no more ape-like than the Taung child, and he had limb bones which demonstrated that they were bipedal. Their place in human evolution was established.

♛   ♛   ♛

Broom's work paved the way for many additional australopith discoveries in South Africa, and the total sample now numbers more than thirty-two skulls or partial skulls, roughly one hundred jaws or partial jaws, hundreds of isolated teeth, and more than thirty bones of the limbs, spine, and pelvis. In addition to Taung, Sterkfontein, and Kromdraai, the fossils come from ancient caves at Swartkrans, Gladysvale, and Drimolen, all clustered near Krugersdorp, and from the Makapansgat Limeworks Cave, about 300 kilometers (180 miles) to the north (Figure 2.1). Undoubtedly, there are more caves to be found, and the sample will continue to grow.

The fossils from Taung, Sterkfontein, Gladysvale, and Makapans-gat represent *Australopithecus africanus*, but those from Kromdraai, Swartkrans, and Drimolen come from a second species that specialists variously call *Australopithecus robustus* or *Paranthropus robustus*. *Paranthropus* was the name originally suggested by Broom for the fossils from Kromdraai. It means "alongside man," and those who use it see a greater difference between *africanus* and *robustus* than those who don't.

The South African caves contain no substance that can be reliably dated in years, and their geological antiquity must be judged from animal species that they share with dated sites in eastern Africa. Application of such "faunal dating" shows that *africanus* lived in South Africa from about 3 million years ago until about 2.5 million years ago (Figure 2.3). It could have persisted until 2 million years ago, since no South African cave unequivocally records the interval between 2.5 and 2 million years ago. Based on faunal dating, *robustus* was present from about 2 million until shortly before 1 million years ago.

In many key respects, *africanus* and *robustus* were very similar, and both illustrate the basic nature of the australopiths, or bipedal apes. By modern standards, individuals of both species were very small bodied. The largest probably stood less than 1.5 meters (5 feet) tall, and the heaviest probably did not exceed 50 kilograms (110 lbs.). Females tended to be especially small, and the sexual size difference, known as sexual dimorphism, far exceeded the difference in living humans. It was as great as or greater than in chimpanzees, and it suggests that *africanus* and *robustus* had a chimpanzee-like social organization in which males competed vigorously for sexually receptive females. If so, like chimpanzees, they probably also had a social system in which males and females lived mainly separate lives, neither sharing food nor cooperating to raise the young.

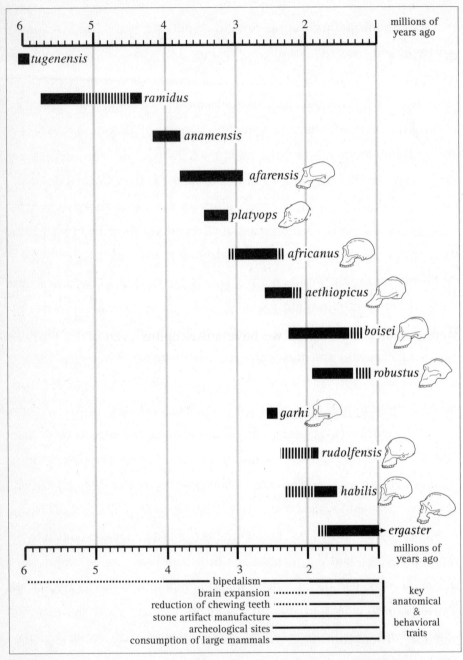

FIGURE 2.3
Top: Time spans of the most commonly recognized human species that existed before 1 million years ago. Bottom: Time spans of some key anatomical and behavioral traits. Broken lines imply less secure or more speculative dating.

Among other ape-like characteristics that *africanus* and *robustus* shared, the most conspicuous was their small brain size. In both species, adult brain volume averaged less than 500 cubic centimeters (cc). This compares to roughly 400 cc in chimpanzees and to 1400 cc in living people. Even when the averages for *africanus* and *robustus* are adjusted for small body size, their brains were less than half the size of ours. Both species also possessed very ape-like upper bodies with long, powerful arms that would have made them agile tree climbers. They differed from apes primarily in their lower bodies, which were shaped for habitual bipedal locomotion on the ground, and in their teeth.

The dental differences are important for two reasons. First, teeth and jaws strongly outnumber other fossil bones, because they are much more durable. They tell us we have australopiths even at sites where limb bones are not preserved. Second, teeth are a window on diet and other aspects of behavior. Chimpanzees and gorillas concentrate on soft foods like ripe fruit and fresh leaves that do not require heavy chewing. Their molar teeth are thus relatively small, and they are encased in relatively thin enamel that soft foods are unlikely to wear away. In their chewing, they do not have to move the jaws from side to side with the mouth nearly closed, and they can therefore have large canines. These are particularly large in males who use them in threat displays and sometimes in violent conflict.

In contrast, *africanus* and *robustus* had greatly expanded molar teeth that were encased in thick enamel (Figure 2.4). The implication is that they often consumed tough, hard, gritty, or fibrous foods that required heavy chewing. Such foods probably included seeds that they found on the ground or bulbs and tubers for which they had to dig. Members of both species also had small canines that would not have

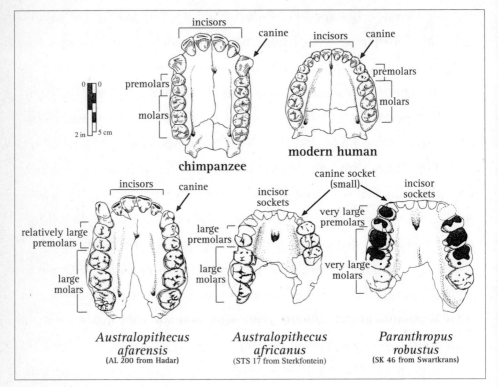

FIGURE 2.4

Upper jaws of a chimpanzee, a modern human, and various australopiths (top redrawn after D. C. Johanson & M. E. Edey 1981, *Lucy: The Beginnings of Humankind.* New York: Simon and Schuster, p. 367; bottom after T. D. White et al. 1981, *South African Journal of Science* 77, fig. 9).

impeded sideways movement of the jaws and that males could not have used in threat displays. This may indicate that dietary change was accompanied by a reduction in male-on-male aggression, or, more generally, by greater social tolerance.

The main differences between *africanus* and *robustus* were in the size of the chewing teeth—the premolars and molars that line the cheeks—and in the power of the chewing muscles. In *robustus*, the molars were huge, the premolars had become almost like molars, and the chewing muscles were extraordinarily well developed. The muscles themselves of course are not preserved, but their bony attachments are, and these include large, forwardly placed, widely flaring cheekbones, and in many individuals, a bony (sagittal) crest along the top of the skull (Figure 2.5). For their huge chewing teeth and rugged skulls, *robustus* and a closely related east African species, *Paranthropus boisei,* have been called the "robust" australopiths. However, they were small-bodied, even petite like *africanus,* and in every essential anatomical respect, including small brain size and ape-like upper body form, they exemplify bipedal apes equally well.

Apes use only the most rudimentary technology, and there is little to suggest that the australopiths were different. Flaked stone tools that show a technological advance beyond the ape level appear for the first time around 2.5 million years ago, and the robust australopiths might have produced some. Several findings, however, implicate an early member of the genus *Homo* as the more likely maker. Perhaps like some chimpanzees, *africanus* and *robustus* modified twigs to probe termite nests or they employed naturally occurring rocks or pieces of wood to crack nuts, but such tools would be archeologically invisible. And if the tools were as simple as their chimpanzee counterparts, their use could have been lost and reinvented many times, with minimal impact on the species. In strong contrast, human technology accumulates progressively, it could not be easily reinvented from scratch, and its loss would imperil the species. Even the earliest stone tool makers would probably have quickly vanished if they had somehow forgotten how to flake.

Dart proposed that the australopiths carried the bones of australopiths and other mammals into the South African caves. If this were true, it might follow that they possessed a typically human interest in

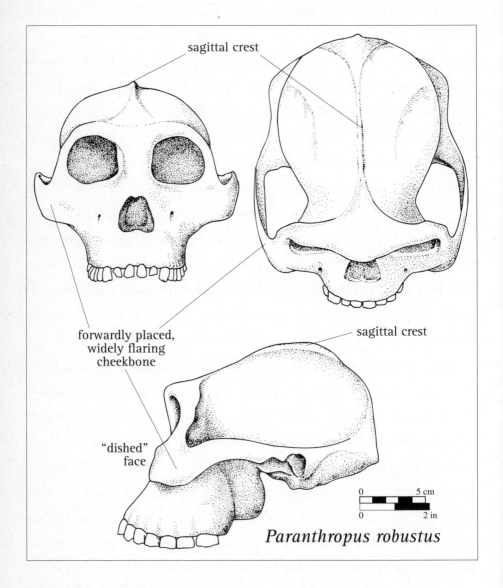

sagittal crest

forwardly placed,
widely flaring
cheekbone

sagittal crest

"dished"
face

0   5 cm
0   2 in

Paranthropus robustus

FIGURE 2.5
A reconstructed skull of *Paranthropus robustus* (redrawn after F. C. Howell 1978, in *Evolution of African Mammals*, Harvard University Press: Cambridge, MA, fig. 10.7).

meat and marrow. C. K. Brain, who excavated at Swartkrans Cave for twenty years and carefully studied the bones, has argued alternatively that large cats or other large carnivores probably introduced the bones of australopiths and other creatures. His most gripping clue is a *robustus* skull fragment with puncture marks that are the right form and distance apart to have been made by a leopard's canines. Like baboons, the australopiths probably sometimes sheltered in caves at night, where they would have provided tempting targets for leopards or extinct saber-tooth cats. If a successful predator consumed its victim on the spot, many of the bones would have fallen to the floor, to become part of the cave deposit. Perhaps like chimpanzees, *africanus* and *robustus* sometimes hunted monkeys or other small mammals, but the South African caves indicate that they were more often the hunted than the hunter.

Since *africanus* lived in South Africa before *robustus,* it could have been its ancestor, and teeth and skulls of *africanus* anticipate those of *robustus* in some respects. The history of the robust australopiths, however, extends to 2.5 million years ago in eastern Africa, where *africanus* is unknown, and the ancestry of *robustus* probably lies there. Robust australopiths are unlikely ancestors for true humans, because their teeth and skulls were so specialized and because they coexisted with more plausible ancestors after 2.5 million years ago. The robust australopiths became extinct by 1 million years ago, perhaps because they could no longer compete with evolving true humans or because they could not adjust to a decline in rainfall that occurred about the same time. *Africanus* is a different matter. In both its anatomy and its presence before true humans, it remains a possible human ancestor, and some anthropologists believe that if it was not, it closely resembled whoever was. To address this important issue and to continue the story of the bipedal apes, we must now turn to eastern Africa.

♛   ♛   ♛

Both laypeople and anthropologists know that eastern Africa is vital to our understanding of early human evolution. It is no exaggeration to say that this is due largely to the extraordinary dedication and talent of Louis and Mary Leakey. Beginning in 1935, from their base in Nairobi, Kenya, the Leakeys repeatedly traveled to northern Tanzania (known as Tanganyika before independence), where they scoured Olduvai Gorge for traces of early people. They always found artifacts and fossil animal bones, but it was only in 1959 that they recovered their first significant human fossil. This was the well-preserved skull of an adolescent "robust" australopith. We now assign it to the species *Paranthropus* (or *Australopithecus*) *boisei,* although *boisei* may have been simply an east African variant of South African *Paranthropus robustus.* Bones of *boisei* have been found at eight other east African sites, from Ethiopia on the north to Malawi on the south.

The Leakeys' success in 1959 brought them richly deserved financial support, and they excavated much more deposit over the next fourteen years at Olduvai than they had in the previous thirty. They recovered many additional human fossils, and they showed that *boisei* had coexisted with early true humans after 2 million years ago, just as *robustus* had in South Africa. They also illuminated the course of human evolution after *robustus* and *boisei* became extinct and only true humans survived.

The Leakeys' research revolutionized paleoanthropology not only because it provided key fossils and artifacts at Olduvai, but because it encouraged others to tap the great paleoanthropological potential of eastern Africa. The expedition leaders came from many countries, and the long list includes the Leakeys' son Richard from Kenya and his wife, Meave, Clark Howell, Donald Johanson, William Kimbel, and Tim White from the United States, Berhane Asfaw from Ethiopia, Yves Coppens and Maurice Taieb from France, and Gen Suwa from Japan. The expeditions have met their greatest success at sites near Lake Turkana straddling northern Kenya and southern Ethiopia and along the margins of the Awash River in north-central Ethiopia. In their quest, the fossil hunters have followed an important precedent that Mary Leakey established at Olduvai and at the older site of Laetoli nearby. She knew that ancient fossils and artifacts have little value if their stratigraphic position is not carefully recorded, and she therefore collaborated closely with the geologist Richard Hay, whose careful geologic mapping ensured the correct stratigraphic ordering. It also allowed him to reconstruct the landscape in which early people lived. Other fossil expeditions have routinely engaged field geologists for the same purpose, and like the Leakeys, they have also relied on geochemists to date the deposits in years and on paleontologists to identify the animal remains for both dating and environmental reconstruction. In short, research into early human evolution in eastern Africa has succeeded because it has been truly multidisciplinary, and it was the Leakeys who provided the model.

Eastern Africa has two distinct advantages over South Africa for the study of human evolution. First, the east African fossils often occur in relatively soft river or lake deposits that can be excavated with trowels, brushes, and other standard archeological tools. In contrast, the rock-hard South African cave breccias commonly require dynamite and pneumatic drills. Second, the east African sites often contain layers of lava or volcanic ash (tiny particles of lava that were erupted into the atmosphere and later settled to Earth). Lava and ash cool in a geologic eye-blink, and the time when they cooled can be estimated by the potassium/argon technique. This depends on the observation that rocks commonly contain small amounts of naturally occurring radioactive potassium-40 and of its daughter (decay) product argon-40. Argon-40 is a gas that disappears from molten rocks and that reaccumulates in cooled rocks in direct proportion to the known decay rate ("half-life") of potassium-40. The ratio of potassium-40 to argon-40 thus tracks the time of cooling in years, and the time when lava or ash cooled can be used in turn to date fossils and artifacts that are stratified within the same deposits. The South African cave breccias contain neither lava nor ash, and the South African australopiths must thus be dated mostly by associated animal species whose time ranges have been established at east African sites.

The twin advantages of the east African sites reflect their proximity to the eastern branch of the Great Rift Valley (Figure 2.1). This is essentially a gigantic geologic fault that marks the boundary between two massive continental plates. Tension and compression along the fault have forced its bottom down and its sides up, creating a trough more than 2000 kilometers (1200 miles) long and 40 to 80 kilometers (25 to 50 miles) wide. Repeated crustal movements in and around the Rift have often blocked streams to create lake basins that trapped and preserved fossil bones and artifacts. When later earth movements caused the lakes to drain, sparse vegetation and episodically violent rainfall encouraged erosion that exposed fossils for discovery. Rifting also promoted the volcanic activity that supplied lava and ash for dating. In contrast, the landscape of southern Africa was stable over the entire course of human evolution. It provided few internal basins to trap fossils and no active volcanoes. The result is that we have only the cave breccias and the challenge they present to excavation and to dating.

W W W

East African discoveries have not only extended the geographic range of the australopiths, they have also pushed the australopith record back beyond 4 million years ago (Figure 2.3). Ultimately, they will push it back to between 7 and 5 million years ago, the time when geneticists estimate that people and chimpanzees last shared a common ancestor. Two teams—one French and the other Ethiopian/American—already claim to have done this. Early in the winter of 2001, the French team announced the discovery of thirteen tantalizing, fragmentary fossils from deposits dated to 6 million years ago in the Tugen Hills of northern Kenya. They assigned the fossils to the new species *Orrorin tugenensis,* from the location of the site and the word "orrorin," meaning "original man" in the local Tugen language. Then in the summer of 2001, the Ethiopian/American team reported eleven fossils dated to between 5.8 and 5.2 million years ago from the arid margin of the middle stretch of the Awash river, about 300 kilometers (180 miles) northeast of Addis Ababa, Ethiopia. The Ethiopian/American team tentatively assigned their specimens to an older variant of the previously known species, *Ardipithecus ramidus,* whose discovery at the site of Aramis we recount below.

Neither the Kenyan fossils nor the Ethiopian ones include bones that unequivocally demonstrate bipedalism, and team members and other specialists are currently debating which species is more likely to be an early australopith as opposed perhaps to an ancestral chimpanzee. Conceivably, one or the other might even represent the last shared ancestor of australopiths and chimpanzees. Their status cannot be resolved without additional, more complete fossils, and in the meanwhile, the oldest widely accepted australopith comes from the site of Aramis, also in the Middle Awash Valley. We expand on Aramis here, for it nicely illustrates both the difficulties and rewards that fossil hunters can encounter in eastern Africa.

Aramis today is an inhospitable patch of sparse vegetation and ultrahigh temperatures. Ticks, vipers, and scorpions call it home, and at first glance, it looks like an unlikely place to seek fossils. Yet an international team of scientists who began working at the site in 1992 showed that when they look hard, sometimes crawling on their hands and knees, shoulder to shoulder, for days on end, they can recover fascinating traces of ancient life: seeds, fossilized wood, insect remains, and bones of birds, reptiles, and mammals. Potassium/argon analysis of volcanic ash shows that the fossils accumulated at Aramis about 4.4 million years ago.

The hard-won finds from Aramis reveal a far less forbidding ancient landscape. A dense forest lined the river. Acrobatic colobus monkeys clambered through the trees, and spiral-horned kudu antelopes browsed on leaves near ground level. Monkeys and kudus seem to have been the most common animals, but many other species were also present. These ranged in size from tiny rodents and bats to hippos, giraffes, rhinos, and elephants. The carnivores included large cats, hyenas, and other species that we would expect in Africa, and a bear that seems oddly out of place. The same bear occurs at other ancient African sites as far south as the Cape of Good Hope, and its presence underscores how much Aramis—and Africa—have changed over the past four million years.

The carnivores that hunted and scavenged near the river often chewed and crushed bones, and few specimens have survived intact. Partial skeletons are particularly rare, with one prominent exception. This represents a creature who, to the great fortune of paleontologists, died as floodwaters rose and covered its body with a layer of silt—a crucial step on the path to bone preservation.

In November 1994, University of California graduate student Yohannes Haile-Selassie was crawling across the surface at Aramis when he spotted some broken hand bones eroding from below. When he and his coworkers scraped the subsurface, more of the skeleton appeared: a tibia or shin bone, a heel bone, part of the pelvis, forearm bones, hand and wrist bones, and part of the skull. The bones were very fragile, and a careless touch could have turned them to powder, so the excavators softened the deposit with water, and they worked with surgical precision. Their painstaking efforts eventually retrieved more than one hundred pieces of the skeleton, including a nearly complete set of wrist bones and most of the finger bones from one hand. They recovered a lower jaw nearby.

The new skeleton proved to come from the same 4.4-million-year-old australopith species that Tim White, Gen Suwa, and Berhane Asfaw had described from other find spots at Aramis just two months before. Their description, in the journal *Nature*, was based on seventeen fossils, including a lower jaw, isolated teeth, pieces of skull, and three left arm bones. The species was roughly one-half million years older than any previously known australopith, and it was significantly more ape-like. To signal its position near the bottom of the human family tree, White and his colleagues named it *Australopithecus ramidus,* from "ramid," meaning "root" in the language of the local Afar people. Later, they concluded that it was so distinct that it deserved its own genus, and they renamed it *Ardipithecus ramidus.* Ardi means "ground or floor" in the Afar language, and the new name reinforced both the basal position of the species in human ancestry and the likelihood that it spent much of its time on the ground.

In the parts that have been described, *ramidus* was remarkably ape-like even for a bipedal ape. Its canines, for example, were exceptionally large relative to its molars, and its teeth were covered by thin enamel. It was also decidedly ape-like in the power of its arms, and it probably even possessed the ability to lock the elbow joint for added stability during climbing. If the teeth and arm bones were all we had, we might conclude that *ramidus* was only an ape, but a fragment from the base of the skull suggests that it carried its head in the human (bipedal) position. We will know just how bipedal when White and his colleagues describe the leg and foot bones of the partial skeleton.

Bipedalism is amply documented for the next youngest australopith, which Meave Leakey and her paleoanthropologist colleague Alan Walker described in 1995 from the sites of Kanapoi, southwest of Lake Turkana, and Allia Bay on the lake's eastern margin. They named the species *Australopithecus anamensis,* from "anam," meaning "lake" in the language of the local Turkana people. Potassium/argon dating shows that *anamensis* lived near Lake Turkana between 4.2 and 3.8 million years ago (Figure 2.3). Accompanying animal fossils show that the environs were wooded, but trees were probably sparser than they were at Aramis.

The bone sample of *anamensis* includes thirteen partial jaws, fifty isolated teeth, a piece of skull from around the ear region, two bones of the arm, a hand bone, a wrist bone, and the *pièce de résistance,* a tibia or shin bone. The jaws and teeth show that *anamensis* retained relatively large canines, but it also had the broadened molars and thickened enamel that mark virtually all later australopiths. The arm bones suggest that it preserved an ape-like ability to climb, but the tibia shows even more clearly that it was habitually bipedal on the ground. In people, in contrast to chimpanzees, the flat, articular surface at the knee end of the tibia is almost perpendicular to the shaft, and the shaft itself is heavily buttressed near both ends (Figure 2.6). These and other features allow people to shift their weight from one leg to the other during bipedal movement, and they are all present in the *anamensis* tibia. Together, then, the teeth, the arm bones, and the tibia unequivocally finger *anamensis* as a bipedal ape.

On known parts, *anamensis* closely resembled *Australopithecus afarensis,* which occurred in the immediately succeeding time period, and when *anamensis* becomes better known, it may turn out to be simply an early version of *afarensis.* Since *afarensis* was recognized first, its name would be applied to both species.

Afarensis illustrates the bipedal ape character of the australopiths more clearly than any other species, because it is known from virtually every bone of the skeleton, often in multiple copies. That we know *afarensis* so well is due almost entirely to the efforts of Donald Johanson and his coworkers beginning in 1973 at Hadar, immediately north of Aramis in Ethiopia, and to the work of Mary Leakey between 1974 and 1979 at Laetoli, 45 kilometers (27 miles) south of Olduvai Gorge in northern Tanzania. At one small site, Johanson's team recovered forty percent of the skeleton of a single individual (Figure 2.7), whom they immortalized as "Lucy," from the lyrics of a Beatles tune

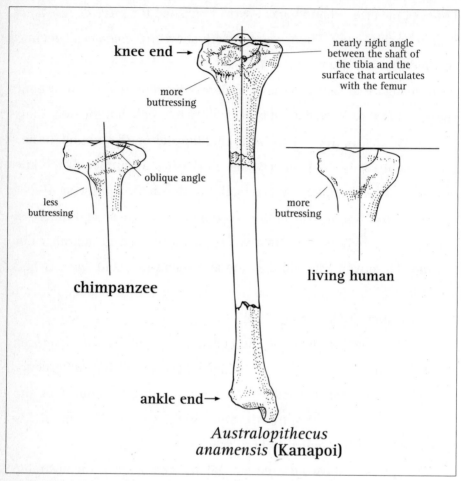

knee end →

nearly right angle
between the shaft of
the tibia and the
surface that articulates
with the femur

more
buttressing

oblique angle

less
buttressing

more
butressing

chimpanzee

living human

ankle end→

*Australopithecus
anamensis* (Kanapoi)

FIGURE 2.6
Front views of tibias (shin bones) of a chimpanzee, *Australopithecus anamensis,* and of a
living human (redrawn after M. G. Leakey 1995, *National Geographic* 190 (9), p. 45).

that was popular at the time. A partial skeleton is worth far more than
the sum of its parts, because unlike isolated bones, it permits anthropologists to reconstruct bodily proportions, including, for example, the
length of the arms relative to the length of the legs. At another small
site, Johanson's team found more than two hundred bones from at least
nine adults and four juveniles who have been dubbed the "First Family."

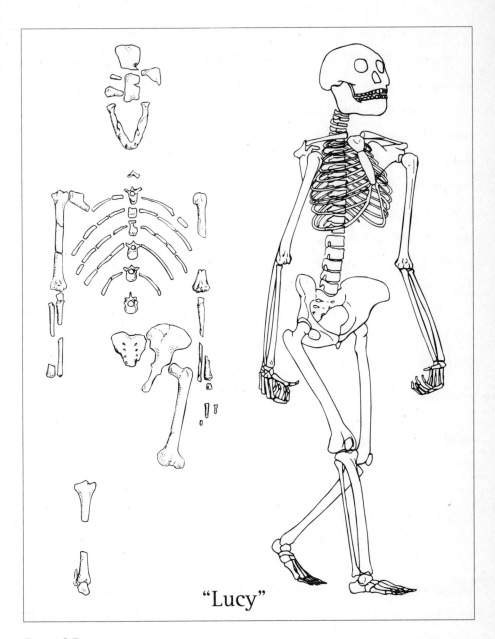

FIGURE 2.7
Left: The forty-percent-complete skeleton of "Lucy" (*Australopithecus afarensis*) from Hadar, Ethiopia (drawn from a photograph in M. H. Day 1986, *Guide to Fossil Man*. Chicago: University of Chicago Press, p. 250). Right: a reconstruction of the entire skeleton based on mirror-imaging and on other specimens of the same species (drawn after K. F. Weaver, 1985, *National Geographic* 168, p. 564).

Together with fossils from other sites, they allow highly reliable esti- mates of variability within *afarensis,* including the degree of sexual dimorphism.

Based on the Hadar and Laetoli samples, Johanson, Tim White, and Yves Coppens defined *afarensis* in 1978, and they took the name from the Afar region of Ethiopia that includes Hadar, Aramis, and other key fossil sites. Potassium/argon analysis shows that Hadar fossils of *afarensis* accumulated between about 3.4 and 2.9 million years ago and that the Laetoli fossils are somewhat older. They take the species back to roughly 3.8 million years ago (Figure 2.3). Thus, even if *anamensis* is kept separate, *afarensis* spanned an interval of about a million years, and it changed little over this long span. At Laetoli, it occupied a dry environment, with few trees, but at Hadar it enjoyed generally moister, more wooded conditions. It was thus flexible in its environmental requirements.

Afarensis had a small ape-sized brain that may have been even smaller on average than the brains of *africanus* or *robustus.* It shared their relatively small body size, but it was much more dimorphic. Males not only averaged perhaps fifty percent taller and heavier than females, they also had significantly larger canines. In both males and females, the jaws protruded farther forwards below the nose than in any other known member of the human family, and body proportions were inter- mediate between those of apes and later humans. Thus, the arms were very long relative to the legs, and the forearm was particularly long and powerful. Combined with ape-like curvature of the finger and toe bones (phalanges), the arms imply an ape-like agility in the trees.

At the same time, in all key respects, the pelvis, the leg, and the foot demonstrate bipedalism (Figure 2.8). The pelvis was shortened from

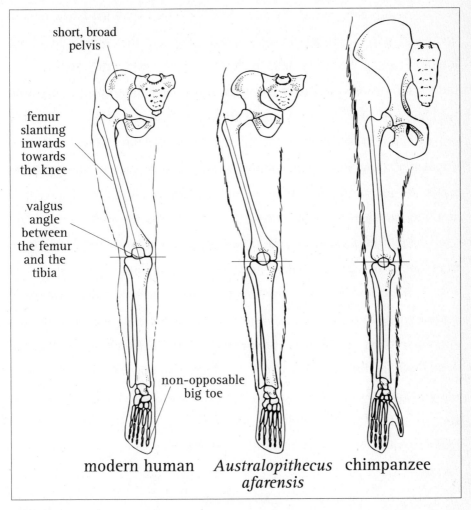

short, broad pelvis

femur slanting inwards towards the knee

valgus angle between the femur and the tibia

non-opposable big toe

modern human *Australopithecus afarensis* chimpanzee

FIGURE 2.8
Lower limbs of a modern human, of *Australopithecus afarensis*, and of a chimpanzee (redrawn after D. C. Johanson & M. E. Edey 1981, *Lucy: The Beginnings of Humankind*. New York: Simon and Schuster, p. 157).

top to bottom and broadened from fore to rear to center the trunk over the hip joints and thereby reduce fatigue during upright, bipedal locomotion. The femur slanted inwards towards the knee and formed a distinct (valgus) angle with the tibia so that the body could balance on one leg while the other was off the ground. And the foot had the expanded heel, upward arch, and non-divergent (non-opposable) big toe that are essential for human walking. In humans, each step involves a heel strike, followed by the planting of the foot over the arch, and finally by a pushing off from the big toe. If there were any doubt about this sequence in *afarensis,* Mary Leakey laid it to rest in what for anyone else would have been the discovery of a lifetime. In her excavations at Laetoli, her team uncovered a 27-meter (89-foot) long trail of footprints left by two *afarensis* individuals strolling together on a mushy surface that hardened about 3.6 million years ago. In heel strike, arch, and non-divergent big toe, the prints match ones that living humans make when they walk barefoot on a soft substrate.

If paleontologists wanted to construct a bipedal ape from scratch, they could probably not produce a more persuasive species than *Australopithecus afarensis,* and nothing could provide more compelling evidence that humans descend from apes. For opponents of this idea, *afarensis* is an even more formidable foil than the flamboyant Clarence Darrow, who found himself defending evolution in a Tennessee court half a century before *afarensis* was discovered.

♛ ♛ ♛

A reader who has reached this point may be thinking "OK, bipedal apes, but why bipedal?" What natural selective force could have prompted an ape to become bipedal and what advantage would bipedalism have conferred? These questions are not trivial, but they are also not easy to answer. With regard to what stimulated the shift to bipedalism, the most likely cause is environmental change. Between 10 million and 5 million years ago, global climate became cooler and drier, and grasslands expanded while forests shrank or thinned out. The change spelled doom for many forest-adapted species, including a variety of apes that lived in Africa and Eurasia before 10 million years ago. In equatorial Africa, however, one ape species adapted to the changing conditions by spending an increasing amount of time on the ground. Life on the ground presented new challenges and opportunities that favored those individuals whose anatomy and behavior gave them a reproductive edge, however slight, over their peers. In retrospect, it appears that the most important anatomical advantage was an enhanced ability to walk and run bipedally.

The shift to a lifestyle grounded in bipedalism may have progressed gradually over a long interval, or it may have occurred abruptly, as African environments changed in response to a particularly dramatic decline in global temperature and humidity between 6.5 and 5 million years ago. During this interval, periodic growth in the Antarctic ice cap sucked so much water from the world ocean that the Mediterranean Sea was drained. The loss of moisture from the Mediterranean accelerated forest contraction on the adjacent continents, and animal communities responded. In Africa, the antelopes burgeoned into the wide variety we know historically, and the human line may have emerged at the same time. If so, its origin would constitute a punctuational event. For the moment this idea must remain conjectural, but ongoing research in eastern Africa will one day provide the fossils to test it.

As to the advantages that bipedalism would have offered a ground-dwelling ape, the first and perhaps most obvious is that the arms and hands could now be used to carry food to widely scattered trees or to other group members. In addition, as Darwin noted more than a century ago, the hands would now be freer for tool manufacture and use. Today, this idea is less compelling, because archeology shows that tool use beyond the level of living apes occurred only about 2.5 million years ago, long after bipedalism. Among other less obvious natural selective advantages, bipedalism may have reduced the energy that ground-dwelling apes needed to travel between widely scattered trees or tree clumps, and it could have lessened their danger of heat stroke, if they were often forced to forage in the open at midday. This is because the sun's most intense rays would have fallen only obliquely on upright backs.

Modern experiments have failed to confirm that bipedalism increases energy efficiency, while animal and plant fossils show that the bipedal apes, particularly the earliest ones, lived in environments where shade trees were plentiful. It was only about 1.7 million years ago that people invaded savannas where shade may have been sparse, and they evolved a different body form to meet the challenge. Novel explanations of bipedalism are thus still welcome, and Nina Jablonski and George Chaplin of the California Academy of Sciences have offered a particularly intriguing one. It draws on the observation that free-ranging chimpanzees and gorillas stand upright mainly to threaten each other over food or mates. In the process, they wave their arms, beat their chests, and sometimes even brandish branches to enhance their displays. When male gorillas feel threatened, they often stand erect before charging, while chimpanzees swagger and raise their hair so that they seem even more imposing. When an opponent fails to back down, violent, deadly struggles may ensue. Humans of course also signal their status or intentions with posture, and Jablonski and Chaplin propose that an increase in bipedal displays for dominance and appeasement—standing up or backing down—may have been important to reduce violent aggression among early bipedal apes. The potential for aggression may actually have increased, if forest fragmentation had concentrated the most desirable food in small, dense patches. Individuals who learned to defuse tense situations with bipedal displays could have reduced their risk of injury or death and thus, by definition, improved their reproductive chances. In this scenario, bipedalism may have been important for promoting social tolerance even before it facilitated carrying or tool use.

♙ ♙ ♙

The initial advantages of bipedalism may always remain a matter for speculation, but they must have been significant, for the bipedal apes not only survived, they eventually proliferated. Anthropologists disagree on whether *ramidus* is a likely ancestor for *anamensis* and *afarensis,* but most agree that between 3.5 and 2.5 million years ago, multiple bipedal species appeared (Figure 2.3). By 2.5 million years ago, there were at least two highly distinct bipedal lines—one that produced the later robust australopiths and another that led to true people of the genus *Homo* and ultimately to ourselves.

The robust line is better documented, mainly thanks to a spectacular skull that Alan Walker and his colleagues described in 1986 from a site to the west of Lake Turkana in northern Kenya. As it lay in the ground, the skull had been permeated with manganese which turned it blue-black, and it is thus been dubbed the "Black Skull" (Figure 2.9). It had a face like that of *afarensis,* in which the jaws projected far forward, but it also had very large chewing teeth and a powerfully developed sagittal crest like those of *robustus* and *boisei.* It is now commonly

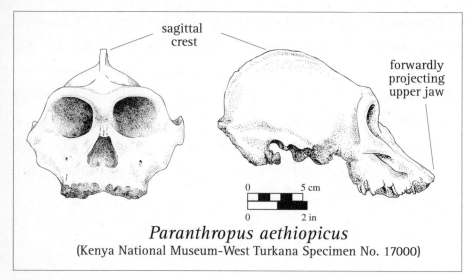

sagittal crest

forwardly projecting upper jaw

0   5 cm

0   2 in

Paranthropus aethiopicus
(Kenya National Museum-West Turkana Specimen No. 17000)

FIGURE 2.9
The "Black Skull," *Paranthropus aethiopicus,* from West Turkana, Kenya (drawn by Kathryn Cruz-Uribe from photographs) (Copyright Kathryn Cruz-Uribe).

assigned to the species *Paranthropus aethiopicus,* and it is a plausible link between *afarensis* and *boisei/robustus*. Other east African sites that date between 2.5 and 2 million years ago have provided jaws and isolated teeth that may represent either *aethiopicus* or early *boisei*.

The second lineage is sparsely represented before 2 million years ago, but many anthropologists have long assumed that it stemmed from *africanus* or a species like it. Eastern Africa has not yet, however, provided fossils resembling *africanus*. Instead, in 1999, it produced another equally old and totally unexpected species.

Just three years after he discovered the partial skeleton of *Ardipithecus ramidus* at Aramis, Yohannes Haile-Selassie spotted a skull fragment on the surface at Bouri, south of Aramis in the Middle Awash Valley. After the Middle Awash team had painstakingly turned over every rock and bone fragment nearby, they were able to reconstruct a remark-able skull (Figure 2.10). A lower jaw from the same deposits at another locality probably represents the same species. Potassium/argon dating demonstrates that the species existed about 2.5 million years ago, which makes it a contemporary of both *Australopithecus africanus* and *Paranthropus aethiopicus*. Yet it differed sharply from both. The part of the skull that contained the brain might have been mistaken for the same part in *afarensis* if it had been found in isolation. In contrast, based on shape and proportions, the jaws and teeth might have been mistaken for those of later humans, except that the teeth were exceptionally large. The premolars and molars equaled or exceeded those of robust australopiths in size, but in contrast to the condition in the robust australopiths, the incisors and canines were also large. "The combination of large teeth and primitive morphology was a surprise," says Tim White. "Nobody expected that." So White and his colleagues decided to call the species *Australopithecus garhi,* from garhi, the Afar word for "surprise." In the April 23, 1999, issue of *Science* magazine, they suggested that "It is in the right place, at the right time, to be the ancestor of early *Homo,* how-ever defined. Nothing about its morphology would preclude it from occupying this position." Possible *garhi* limb bones from Bouri indicate that the forearm remained long relative to the upper arm as in apes, but the thigh was long relative to the upper arm as in humans. In other words, as humans continued to differentiate from apes, it appears that their legs lengthened before their forearms shortened.

We will see that the early *Homo* line may actually include two or even three lines, and if they split by 2.5 million years ago, *garhi* could be ancestral to only one. The east African fossil record between 3 million and 2 million years ago is actually poorer than the record for

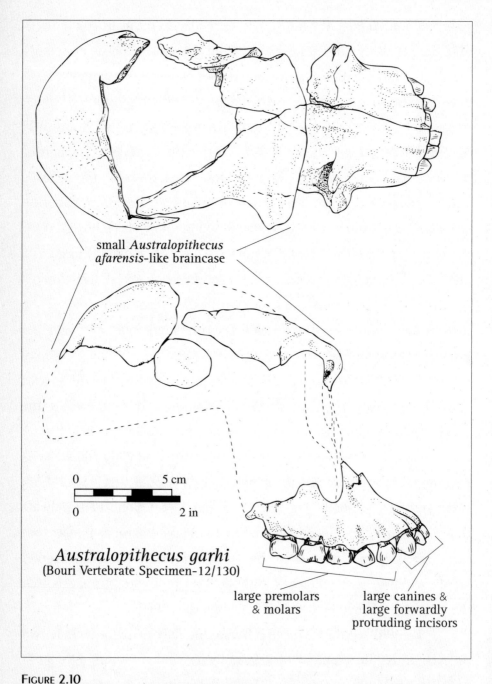

small *Australopithecus afarensis*-like braincase

0   5 cm

0   2 in

Australopithecus garhi
(Bouri Vertebrate Specimen-12/130)

large premolars & molars

large canines & large forwardly protruding incisors

FIGURE 2.10
Skull of *Australopithecus garhi* from Bouri, Middle Awash Valley, Ethiopia (drawn by Kathryn Cruz-Uribe from photographs) (Copyright Kathryn Cruz-Uribe).

the preceding million years, but the difference reflects the vagaries of preservation and discovery, not the likelihood that the australopiths or their descendants had become rarer. The bottom line is that as fossil hunting continues, *garhi* will probably not be the last surprise. Meave Leakey and her team brought this point home in March 2001, when they described a remarkable new skull from 3.5-million-year-old deposits west of Lake Turkana. Prior to the new discovery, most authorities agreed that the relatively well known human fossils from between 4 and 3 million years ago represented only one evolving line—*anamensis* and its immediate descendant *afarensis*. The new skull shares thick dental enamel with both, and like all australopith skulls, it contained a small, ape-size brain. However, its molar teeth were much smaller than those of *afarensis* and *anamensis,* and its face was far flatter and less project-ing. Its individual features can be matched in other australopith species, but it combines them in a unique way, and Leakey and her colleagues have assigned it to a new genus and species, *Kenyanthropus platyops,* or "the flat-faced man of Kenya."

In its flat face and the shape of its brow, *platyops* anticipates a much larger brained 1.9-million-year-old Kenyan skull that is now often assigned to *Homo rudolfensis.* However, the facial resemblance could be simply a matter of chance, and many new fossils will be necessary to clarify the relationships of *platyops* to *Homo* and to other australopiths. For the moment, *platyops* is important because it shows that like the monkeys, the antelopes, and other mammal groups, early humans had diversified into multiple contemporaneous forms early on. In a few short years anthropologists may be worrying less about why bipedalism was successful and more about how it could have promoted such a prolifer-ation of species.

♛ ♛ ♛

3
THE WORLD'S OLDEST WHODUNIT

magine camping on an east African savanna without the benefit of tents, tools and utensils, a four-wheel-drive vehicle, or even a camp-fire. You're small, naked, and bipedal, and your intelligence is crammed in a brain less than half the size of the one you're using to read these words. A nearby river or a waterhole provides a reliable source of water, and when danger looms your long arms can quickly propel you into the trees. Your climbing ability is crucial, because you cannot out run the large cats, hyenas, and other predators who see you as food. But what will you eat? How will you find enough to survive?

Around 2.5 million years ago, some scrawny bipedal creature made a revolutionary discovery that greatly increased its chances for survival. It lived in woodlands or savannas where predators, accidents, disease, or starvation often killed antelopes, zebras, wild pigs, and other large mammals. Carnivores and scavengers did not claim all the available flesh or marrow, and therein lay an opportunity. What our spindly biped found was that if it struck one stone against another in just the right way, it could knock off thin, sharp-edged flakes that could pierce the hide of a dead zebra or gazelle. It could use the same flakes to slice through the tendons that bind muscle to bone. In effect, it had found a way to substitute stone flakes for the long slicing teeth that cats and other carnivores employ to strip meat from a carcass. Our primitive inventor also discovered that it could use heavy stones to crack bones for their nutritious, fatty marrow, and in this, it unwittingly imitated hyenas who employ hammer-like premolars for the same purpose. Its use of stone tools conferred a reproductive advantage over individuals who could not do likewise, and those who could soon increased in number. In extending their anatomy with tools so that they could behave more like carnivores, they set in train a co-evolutionary interaction between brain and behavior that culminated in the modern human ability to adapt to a remarkable range of conditions with culture alone.

♛ ♛ ♛

It should come as no surprise that the world's oldest known stone tools come from the Awash Valley of north-central Ethiopia, famous for its early australopith fossils. In one locality or another, the Awash Valley contains ancient river or lake deposits that span the entire range of human evolution, from before 6 million years ago until recent times. Fossil and artifact hunters look for places where fossils or artifacts have eroded from ancient deposits. When they find what they are seeking, they first attempt to establish the layer of origin, and if the layer remains intact nearby, they often excavate to recover objects that are "*in situ,*" that is, still sealed in their original resting places.

The most ancient artifacts come from the drainage of the Gona River, a tributary of the Awash, between Hadar on the north and Bouri and Aramis on the south (Figure 3.1). Rutgers University archeologist Jack Harris made the first discovery in 1976, but it was only between 1992 and 1994 that a team including Harris and his Ethiopian colleague, Seleshi Semaw, excavated a large number of pieces *in situ* and firmly established their geologic age. The excavated sample numbers more than 1000 pieces from two separate sites, and it is supplemented by about 2000 pieces that had eroded onto the surface near to the excavations.

For raw material, the Gona artifact makers selected volcanic pebbles or cobbles from ancient streambeds, and they left behind sharp-edged flakes, the faceted "cores" from which the flakes were struck, and the battered "hammerstones" that were used to strike the cores. The Gona people clearly understood that to obtain flakes routinely, they had strike the edge of a core forcefully at an oblique angle. When a flake is removed this way, it usually exhibits a distinct swelling or "bulb of percussion" on the inner surface immediately adjacent to the point of impact or "striking platform." Archeologists rely heavily on bulbs to distinguish human flaking from natural fracturing, since collisions between rocks in a stream or under a waterfall tend to be more glancing, and the fracture products rarely show distinct bulbs. The Gona flakes regularly do (Figure 3.2), and they come from silty, low-energy floodplain deposits where natural collisions were unlikely to occur. Their origin as artifacts is thus assured.

The geologic antiquity of the Gona artifacts has been equally well fixed by a combination of potassium/argon and paleomagnetic dating. The potassium/argon method shows that a volcanic ash above

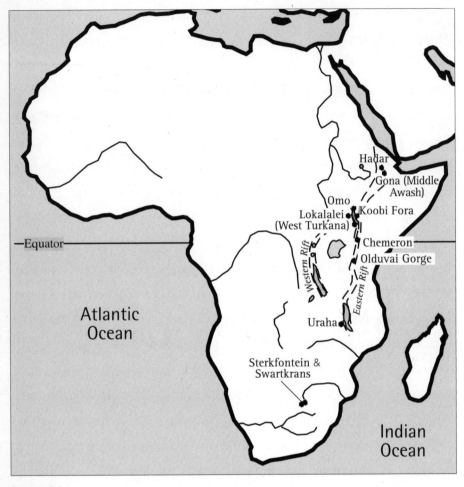

FIGURE 3.1
Locations of the sites with Oldowan tools, fossils of early *Homo*, or both mentioned in the text.

the tool-bearing layer accumulated just before 2.5 million years ago. The paleomagnetic method relies on the repeated tendency of Earth's magnetic field to flip 180 degrees, meaning that the direction a compass needle would point has periodically shifted from north to south and back again. Iron particles in volcanic rocks and in fine-grained sediments like those at Gona retain the ancient direction of the field, and the global sequence of shifts has been dated in volcanic rocks (Figure 3.3). Geophysicists use the term "normal" to refer to a time interval when the magnetic field was oriented north as it is today and "reversed" to refer to an interval when it was oriented south. The Gona deposits record a north-to-south shift just below the tool layer, and such a flip is known to have occurred 2.6 million years ago. Together, then, potassium/argon and paleomagnetism bracket the Gona artifacts between 2.6 and 2.5 million years ago.

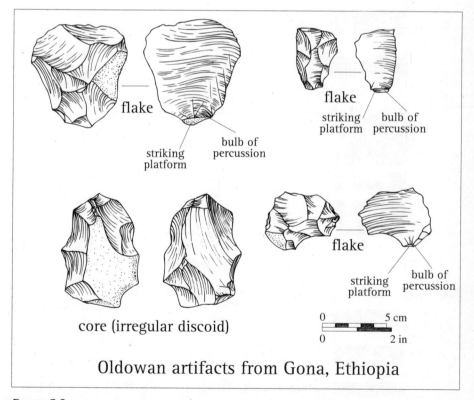

Oldowan artifacts from Gona, Ethiopia

FIGURE 3.2
Oldowan artifacts from the Gona site, Middle Awash Valley, Ethiopia (redrawn after S. Semaw 2000, *Journal of Archaeological Science* 27, fig. 8).

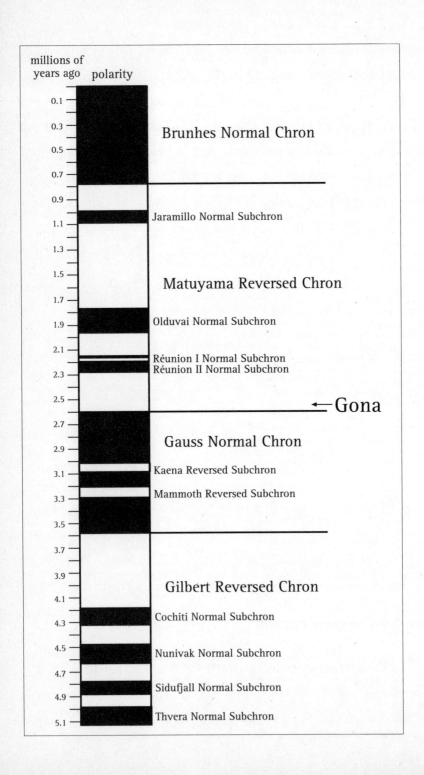

millions of
years ago   polarity

0.1

0.3   Brunhes Normal Chron
0.5

0.7

0.9

1.1   Jaramillo Normal Subchron

1.3

1.5   Matuyama Reversed Chron

1.7

1.9   Olduvai Normal Subchron

2.1

            Réunion I Normal Subchron
2.3   Réunion II Normal Subchron

2.5   ←Gona

2.7

2.9   Gauss Normal Chron

3.1   Kaena Reversed Subchron

3.3   Mammoth Reversed Subchron

3.5

3.7

3.9

4.1   Gilbert Reversed Chron

4.3   Cochiti Normal Subchron

4.5   Nunivak Normal Subchron

4.7

4.9   Sidufjall Normal Subchron

5.1   Thvera Normal Subchron

Older artifacts may exist, but southern African and other eastern African sites indicate that they cannot be much older. Deposits that are about 2 million years old at the *robustus* cave of Swartkrans in South Africa contain flaked stone artifacts, but deposits dated between roughly 3 million and 2.5 million years ago at the *africanus* caves of Sterkfontein and Makapansgat do not. Similarly, deposits at Hadar with abundant remains of *afarensis* dated between 3.4 and 2.8 million years ago have produced no artifacts, but a younger site dated to 2.33 million years has. This younger site is particularly important, because it has also provided a fossil that may represent the artifact maker. Together, observations in South Africa, at Hadar, and at other east African sites indicate that the Gona date of 2.6 to 2.5 million years ago must closely approximate the actual time when stone flaking began.

♛ ♛ ♛

Artifacts resembling those from Gona have been dated to 2.4 to 2.3 million years ago at Hadar, at Omo just north of Lake Turkana in southern Ethiopia, and at Lokalalei west of Lake Turkana in northern Kenya. Similar artifacts also occur at eleven east and South African localities that date between 2 million and 1.7 to 1.6 million years ago. The South African artifacts come from Swartkrans Cave and from deposits at Sterkfontein Cave that overlie those with *africanus* fossils. The most

FIGURE 3.3

The global geomagnetic stratigraphy for the past 5 million years and the geologic age of the Gona site. Black rectangles designate past intervals when polarity was normal, white rectangles intervals when it was reversed. Geophysicists refer to long intervals of normal or reversed geomagnetic polarity as chrons and to shorter intervals as subchrons.

important east African sites are at Koobi Fora on the eastern shore of Lake Turkana and at Olduvai Gorge in northern Tanzania. As a group, the east and South African sites show that artifact technology remained remarkably stable for nearly a million years after it began.

The Olduvai artifact assemblages are particularly large and thoroughly described, thanks again to the dedication of Louis and Mary Leakey. Archeologists group similar stone tool assemblages within an "Industry," an "Industrial Complex," or a "Culture," and Louis suggested the name Oldowan Industry to encompass the most ancient Olduvai artifacts. Since all other assemblages before 1.7 to 1.6 million years ago closely resemble those from Olduvai, they are now also assigned to the Oldowan. In Mary Leakey's pioneering descriptions of Oldowan tools, she made a basic distinction between core forms shaped by the removal of flakes and the flakes themselves. She then divided both core forms and flakes among different types depending mainly on size, shape, and the degree of working (Figure 3.4). Thus, she used the term "scraper" for a flake that had been modified (or "retouched") by the removal of yet additional, smaller flakes on one or more edges. She distinguished between small scrapers, which she called "light duty," and large scrapers, which she called "heavy duty." She divided core forms between "choppers," on which flaking was restricted to one edge, and "discoids," "spheroids," and "polyhedrons," on which flaking was more extensive and produced pieces shaped like discs, spheres, and cubes. Choppers could be either "unifacial," with the flaking restricted to just one surface, or "bifacial," with the flaking spread out over both surfaces. A "bifacial chopper" on which the flaking extended around the entire periphery became a "protobiface," and protobifaces graded into true bifaces (or hand axes) on which the flaking covered both surfaces. Bifaces are unknown in the

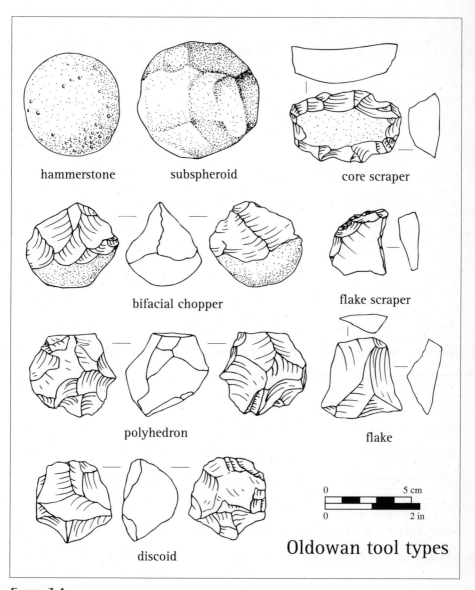

hammerstone   subspheroid   core scraper

bifacial chopper   flake scraper

polyhedron   flake

discoid

Oldowan tool types

0   5 cm

0   2 in

FIGURE 3.4
Representative types of Oldowan stone tools recognized by Mary D. Leakey and other special-
ists (redrawn after originals by Isaac and J. Ogden in N. Toth 1985, *Journal of Archaeological
Science* 12, fig. 1).

Oldowan proper, but they are the hallmark of the subsequent Acheulean
Industry which emerged from it about 1.7 to 1.6 million years ago.

Specialists have sometimes defined yet further tool types or subtypes, but even the basic list probably exaggerates the formality of Oldowan assemblages. Anyone who has tried to sort Oldowan tools knows that many fail to conform to predefined types. Individual pieces often have attributes of two or more types, and they can be pigeonholed only after much subjective head-scratching. Gary Larson captured the essence of the problem in a cartoon showing an early human trying to crack a boulder with a roughly shaped stone. In exasperation, the would-be boulder breaker turns to his tool-box-toting assistant and says, "So what's this? I asked for a hammer! A hammer! This is a crescent wrench. Well, maybe it's a hammer. Damn these stone tools."

Archeologist Nicholas Toth of Indiana University has conducted experiments that explain why attempts to pigeonhole Oldowan tools are so frustrating. Toth is skilled at stone flaking, and his efforts to replicate Oldowan core forms show that their final shape depends not on a template in the maker's head, but on the shape of the raw pebble or other unmodified rock fragment with which the maker starts. The result is that experimental products tend to intergrade in shape, just like genuine Oldowan core forms.

Archeologists have often assumed that Oldowan people were more interested in core forms than in flakes, but Toth believes that the core forms were mainly byproducts of flake manufacture. Butchering experiments show that heavier core tools with long cutting edges and large gripping surfaces can be useful for dismembering large carcasses or for smashing bones to get marrow. But for entering a carcass and removing muscle masses, nothing that Oldowan people made could surpass a fresh lava or quartz flake. And when a flake became dull from use, a butcher could always strike a fresh one and continue on.

Cut-marked animal bones demonstrate that Oldowan people often employed stone flakes just as Toth proposes. In their stone working, they mainly focused on sharp edges, and they probably cared little about the final shape of the core.

By later human standards, Oldowan stone-working technology was remarkably crude, and an observer might reasonably ask if it exceeded the capability of a chimpanzee. The answer is probably yes, based on research that Toth and his colleagues have done with Kanzi, a bonobo at the Yerkes Regional Primate Center in Atlanta, Georgia. (Bonobos differ from "common" chimpanzees in body proportions and in aspects of social behavior. They are geographically separated from common chimpanzees in the wild, and they are usually placed in a separate species, although they readily interbreed with common chimpanzees in captivity.) When Kanzi was still an infant, psychologist Sue Savage-Rumbaugh and her colleagues began to investigate his ability to communicate with symbols, and they found that he was an unusually talented subject. Toth had taught scores of students to make stone tools, and he reckoned that if he could teach any ape, Kanzi was the one. In the spring of 1990, when Kanzi was nine years old, Toth showed him how to strike a sharp stone flake from a core and how to use the flake to sever a nylon cord encircling a box containing an edible treat. Kanzi got the point immediately, but he had great difficulty producing flakes in the standard human way by striking a core with a hammerstone. In his frustration and perhaps to his credit, he soon devised an alternative method: hurling a core against a concrete floor.

Kanzi sometimes did obtain the sharp-edged pieces he needed, but even after months of practice, neither his cores nor his flakes came up to Oldowan standards. The cores have a battered look, reflecting Kanzi's many unsuccessful attempts to strike flakes, and his flakes are mostly tiny and difficult to distinguish from naturally fractured pieces. In sum, despite having the best possible human mentor, Kanzi has never mastered the mechanics of stone flaking, and if his products turned up in an ancient site, archeologists would probably not accept them as unequivocal artifacts. Kanzi's younger sister, Panbanshiba, has now also been encouraged to flake stone, and there are plans to involve common chimpanzees. Archeologists await the results with interest, but the evidence so far suggests that even an especially intelligent and responsive ape cannot grasp the mechanics of stone flaking.

♛　♛　♛

Oldowan tool makers did much more than flake stones. At Gona, Koobi Fora, Olduvai, and other sites, they accumulated the flakes and core forms in clusters that mark the world's oldest known archeological sites. Where soil conditions were favorable, the clusters also preserve fragmentary animal bones. The bones commonly come from antelopes, zebras, pigs, and other animals that are far larger than any on which chimpanzees feed, and it is tempting to regard each cluster as a campsite where Oldowan people converged each night to exchange food, have sex, or simply socialize, just as modern hunter-gatherers often do. Such an interpretation may be too far-reaching, however, and the clusters could represent something far more prosaic, like clumps of trees in which individuals congregated to feed in safety. So far, no cluster has provided unequivocal traces of fireplaces or of structures that would imply anything more.

Cut and bash marks show that Oldowan people handled the bones at their sites, but carnivore-damaged specimens are also common, and this raises the question of how the people obtained the bones. Some archeologists argue for hunting or for confrontational scavenging in which groups of people drove carnivores off still-fleshy carcasses. Others argue for more passive scavenging from carcasses that carnivores had largely consumed. In advance, the simplicity of Oldowan technology may favor passive scavenging, but direct evidence is sparse, and naturalistic and experimental observations can be used to support hunting or scavenging. We know, for example, that carnivores largely ignore limb bone shafts that people have smashed, because the marrow is gone and the shaft fragments themselves have little food value. In Oldowan sites, limb bone midshaft fragments from antelopes and other animals often show numerous carnivore tooth marks, and this may mean that the people mainly scavenged from carcasses on which carnivores had already fed. Yet, we also know that carnivore feeding tends to remove the most nutritious skeletal elements first. These are bones of the upper fore limb (humeruses and radioulnas) and upper rear limb (femurs and tibias) that are especially rich in meat, marrow, and grease. Compared to less desirable parts, such bones tend to be common in Oldowan sites, and this might mean that the people often got to carcasses first and did not have to settle for scraps—in short, that they were hunters or confrontational scavengers.

Passive scavenging could still have been the rule, however, if we assume that Oldowan people favored environments with few hyenas, so that they could scavenge directly from lions or other large cats. Lions deflesh limb bones but often leave the shafts intact, and in the absence of hyenas, scavenging people might still have been able to obtain numerous marrow-rich, meatless arm and leg bones. Marrow alone, however, provides relatively little food value, particularly when the effort to remove it is considered, and scavenging focused on marrow would provide little sustenance, unless lion kills were far more abundant than they are in most historic African environments. In addition, the most nutritious limb bones at Oldowan sites often show cut marks from flesh removal, which suggests that the people got the bones before someone else picked them bare.

The bottom line is that the available evidence can be read to favor either hunting or passive scavenging, and the surviving data may never allow a firm choice. Still, the uncertainty over hunting vs. scavenging should not be allowed to obscure a far more fundamental point. About 2.5 million years ago, bipedal creatures that were probably no more technological or carnivorous than living chimpanzees evolved into ones who mastered the physics of stone flaking and then used their newfound knowledge to add an unprecedented amount of meat and marrow to their traditional vegetarian diet.

w w w

At this point, the reader is surely wondering just who these Oldowan people were. What species did they belong to and what did they look like? To address this question, we must return briefly to the australopiths and their evolutionary history. Anthropologists disagree on the relationships among the australopith species that existed before 2.5 million years ago, and the recent discovery of *Kenyanthropus platyops* can only fuel the debate. Before *platyops* was found, most authorities agreed that *Australopithecus afarensis* was the only human species between 3.5 and 3 million years ago and that it was ancestral to all later people. It may still be the most plausible ancestor for some or all, but *platyops* provides an alternative that cannot be ruled out a priori. Equally important, it suggests that fresh finds may only expand the choices, if like *platyops* they reveal yet additional, unexpected australopith species. What remains clear is that when Oldowan tools appeared around 2.5 million years ago, people were divided between at least two distinct evolutionary lines. One led to the later robust australopiths and the other to the genus *Homo* (Figure 3.5).

We do not know when the two lines separated, but a reasonable working hypothesis is that they diverged abruptly between 2.8 and 2.5 million years ago, when a climatic inflection reduced moisture across much of Africa and sparked extinctions and new species in antelopes and other mammalian groups. The key point here is that the lines were already separate when Oldowan tools appeared, and we must therefore contemplate more than one potential tool maker. No one doubts that early representatives of *Homo* produced stone tools, but what about the robust australopiths? The question is not hypothetical, since flaked stones have been found with *robustus* at Swartkrans Cave in South Africa and with its east African cousin, *boisei,* at Olduvai Gorge and other sites in eastern Africa.

Anthropologist Randall Susman of the State University of New York at Stony Brook has proposed a rule of thumb for determining whether robust australopiths produced Oldowan artifacts. He notes that chimpanzees have curved, narrow-tipped fingers and short thumbs. This hand structure promotes a power grip that is helpful for grasping tree limbs. Humans, in contrast, have shorter, straighter fingers with broad tips and larger, stouter thumbs. The human hand promotes a

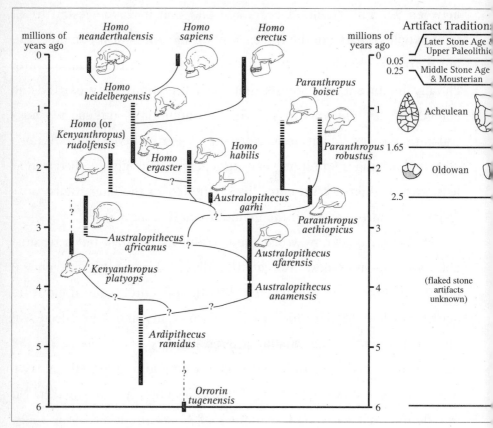

FIGURE 3.5

A tree diagram (phylogeny) linking human species. Dotted bars indicate tentative time ranges. The broad outline of the tree is established, but new discoveries may alter the proposed connections between the branches.

precision grip that is well suited for opening a jar, writing with a pencil, or flaking stone. The chimpanzee/human difference is manifest in the first or thumb metacarpal, the bone at the edge of the palm that runs between the wrist and the thumb itself. In chimpanzees, the thumb metacarpal is relatively short, and it is narrow, particularly at the end where it articulates with the first bone (phalange) of the thumb (Figure 3.6). In humans, it is relatively longer and broader, and in combination

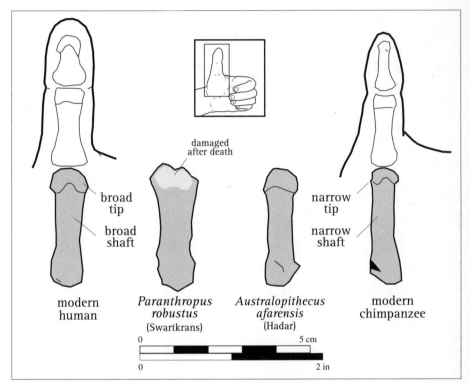

FIGURE 3.6
Thumb metacarpals of a modern human, *Paranthropus robustus, Australopithecus afarensis,* and a chimpanzee (redrawn after R. L. Susman 1994, Science 265, fig. 3).

with a broader thumb tip, it provides attachment for three muscles that chimpanzees lack and that promote precision grasping in humans.

No tools are associated with *Australopithecus afarensis,* and Susman's criterion suggests that none were to be expected, since *afarensis* had a chimpanzee-like thumb metacarpal. Tools abound with much later *Homo erectus* and *Homo neanderthalensis,* and again in keeping with advance expectations, both had typically human thumb metacarpals. Tools also occur at robust australopith sites, but in this instance, no prediction is possible because the same sites usually contain bones of early *Homo*. And therein lies a dilemma. Early *Homo* and robust australopiths can be cleanly separated only on their teeth and skulls. The isolated limb bones that occur at most sites could come from either. At Swartkrans, these bones include a thumb metacarpal that Susman assigns to *robustus*, because unequivocal *robustus* teeth and skull parts heavily outnumber those of *Homo*. In form, the metacarpal is typically human, and if Susman's assignment is accepted, it could imply that *robustus* made some or all of the Swartkrans stone tools. The problem is that the metacarpal could represent *Homo*, and this might even seem likely, since it strongly resembles thumb metacarpals in much later humans. In short, thumb metacarpal form does not unequivocally finger *robustus* as a stone tool maker.

It remains possible, of course, that both *robustus* and early *Homo* made stone tools, but if so, we might expect two distinct tool traditions between 2.5 million years ago and the time when *robustus* and its east African relative, *boisei,* became extinct, at or shortly before 1 million years ago. Oldowan tools may be too crude to reveal separate traditions, but tools of the Acheulean Industry or Culture that replaced the Oldowan 1.7 to 1.6 million years ago were more formal, and they suggest only one evolving tradition. No one questions that *Homo* alone produced the Acheulean tradition, since it persisted long after the robust australopithecines had disappeared.

This is not to say that *robustus* made no tools, and it could be responsible for some polished bone fragments found at Swartkrans and at nearby Drimolen Cave. Experiments with modern replicas indicate that the polish formed when someone used the fragments to open termite nests. Chimpanzees savor termites, and in some groups, individuals routinely probe nests with modified branches. If *robustus* had developed a more aggressive twist on this basic strategy, its success could explain a peculiarity in the carbon composition of its dental enamel. Carbon comes in two naturally occurring non-radioactive forms (isotopes)—carbon 12 (^{12}C) and carbon 13 (^{13}C)—and in tropical or subtropical environments like those that *robustus* inhabited, grasses tend to be significantly richer in ^{13}C than leaves, tubers, fruits, or nuts. The ratio of ^{13}C to ^{12}C in the tooth enamel of an animal reflects the ratio in its preferred foods, and a team of geochemists led by Julia Lee-Thorp of the University of Cape Town has shown that *robustus* enamel is relatively enriched in ^{13}C. *Robustus* individuals must thus have been feeding fairly heavily on grasses or on grass-eating animals. Grass-eating itself can be ruled out, because grasses contain small, hard particles (phytoliths) that score teeth in a distinctive way, and *robustus* teeth lack the signature scratches. Feeding on grass-eating antelopes or other mammals cannot be dismissed, but focusing on grass-eating termites or other invertebrates would have been far less risky.

♛ ♛ ♛

If we eliminate robust australopiths, it may seem a simple matter to determine who made Oldowan tools. Unfortunately, it is not, and to explain why, we have to back up a little and expand on the history of the Leakeys' research at Olduvai Gorge. Recall that their first human fossil represented the robust australopith, *Paranthropus boisei*. They found it in 1959 at site FLKI near the very bottom of the Gorge, where it was accompanied by numerous Oldowan tools and fragmentary animal bones. Understandably, they assumed that *boisei* made the tools and collected the bones. (They initially spoke of *Zinjanthropus boisei* or "Boise's east African man" in honor of one of their financial sponsors. The species was subsequently reassigned to *Paranthropus,* but *Zinjanthropus* or "Zinj" lives on in the vernacular, and FLKI is often known alternatively as FLK-Zinj.) In 1961, the paleoanthropological world was electrified when Louis, Jack Evernden, and Garniss Curtis, two pioneers in potassium/argon dating from the University of California at Berkeley, announced that "Zinj" and his tools were 1.75 million years old. The date itself stirred a revolution, since to that point, many authorities, Louis Leakey included, assumed that human evolution might have spanned no more than a million years. Suddenly there was a lot more time to accommodate both biological and behavioral change.

The discovery of "Zinj" enabled the Leakeys to obtain funding to excavate other 1.8- to 1.6-million-year-old Olduvai sites, and they soon recovered remains of a second, larger-brained, smaller-toothed, bipedal species. Louis and his anatomist colleagues Phillip Tobias and John Napier formally described it in *Nature* in 1964, and they dubbed it *Homo habilis,* or "handy man" to signal their belief that it—and not Zinj—was the Oldowan tool maker. They and others reasoned that brain enlargement fostered tool-making and that tools to process food fostered smaller chewing teeth. In reducing "Zinj" to non-technological status, they anticipated the position we have taken here. However, the years have not been kind to *habilis,* and there is now reason to question its status as a species and as a tool maker.

In a nutshell, the difficulty for *habilis* comes down to this. Between 1969 and 1975, a team led by the Leakeys' son Richard recovered numerous skulls, jaws, and other bones from deposits dated between 1.9 and 1.6 million years ago at Koobi Fora on the eastern margin of Lake Turkana in northern Kenya. The time interval was the same one the Leakeys had established for *boisei* and *habilis* at Olduvai. Some of the Koobi Fora specimens clearly represented *boisei*, and for present purposes, they can be placed aside. Others come from something more *Homo*-like, but if they are lumped with the Olduvai *habilis* sample, *habilis* becomes extremely variable. Some individuals (from Koobi Fora) had relatively large skulls and large australopith-size teeth, while others (from both Koobi Fora and Olduvai) had small australopith-size skulls and small *Homo*-sized teeth (Figure 3.7). Brain volume, estimated from eight Olduvai and Koobi Fora skulls, averaged 630 cubic centimeters (cc), but it ranged from a low of 510 cc to a high of 750 cc. The smallest and largest skulls both come from Koobi Fora, and limb bones in the same deposits imply equally large differences in body size. To some specialists, the differences suggest a persistence of the high degree of sexual dimorphism that characterized the australopiths, but to others they indicate that *habilis* actually confounds two species. The smaller-brained, smaller-toothed species could still be called *habilis*, since it more closely matches the definition that Louis Leakey and his colleagues offered in 1964. Its larger-brained, larger-toothed contemporary would require a new name, for which advocates have proposed *Homo rudolfensis*, based on "Rudolf," the now obsolete colonial name for Lake Turkana.

If we accept two species, only one could be ancestral to later humans including ourselves, and the choice is not easy. If brain expansion is emphasized, then *rudolfensis* is the clear winner, but if dental and facial reduction are accentuated, then *habilis* is the better candidate. Limb bones may favor *rudolfensis*, if we assume that some larger isolated thigh bones (femurs) represent this species. In size and shape,

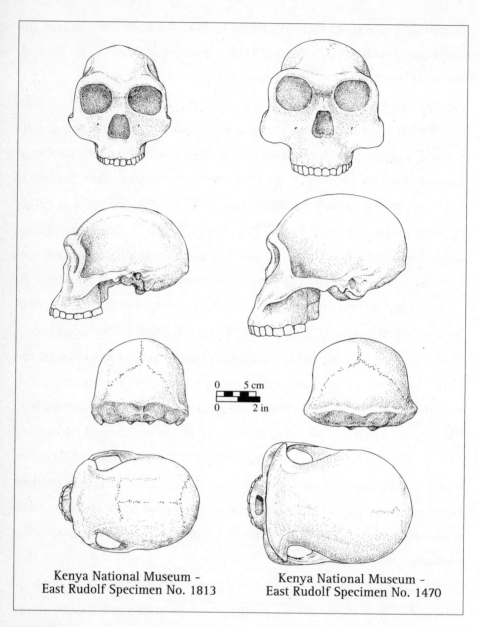

Kenya National Museum -
East Rudolf Specimen No. 1813

Kenya National Museum -
East Rudolf Specimen No. 1470

FIGURE 3.7

Reconstructed skulls of *Homo habilis* from deposits east of Lake Turkana (formerly Lake Rudolf), northern Kenya (redrawn after F. C. Howell 1978, in *Evolution of African Mammals*, Harvard University Press: Cambridge, MA, fig. 10.9). Specialists who want to divide *Homo habilis* between two species would keep the skull on the left within *Homo habilis*, but they would assign the skull on the right to a new (second) species, *Homo rudolfensis*.

they closely resemble the thigh bones of later humans, and they suggest that *rudolfensis* was significantly larger than any known australopith. In contrast, two highly fragmentary partial skeletons that are thought to represent *habilis* in the strict sense suggest tiny bodies (one individual may have been no more than 1 meter or 3'3" tall) and arms that may have been remarkably long compared to the legs. Given the australopith-like dentition of *rudolfensis* and the australopith-like body and small brain of *habilis,* some authorities have suggested that they should both be removed from *Homo* and placed in *Australopithecus.* This is ultimately a matter of definition, and an answer won't help us to decide whether *habilis, rudolfensis,* or both produced the Oldowan tools that occur in the same deposits at Olduvai and Koobi Fora. Unfortunately, for the moment, there is no way to tell, and if they actually were separate species, we can only speculate on how they differed behaviorally and ecologically.

♛ ♛ ♛

The *habilis/rudolfensis* conundrum might be resolved if fossil hunters could recover enough additional bones to determine conclusively how many anatomical or size modes existed 1.9 to 1.6 million years ago. If future discoveries confirmed that there were only two, the implication would be for a single species marked by an extraordinary degree of sexual dimorphism. If new discoveries suggested four modes, we might conclude that there were two species, each predictably with two sexes. The problem might also be resolved if field workers were to recover additional, more complete skeletons to confirm body size and proportions in one or both species. But these are big "ifs," and the pace of fossil discovery suggests that they are unlikely to be satisfied soon.

It's obviously also crucial to know the history of *habilis/ rudolfensis* before 2 million years ago. In some features of face and brow, *rudolfensis* recalls 3.5-million-year-old *Kenyanthropus platyops,* and if the resemblance implies an ancestor-descendant relationship, *rudolfensis* could be removed from *Homo* to *Kenyanthropus.* This would reduce the puzzling variability in early *Homo,* but there are no fossils between 3.5 and 1.9 million years ago to link *platyops* and *rudolfensis,* and the differences between them in brain size, tooth size, and other aspects are profound. For the moment then, it seems wise to withhold judgment on a possible connection. What is certain is that the line (or lines) that produced *habilis/rudolfensis* were distinct by 2.5 million years ago, because the collateral robust australopith lineage had already emerged by this time.

Unfortunately, *platyops* aside, so far, there are only three fossils that may document *habilis/rudolfensis* before 2 million years ago. These are a skull fragment from Chemeron, Kenya, a lower jaw from Uraha, Malawi, and an upper jaw from Hadar, Ethiopia (Figure 3.8). The Hadar jaw is the most important, because it is more obviously from *Homo* than the Chemeron skull fragment and it is more firmly dated than the Uraha jaw. Potassium/argon analysis of overlying volcanic ash places the Hadar jaw just before 2.33 million years ago, and it resembles *Homo* in multiple features, including its narrowed molars, its limited forward projection (prognathism) below the nasal opening, and the parabolic shape of its dental arcade—the path that the tongue describes as it passes over each tooth beginning with the third molar on one side and ending with the third molar on the other. In the australopiths, the molars tend to be significantly broader, the upper jaw protrudes further forwards below the nose, and the dental arcade is more U-shaped. On the ground near the

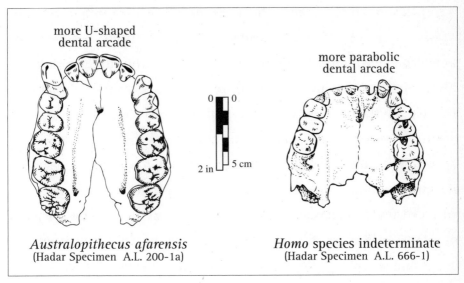

more U-shaped
dental arcade

more parabolic
dental arcade

2 in — 5 cm

Australopithecus afarensis
(Hadar Specimen A.L. 200-1a)

Homo species indeterminate
(Hadar Specimen A.L. 666-1)

FIGURE 3.8

Upper jaws of *Australopithecus afarensis* and early *Homo* from Hadar, Ethiopia (drawn by Kathryn Cruz-Uribe from photographs).

jaw, a Hadar team led by William Kimbel found three Oldowan choppers and seventeen flakes that had eroded from the same deposit, and when they excavated they recovered another core tool and thirteen more flakes. They also found fragments of animal bones, including one that bore a possible stone tool mark. So far, the artifacts are the oldest to have been recovered in direct association with a human fossil.

Neither the Hadar jaw nor the other two fossils that may represent *Homo* before 2 million years ago inform on brain size, but if stone flaking and brain expansion were closely linked, then brain expansion must have begun by 2.5 million years ago. Future discoveries may confirm this—or they may not. The *Australopithecus garhi* skull from Bouri, Ethiopia, which we described in the last chapter, provides fodder for doubters. This is because it anticipates *Homo* in its dentition, but not in the enclosure for the brain, which was no larger than in australopiths. The Bouri deposits have not yielded any stone artifacts, but they have provided animal bones that were cut and broken with stone tools. Unlike nearby Gona, Bouri lacked cobbles or other rock fragments that were suitable for flaking, and when the tool makers visited, they may have carefully conserved their implements until they could return to a locality like Gona. If so, they were thinking ahead in a way that is decidedly human. The bones they damaged include an antelope tibia shaft that was repeatedly cut, bashed, and chopped to get at the marrow, the femur of a three-toed horse that was cut when it was separated from adjacent bones and stripped of flesh, and an antelope lower jaw that was cut on the inner surface when the tongue was removed.

The implication may be, as *Time Magazine* suggested in April 1999, that *garhi* was "the first butcher." Tim White, whose team found the *garhi* skull and the tool-marked bones, is more cautious: "It's circumstantial evidence, and not as strong as it might be. It's possible that some [other] hominid came by and left the tools. Then a year later, a carnivore dropped the carcass of a different kind of hominid [*garhi*] in the same place." He continues: "What it tells you, though, is that there was a hominid in these habitats with stone tools [who was] engaged in large mammal carcass processing. That's very important. The behavior is, in some ways, more important than whether it was *garhi* engaging in the behavior." White calls the bone-processor a "superomnivore" to distinguish it from its predecessors who were probably more ape-like in both diet and behavior.

White and his team have scoured all the Bouri exposures for fossils and artifacts, and it will be many years, perhaps decades or centuries, before fresh erosion at Bouri provides new clues. Still, there are other like-aged east African sites to explore, and one may yet provide a larger-brained species dated to 2.5 million years ago. The discovery will satisfy those who believe that brain enlargement and stone flaking originated in an evolutionary feedback loop. If *garhi,* however, coexisted with a larger-brained companion, then there must have been at least three distinct human types by 2.5 million years ago—an early robust australopith, *garhi,* and the putative larger-brained species. We could even argue for four types, if we accept, as seems increasingly likely, that *Australopithecus africanus* was restricted to South Africa and disappeared there without issue before 2 million years ago.

In short, the proper metaphor for human evolution between 3 and 2 million years ago may turn out to be a bush, and the high degree of variability in *habilis/rudolfensis* between 1.9 and 1.6 million years ago may actually represent the tips of multiple branches that the fossil record will eventually reveal. If there was such a bush, though, natural selection had severely pruned it by 1.6 million years ago, and thereafter only two branches survived—the robust australopiths and the line that ultimately led to ourselves (Figure 3.5). By 1.7 million years ago, this line had produced a species that departed sharply from the australopiths in anatomy, behavior, and ecology, and there is no question about its assignment to *Homo.* Its members have been called the first "true humans," and we explore next the important step they represent on the long road to human culture.

♛ ♛ ♛

4
THE FIRST TRUE HUMANS

We have suggested that human evolution was characterized by a series of short, abrupt steps or punctuations, separated by long periods with little or no change. So far, we have described a possible first punctuation, which occurred between 7 and 5 million years ago and produced bipedal apes, and a better-evidenced second event, which occurred between 3 million and 2 million years ago and produced the first stone tool makers. The abruptness of each step is debatable, but the stability that followed is patent. Thus, the anatomy of the bipedal apes changed little over intervals that lasted a million years or more. The anatomy of the earliest tool makers is poorly known, but they were probably equally conservative, judging by a remarkable lack of change in the tools they produced. They may have had larger brains than the bipedal apes, but they may also have retained an ape-like upper body form and a high degree of size difference between the sexes. If so, it's probable that they continued to rely heavily on trees for food and refuge and that they had an ape-like social organization that involved little or no cooperation between the sexes. When we know them better, we may decide that for all effects and purposes, they were "technological apes."

We turn now to a third step that occurred about 1.8 to 1.7 million years ago. It is more fully documented than its forerunners, and it was at least as momentous, for it produced a species that anticipated living people in anatomy, behavior, and ecology, save mainly for its smaller brain. With this caveat in mind, its members can reasonably be labeled the first "true humans," and this is how we will refer to them here. Early on, the first true humans authored a major advance in stone flaking technology, but thereafter, both their anatomy and their artifacts appear to have remained remarkably stable for a million years or more. In this respect, they were marching to the same drummer as their predecessors.

In late August 1984, Kamoya Kimeu was prospecting for fossils along the south bank of the Nariokotome River, west of Lake Turkana in northern Kenya. Kimeu had long assisted Richard and Meave Leakey in their quest for ancient human bones, and before his retirement in 1993, he had probably found more than anyone else. On this occasion, his team had been in the field for two weeks, but their extensive fossil haul included no human specimens. They planned to move camp the next day, but while others rested or did chores, Kimeu continued the hunt. He picked a difficult, unpromising spot, a slight rise protected by an acacia tree within a sun-baked gully. The surface was littered with black lava pebbles, and any fossils that had eroded out were likely to have been trampled by local herds of goats and camels. Kimeu's chances seemed slim, but he had overcome such odds before, and he did so again now. He soon spotted a match-book-sized piece of black bone, hardly distinguishable from the surrounding pebbles, and when he picked it up, he knew that it came from the forehead of an extinct kind of human.

Kimeu's assessment drew the Leakeys and their paleoanthropo-logical colleague, Alan Walker, to the find spot, and over the next four years, they led parties that meticulously excavated the deposits nearby. In the end, they not only managed to piece together a complete skull, they also recovered most of the skeleton that went with it. The skele-ton turned out to represent an adolescent male, whom his discoverers affectionately dubbed the "Turkana Boy." Analysis of the enclosing sediments showed that the boy had died and been rapidly buried on the edge of a marsh about 1.5 million years ago. His skeleton was even more complete than Lucy's, found a decade earlier in deposits that were 1.8 million years older, and it is still the most complete skeleton from any human who lived before 120,000 years ago. Its significance matches that of Lucy, for if she left no doubt that her kind were bipedal apes, the Turkana Boy showed just as clearly that his kind were true humans.

Recall that Lucy was tiny—probably only about one meter (3' 3") tall, and she had very long arms relative to her legs. She also had an ape-like cone- or funnel-shaped trunk, which narrowed upwards from her pelvis to her shoulders (Figure 4.1). From a distance, a mod-ern observer might have mistaken her for a kind of chimpanzee. The Turkana Boy was tall—about 1.62 meters (5'4") at time of death and

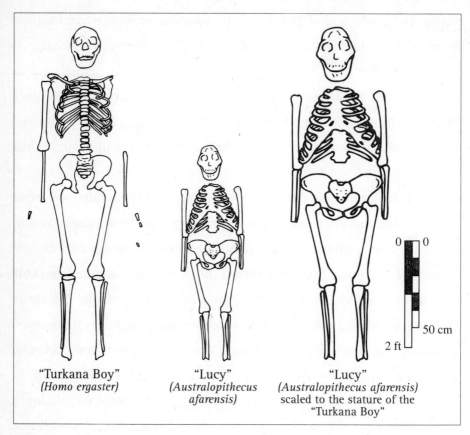

0

0

50 cm

2 ft

"Turkana Boy"
(Homo ergaster)

"Lucy"
*(Australopithecus
afarensis)*

"Lucy"
(Australopithecus afarensis)
scaled to the stature of the
"Turkana Boy"

FIGURE 4.1

Stature and body proportions in the "Turkana Boy" and in "Lucy" (redrawn after C. B. Ruff 1993, *Evolutionary Anthropology* 2, p. 55).

destined to reach 1.82 meters (6') or more if he had survived to adulthood. His arms were no longer, relative to his legs, than in living people, and he had a barrel-shaped chest over narrowed hips. From a distance our time-traveler might have confused him for one of the lanky Turkana herders who live around Nariokotome today.

Close up, our observer would soon realize his error, for the Turkana Boy had a skull and face that would startle any living human (Figure 4.2). His brain was nearly full grown, but its volume was a mere

880 cubic centimeters (cc), only 130 cc greater than the maximum in *Homo habilis* (including all of its possible constituents) and 450 to 500 cc below the average in living people. The size increase from *habilis* all but melts away when the Turkana Boy's larger body size is considered. His braincase—the part of the skull that enclosed his brain—was long and low, and the skull walls were exceptionally thick. It was the thickness of the forehead fragment that first alerted Kimeu to the kind of human he had found. The boy's forehead was flat and receding, and it descended to merge at an angle with a bony visor or browridge over his eyes. His nose was typically human in its forward projection and downwardly oriented nostrils, and in this he differed from the australopiths and *habilis* who had ape-like noses that were flush against the face. The nose aside, however, his face was striking for its great length from top to bottom, and his jaws projected far to

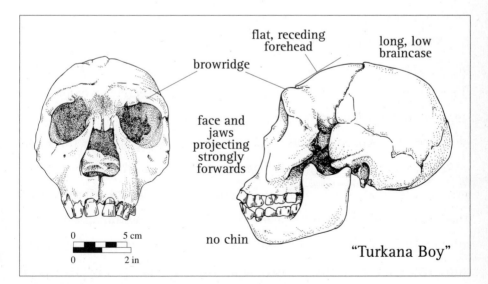

FIGURE 4.2
The skull of the "Turkana Boy" (drawn by Kathryn Cruz-Uribe from photographs and casts) (Copyright Kathryn Cruz-Uribe).

the front. His lower and upper jaws were massive, and they contained chewing teeth that were significantly larger than our own, even if they were smaller than the average in *habilis* or the australopiths. The bone below his lower front teeth slanted sharply backwards, meaning that he was completely chinless.

On reflection, contemplating a seemingly improbable combination of modern body and primitive head, our hypothetical observer might wonder if his companion was a visitor from an alternative universe or perhaps the product of some strange genetic experiment. In a sense, he was both, but the alternative universe was our own world long ago, and the experimenter was nature.

♛ ♛ ♛

The Turkana Boy's skeleton provided unique insight into the body structure of his people, but in the early and middle 1970s, teams from the Kenya National Museum had already recovered two skulls, nine partial lower jaws, a much less complete skeleton, and some isolated limb bones that all closely resembled his. The specimens came from deposits dated between 1.8 and 1.6 million years ago at Koobi Fora on the eastern shore of Lake Turkana, and from the time of their discovery, they were likened to east Asian fossils that are assigned to the primitive human species *Homo erectus*. The antiquity of the Asian specimens is disputed for reasons we discuss below, but most if not all are probably younger than a million years. If then, as many authorities believe, the Koobi Fora, Nariokotome, and east Asian specimens should be placed in the same species, *erectus* would have an African origin.

The similarities between the east African and Asian fossils are unquestionable, but some specialists have also pointed to subtle and potentially significant differences. Thus, on average, the African skulls tend to be somewhat higher-domed and thinner-walled than their east Asian counterparts, and they have less massive faces and browridges. In these respects and others, they are more primitive or less specialized, and they may tentatively be assigned to a separate species for which the name *Homo ergaster* has been proposed. The name translates roughly as "working man," and it was first applied to some of the Koobi Fora fossils that came from deposits that also contained flaked stone tools.

The removal of the east African fossils from *erectus* to *ergaster* would be trivial if we accepted the once common notion that *erectus* was directly ancestral to *Homo sapiens,* for *ergaster* would then be simply an early stage of *erectus.* Fossils that date from after 500,000 years ago, however, now indicate that *sapiens* evolved in Africa while *erectus* continued on largely unchanged in eastern Asia (Figure 4.3). In form and geologic age, *ergaster* is well positioned to be the ancestor not only of *erectus* but also of *sapiens,* and this is the view we adopt here.

The ancestry of *ergaster* is murky, but it may have originated suddenly from *habilis* (or from one of the variants into which *habilis* may eventually be split) in adaptive response to a sharp increase in aridity and rainfall seasonality that occurred across eastern Africa about 1.7 million years ago. Alternatively, at the end of the last chapter, we noted that future research may reveal a bush of human species between 3 million and 2 million years ago, in which case *ergaster* could represent a branch totally separate from the variants of *habilis.*

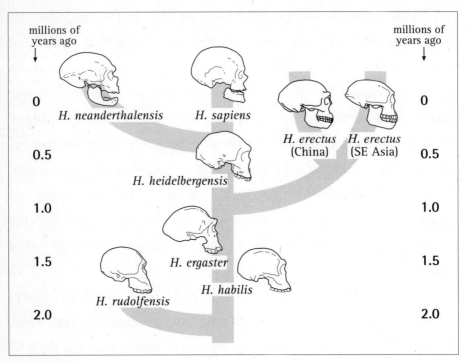

FIGURE 4.3
A tree diagram showing the suggested relationships between *Homo ergaster* and later human species.

At Olduvai Gorge, *habilis* or one of its variants may have persisted until 1.6 million years ago, but thereafter *ergaster* survived alone. Its history after 1 million years ago is debatable, because few relevant fossils are known, but on present evidence it may have persisted largely unchanged until about 600,000 years ago, when brain size increased rapidly and new, more advanced human species arose.

♛ ♛ ♛

Sometimes it seems as if controversies over species assignments and ancestor-descendant relationships dominate paleoanthropology, but in fact paleoanthropologists know that their first priority must be to understand how ancient people looked and behaved. Alan Walker and Richard Leakey, who co-directed the excavation of the Turkana Boy's skeleton with Meave Leakey, realized that it provided a unique opportunity to explore the biology of a primitive human species. They thus invited anatomist colleagues to study it with them, and the result was a comprehensive, stimulating monographic description that fleshes out our knowledge of *ergaster*.

On average, brain volume in *ergaster* was only about 900 cc, large enough to invent the new kinds of stone tools with which it is associated, but also small enough to explain why the tools then changed little over the next million years or so. Based mainly on dental development, the Turkana Boy was probably about 11 years old at time of death, but his stature compared more closely with that of a modern 15-year-old and his brain with that of a modern 1-year-old. The sum has led Walker to conclude that "While he may have been smart by ape standards, relative to [living] humans the Turkana Boy was tall, strong, and stupid." The same statement might apply equally well to everyone who lived between 1.8 million and 600,000 to 500,000 years ago, before a spurt in brain volume brought it much closer to the modern average.

Body form and size tell a different story, and in this regard *ergaster* was as human as anyone alive today. The shortening of its arms relative to its legs signals the final abandonment of any ape-like reliance on trees for feeding or refuge. A greater commitment to life on the ground meant an even greater emphasis on bipedalism, and this could explain the narrowing of the hips (pelvis) and the concomitant development of a barrel-like chest. The narrowed pelvis increased the efficiency of muscles that operate the legs during bipedal movement, and it would have forced the lower part of the rib cage to narrow correspondingly. To maintain chest volume and lung function, the upper part of the rib cage would have had to expand, and the modern barrel shape would follow. The narrowing of the pelvis also constricted the birth canal, and this must have forced a reduction in the proportion of brain growth that occurred before birth. Infant dependency must then have been prolonged, foreshadowing the uniquely long dependency period that marks living humans.

Pelvic narrowing must also have reduced the volume of the digestive tract, but this could have occurred only if food quality improved simultaneously. Direct archeological evidence for new foods is lacking or ambiguous, but the choices are larger quantities of meat and marrow, greater numbers of nutritious tubers, bulbs, and other underground storage organs, or both. Cooking might also be implied, since it would render both meat and tubers much more digestible, but so far, persuasive fireplaces or hearths are unknown before 250,000 years ago, by which time *ergaster* had been replaced by more advanced species.

Archeology shows that *ergaster* was the first human species to colonize hot, truly arid, highly seasonal environments in Africa, and this may partly explain why the Turkana Boy was built like a modern equatorial east African, with a lanky body and long limbs. As the trunk thins, body volume decreases more rapidly than skin area, and greater skin area promotes heat dissipation. Long limbs provide the same benefit. In people like the Inuit or Eskimo who must conserve heat, we see the reverse—stocky bodies and short limbs that reduce heat loss. Adaptation to hot, dry conditions can also explain why *ergaster* was the first human species to have a forwardly projecting, external nose.

In living humans, the external nose is usually cooler than the central body, and it thus tends to condense moisture that would otherwise be exhaled during periods of heightened activity. Finally, given that *ergaster* was shaped for a hot, dry climate, we can speculate that it was also the first human species to possess a nearly hairless, naked skin. If it had an ape-like covering of body hair it could not have sweated efficiently, and sweating is the primary means by which humans prevent their bodies—and their brains—from overheating.

When the Turkana Boy's skeleton is considered with isolated limb bones from other individuals, it becomes clear that *ergaster* was not only taller and heavier than earlier humans, but also that the sexes differed no more in size than they do in living people. This stands in sharp contrast to the australopiths and perhaps *habilis,* in which males were much larger than females. In ape species that exhibit a similar degree of sexual size difference, males compete intensely for sexually receptive females and male-female relationships tend to be transitory and non-cooperative. The reduced size difference in *ergaster* may signal the onset of a more typically human pattern in which male-male competition was reduced and male-female relationships were more lasting and mutually supportive.

♙ ♙ ♙

A small brain surely means that *ergaster* was less intelligent than living people, and if brain size were all we had to go by, we might wonder if it differed cognitively from *habilis (or habilis/rudolfensis).* But we also have artifacts, and these show that it did. The tools also help us to understand how *ergaster* was able to colonize the more arid, seasonal environments to which it was physiologically adapted and also how it became the first human species to expand out of Africa.

The first tool makers, the Oldowan people, mastered the mechanics of stone flaking, and they were very good at producing sharp-edged flakes that could slice through hides or strip flesh from bone. At the same time, they made little or no effort to shape the core forms from which they struck flakes, and to the extent that they used core forms, it was perhaps mainly to crack bones for marrow. For this purpose, core shape didn't matter very much. *Ergaster,* however, initiated a tradition in which core forms were often deliberately, even meticulously, shaped, and shape obviously mattered a lot.

The characteristic artifact of the new tradition was the hand axe or biface—a flat cobble or large flake that was more or less completely flaked over both surfaces (hence the term biface) to produce a sharp edge around the entire periphery (Figure 4.4). Many hand axes resemble large teardrops, as they narrow from a broad base or butt at one end to a rounded point at the other. Ovals, triangles, and other forms are also common, and in some places, hand axe makers produced pieces with a straight, sharp, guillotine-like edge opposite the blunt butt (Figure 4.5). Archeologists often call such pieces cleavers to distinguish them from hand axes, on which one end tends to be more pointed.

John Frere, the great-great-grandfather of Mary Leakey, is sometimes credited as the first person to recognize the human origin and great antiquity of hand axes. In 1797, he sent a letter to the Society of Antiquaries in London describing two carefully crafted hand axes he had recovered from ancient lake deposits at Hoxne in Suffolk, England. Bones of extinct animals occurred nearby, and Frere concluded that the hand axes had been "used by a people who had not the use of metals"

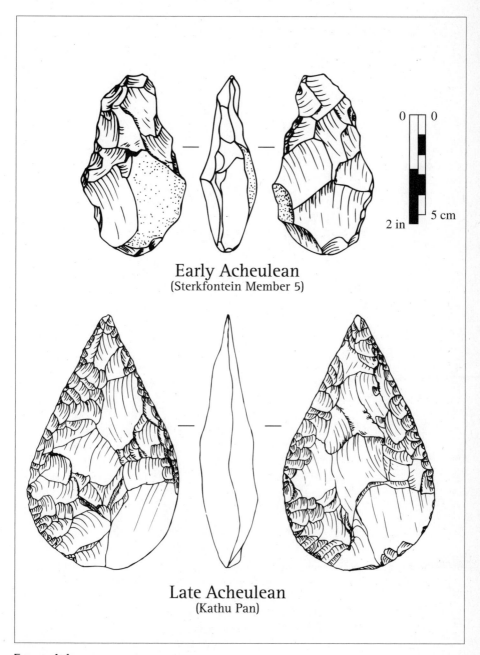

Early Acheulean
(Sterkfontein Member 5)

Late Acheulean
(Kathu Pan)

FIGURE 4.4
An early Acheulean hand axe from Sterkfontein Cave and a late Acheulean hand axe from Kathu Pan (top redrawn after K. Kuman 1994, *Journal of Human Evolution* 27, fig. 6; bottom drawn by Kathryn Cruz-Uribe from the original).

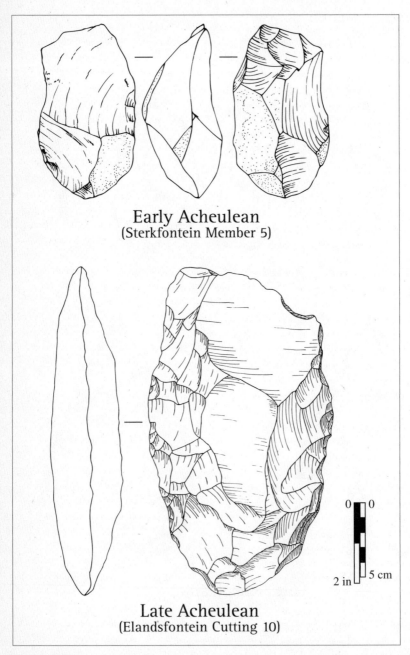

Early Acheulean
(Sterkfontein Member 5)

Late Acheulean
(Elandsfontein Cutting 10)

FIGURE 4.5
An early Acheulean cleaver from Sterkfontein Cave and a late Acheulean cleaver from Elandsfontein Cutting 10 (top redrawn after K. Kuman 1994, *Journal of Human Evolution* 27, fig. 6; bottom drawn by T. P. Volman from the original).

and belonged "to a very ancient period indeed, even beyond the present world." Frere's archeological colleagues largely ignored his opinion, and it was the French customs official Boucher de Perthes who
first forced the issue. Between about 1836 and 1846, de Perthes collected hand axes and bones of extinct mammals from ancient gravels
of the Somme River near the town of Abbeville in northern France. He
concluded that "In spite of their imperfection, these rude stones prove
the [ancient] existence of man as surely as a whole Louvre would have
done." His claims were initially spurned, but they gained credibility in
1854 when Dr. Rigollot, a distinguished and previously vocal skeptic,
began finding similar flint axes in gravels near St. Acheul, a suburb of
Amiens. In 1858, the eminent British geologist Joseph Prestwich visited Abbeville and St. Acheul to check the claims for himself. He came
away convinced, and the case was made. Archeologists subsequently
assigned ancient tool assemblages with hand axes to the Acheulean
Culture or Industry, named for the prolific locality at St. Acheul. Later,
when similar artifacts were recognized in Africa, they were also
assigned to the Acheulean, and we now know that the Acheulean was
present in Africa long before it reached Europe.

The oldest known Acheulean tools are dated to 1.65 million years
ago, and they come from the same west Turkana region of northern
Kenya that provided the Turkana Boy, though not from the same site.
Acheulean artifacts are also well documented at 1.5 to 1.4 million years
ago at Konso in southern Ethiopia, on the Karari Escarpment east of Lake
Turkana in northern Kenya, and at Peninj near Olduvai Gorge in northern Tanzania. In each case, potassium/argon dating has verified their
antiquity just as securely as it demonstrates the presence of *ergaster* by
1.8 to 1.7 million years ago, and the close correspondence between the

oldest *ergaster* and the oldest Acheulean is probably not coincidental. Peninj has provided a lower jaw of the robust australopith, *Paranthropus boisei*, but this shows only that *boisei* persisted after *ergaster* emerged, not that *boisei* made Acheulean tools. Konso has provided an upper third molar and the left half of a lower jaw with four teeth from *ergaster*, and *ergaster* is the more likely tool maker. This is not only because it had a larger brain than *boisei*, but because Acheulean tools continue on largely unchanged after one million years ago, when *boisei* had become extinct.

The Acheulean surely originated from the Oldowan, and the oldest Acheulean assemblages often contain numerous Oldowan-style core forms and flakes alongside Acheulean hand axes. In a broad sense, the Oldowan core forms anticipate Acheulean bifaces, but no Oldowan or Acheulean assemblage contains tools that are truly intermediate between the two, and the biface concept seems to have appeared very suddenly in a kind of punctuational event like the one that may have produced *ergaster*. The earliest biface makers made one other note-worthy discovery that was often tied to biface manufacture—they learned how to strike large flakes, sometimes a foot or more in length, from large boulders, and it was from these that they often made hand axes and cleavers. Ancient stone tool assemblages that contain large flakes can be assigned to the Acheulean even on those occasions when, perhaps by chance, the assemblages lack hand axes.

♔ ♔ ♔

The term hand axe implies that each piece was hand-held and used for chopping. Nonetheless, many hand axes are far too large and unwieldy for this, and their precise use remains conjectural. The puzzle is heightened at sites like Melka Kunturé in Ethiopia, Olorgesailie in Kenya, Isimila in Tanzania, and Kalambo Falls in Zambia, where hand axes occur by the hundreds, often crowded close together and with no obvious signs of use. Such sites have prompted archeologists Marek Kohn and Steven Mithen to propose that the hand axe may have been the Acheulean equivalent of a male peacock's plumage—an impressive emblem for attracting mates. When a female saw a large, well-made biface in the hands of its maker, she might have concluded that he possessed just the determination, coordination, and strength needed to father successful offspring. Having obtained a mate, a male might simply discard the badge of his success, alongside others that had already served their purpose.

The mate selection hypothesis cannot be falsified, but sites with large concentrations of seemingly unused hand axes are less common than ones where hand axes are rarer and sometimes do show signs of use. Since the tools come in a wide variety of sizes and shapes, the probability is that they served multiple utilitarian functions. Some of the more carefully shaped, symmetric examples may have been hurled at game like a discus; other more casually made pieces may have served simply as portable sources of sharp-edged flakes; and yet others could have been used to chop or scrape wood. Experiments have also shown that hand axes make effective butchering tools, particularly for dismembering the carcasses of elephants or other large animals. The truth is that hand axes may have been used for every imaginable purpose, and the type probably had more in common with a Swiss Army knife than with a peacock's tail.

Once in place, the Acheulean Industry was remarkably conservative, and it is often said that it persisted largely unchanged from its inception at roughly 1.65 million years ago until its end at about 250,000 years ago. Harvard archeologist Glynn Isaac, who analyzed the Acheulean artifacts from a deeply stratified sequence at Olorgesailie, Kenya, remarked that the Acheulean displays a "variable sameness" and strikes "even enthusiasts as monotonous." By "variable sameness" he meant that changes in hand axe form from layer to layer or time to time seem to have been largely random and there is no obvious directional trend. Often, where hand axes in one assemblage appear more refined than they do in another, the reason may be that the people had different raw materials at their disposal. Flint or chert, for example, is usually much easier to flake than lava, and where people could get large enough pieces of flint, their hand axes will tend to appear more finely made for this reason alone.

Still, despite the apparent sameness over long periods, early and late Acheulean artifact assemblages do differ in some important respects. Early Acheulean hand axes tend to be much thicker, less extensively trimmed, and less symmetrical (Fig. 4.4). They were commonly shaped by fewer than 10 flake removals, and the flake scars were usually deep. Modern experiments indicate that such scars result from the use of "hard" (meaning stone) hammers. Later Acheulean hand axes are sometimes equally crude, but many are remarkably thin and extensively trimmed, and they are highly symmetric not just in plan form but also when viewed edge on. The final flake scars are shallow and flat, and replication efforts indicate that they were probably produced with "soft" (wooden or bone) hammers.

In addition, later Acheulean hand axes are often accompanied by more refined flake tools that anticipate those of the (Mousterian and Middle Stone Age) people who succeeded the Acheuleans. Like their

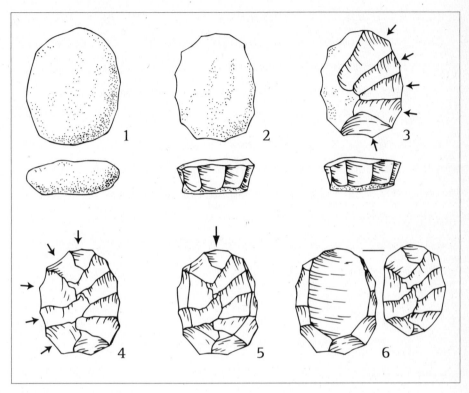

FIGURE 4.6
Stages in the manufacture of a classic Levallois flake whose size and shape have been predetermined on the core (redrawn after F. H. Bordes 1961, *Science* 134, fig. 4).

successors, later Acheuleans also knew how to prepare a core so that it would provide a flake of predetermined size and shape (Figure 4.6). Archeologists call such deliberate core preparation the Levallois technique, named for a western suburb of Paris where prepared cores were found and recognized in the latter part of the nineteenth century. The term Levallois refers strictly to a method of stone flaking, not a culture or tradition, and Levallois flaking was practiced by people of various cultures or traditions, including especially the late Acheuleans and their immediate successors. At any given time, people in some places employed the technique frequently, while people in others hardly used it at all. Most of the variation probably reflects differences in the availability of suitable stone raw material.

Most Acheulean assemblages are only weakly dated within the long Acheulean timespan, but future research may show that there were actually two periods of Acheulean stability, representing the early and late Acheulean respectively. They may have been separated by a short burst of relatively rapid artifactual change roughly 600,000 years ago that resulted in the more refined hand axes of the late Acheulean and that may have coincided with a relatively abrupt increase in human brain size.

♛ ♛ ♛

We have already noted that *Homo ergaster* was the first human species to expand from Africa, but the timing of its dispersal is controversial. To understand why, we must back up a little and address the discovery and dating of its east Asian descendant, *Homo erectus*. The story begins with the Dutch physician and visionary Eugène Dubois.

Dubois was born in 1858, a year before Darwin published his signal classic *On the Origin of Species,* in which he showed how natural selection could drive evolutionary change. Dubois developed a passion for human evolution, and he became the first professional paleoanthropologist when he decided to search full time for human fossils. He focused on Indonesia, which was then a Dutch colony and which he and others reasoned was a logical place to start, since it still contained apes that might broadly resemble protohumans. He obtained a medical appointment in the Dutch East India Army, and he arrived in

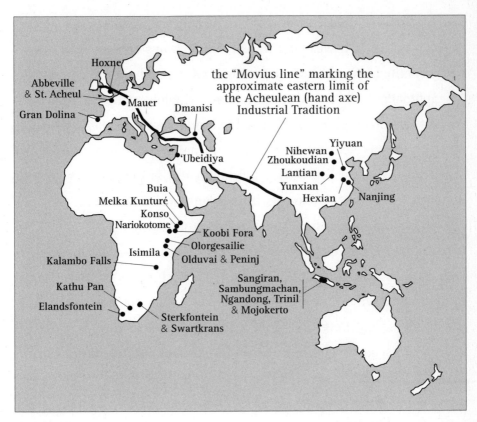

FIGURE 4.7
Locations of the sites mentioned in this chapter.

Indonesia in December 1887. He started his quest immediately, and in October 1891, he hit pay dirt in river deposits near the village of Trinil on the Solo River in central Java (Figure 4.7). Here, together with bones of ancient animals, he found a low-domed, angular, thick-walled human skullcap with a large shelf-like browridge. In August 1892, in what he thought were the same deposits, he recovered a nearly complete human thigh bone that was fully modern in every anatomical respect. The thigh bone and the skullcap convinced him that he had discovered an erect, ape-like transitional form between apes and people, and in 1894, he decided to call it *Pithecanthropus erectus* ("erect ape man"). It was later transferred to *Homo erectus* by scientists who benefited from a much fuller fossil record and a more contemplative approach to the use of species names. The implication of the transfer was that *erectus* did not differ from living people (*Homo sapiens*) as much as Dubois believed. The change in naming is partly a matter of taste, however, and the truly important point is that *erectus* was far removed from its ape ancestors in both anatomy and time.

Dubois's claim for *Pithecanthropus* met broadly the same kind of resistance that Dart's claim for *Australopithecus* did thirty years later. Dubois was discouraged, and after his return to the Netherlands in 1895, he gave up the search for human fossils. He was fully vindicated beginning only in 1936, when G. H. R. von Koenigswald described a second skull of *Pithecanthropus* from Mojokerto in eastern Java. The Mojokerto specimen represented a child between the ages of 4 and 6, but it still exhibited incipient browridges, a flat, receding forehead, an angular (as opposed to rounded) rear profile, and other features that recalled Dubois's Trinil find. Then, between 1937 and 1941, von Koenigswald reported three additional partial adult skulls, some fragmentary lower jaws, and isolated teeth from Sangiran, about 50 kilometers (30 miles) up the Solo River from Trinil in central Java (Figure 4.8). Associated animal bones suggested that two of the Sangiran skulls were about the same age as the Trinil skull and that the third was somewhat older.

Between 1952 and 1977, the deposits at Sangiran produced three additional skulls, some skull fragments, and six partial lower jaws, and there have been sporadic discoveries since. The most recent is a skullcap that turned up in 1999 in a New York City shop that

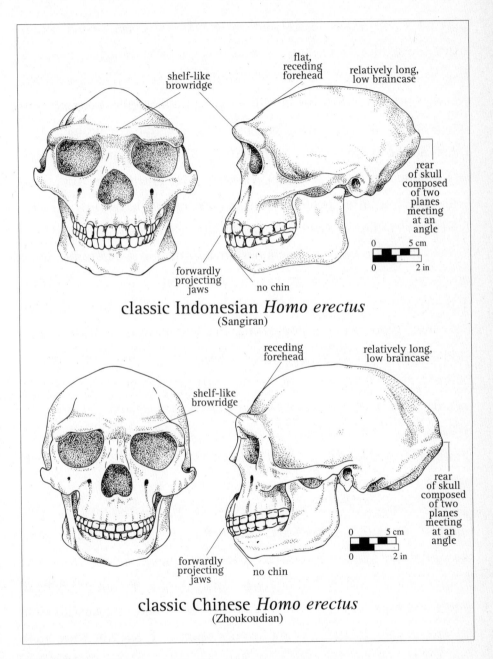

shelf-like
browridge

flat,
receding
forehead

relatively long,
low braincase

rear
of skull
composed
of two
planes
meeting
at an
angle

0   5 cm

0   2 in

forwardly
projecting
jaws

no chin

classic Indonesian *Homo erectus*
(Sangiran)

receding
forehead

relatively long,
low braincase

shelf-like
browridge

rear
of skull
composed
of two
planes
meeting
at an
angle

0   5 cm

0   2 in

forwardly
projecting
jaws

no chin

classic Chinese *Homo erectus*
(Zhoukoudian)

Figure 4.8
Franz Weidenreich's reconstructions of classic Indonesian and Chinese *Homo erectus* skulls
(redrawn by Kathryn Cruz-Uribe partly after originals by Janis Cirulis in W. W. Howells 1967,
Mankind in the Making. New York: Doubleday, pp. 156, 169).

purchases and resells fossils and ancient artifacts. The owner recognized the skullcap for what it was, and he made it available to scientists at the American Museum of Natural History. It was subsequently returned to Indonesia for curation. Still, in the most extreme way imaginable, the New York City discovery illustrates a problem that besets all the Javan fossils, beginning with Dubois's original find—their stratigraphic context was not carefully documented in the field. Sometimes, even the precise find spots are uncertain, because the discoverers were farmers who sold the fossils to scientists.

Java is a land of volcanoes, and in theory, it offers the same potential to date fossils as eastern Africa, since the fossil-bearing deposits often contain volcanic rock fragments or ash layers that are amenable to potassium/argon dating. In some places, the deposits also contain tektites—glassy rocks of meteoritic origin that were molten before they hit Earth and that can be dated in the same way as lava or ash. The dates on various Javan materials range from 2 million to 470,000 years ago, but their meaning is difficult to assess, since the stratigraphic relationship of the materials to the fossils and to each other is largely unknown.

Garniss Curtis, director of the Berkeley Geochronology Center, and his colleague, Carl Swisher, now at Rutgers University, have produced the most credible and most widely publicized dates. Curtis was instrumental in the revolutionary potassium/argon dating of Olduvai Gorge and other east African sites in the 1960s, and he made his first attempt in Java in 1974. He collected a sample of volcanic rock from the vicinity of the Mojokerto site that produced the child's skull in 1936, and he obtained an age of 1.9 million years ago. However, few authorities took this date seriously, mainly because the stratigraphic relationship between the dated sample and the skull was unclear.

In 1992–93, Curtis returned to Java with Swisher for another try. They collected fresh volcanic samples from Mojokerto, and they also examined the Mojokerto skull. They found that volcanic material was still stuck to its base, and Swisher borrowed Curtis' pocket knife to pry some away. The small sample from the skull proved to be too poor in radioactive potassium to provide a reliable age, but in chemical and mineralogical composition it closely matched larger samples collected in the field. When Swisher analyzed the larger samples, he got an age of 1.81 million years, only slightly younger than Curtis's original result.

While Swisher was in Java, he also collected volcanic samples from near Sangiran, which has now provided more than thirty *erectus* fossils, and he obtained an age of 1.65 million years. If the Mojokerto and Sangiran dates are taken at face value, they imply that *Homo erectus* reached Java about the same time that *Homo ergaster* emerged in eastern Africa. In this event, we would either have to abandon the species distinction between *ergaster* and *erectus* or we would have to argue that they shared an even older and as yet unidentified common ancestor. This ancestor could even have lived in eastern Asia rather than eastern Africa.

So why not accept the dates and revise our understanding of human evolution? Mainly because we lack fundamental stratigraphic observations at either Mojokerto or Sangiran. The Mojokerto date is clearly the more persuasive one, because it is based on volcanic material like that still attached to the skull, but experience in eastern Africa shows that older volcanic particles can be introduced by stream action into much younger deposits, and thorough fieldwork is necessary to detect the possibility of such redeposition. To assess the relevance of both the Mojokerto and Sangiran dates, we would need to know, for example, whether volcanic samples from stratigraphically superimposed horizons provide stratigraphically consistent dates, that is, whether deeper layers provide consistently older dates. If not, redeposition is strongly suggested, and the date on any given layer may overestimate the time of its formation, perhaps by a substantial interval.

The 1.81- to 1.65-million-year ages for Mojokerto and Sangiran *erectus* cannot be simply dismissed, but they contradict other age estimates for the same deposits based on animal fossils, paleomagnetism, and fission-track dating. The fission-track method is a cousin of potassium/argon dating that depends on the radioactive decay of naturally occurring uranium within ancient volcanic rocks or tektites, and like the potassium/argon method it estimates the last time the rocks were heated to a very high temperature. If the Javan fission-track dates are correct, the Mojokerto and Sangiran *erectus* fossils are unlikely to be older than 1 million years. Fossils of *erectus* are also known from China, and so far, the oldest reliable Chinese sites are dated to only about 1 million years or slightly before. For the moment then, there is no persuasive reason to doubt the postulated descent of *erectus* from *ergaster*.

♛ ♛ ♛

East Asian *Homo erectus* shows that a human species had left Africa by 1 million years ago, and we believe that this species was *Homo ergaster*. But aside from the issue of the kind of people involved, we may also ask why they left and what route(s) they took. Unlike many other questions in paleoanthropology, these are relatively easy to answer. Archeology shows that about 1.5 million years ago, shortly after *ergaster* emerged in Africa, people more intensively occupied the drier peripheries of lake basins on the floor of the Great Rift Valley, and they colonized the Ethiopian high plateau (at 2300 to 2400 meters or 7600 to 7700 feet above sea level) for the first time. By 1 million years ago, they had extended their range to the far northern and southern margins of Africa. The Sahara Desert might seem to provide an impenetrable barrier to movement northward, but during the long Acheulean time interval, there were numerous periods when it was somewhat moister and more hospitable, and Acheulean people penetrated it readily.

As to how and why people expanded through Africa and beyond, they almost certainly did so automatically, simply because their physiology and technology allowed them to inhabit territories that no one had occupied before. A group on the periphery of the human range would periodically outgrow its resource base, and a splinter party would break off and set up shop in empty territory next door. Such a party probably rarely moved far, but given time, the splintering process would inevitably have brought people to the northeastern corner of Africa. From there, members of a breakaway group would have colonized the southwestern corner of Asia without even knowing they had left Africa. From southwestern Asia, the same process of population budding would inevitably lead other groups eastwards towards China and Indonesia or northwards and westwards towards Europe.

In theory, early African emigrants could also have dispersed across the Strait of Gibraltar, the Bab-el-Mandeb Strait at the southern end of the Red Sea, or even by island hopping across the central part of the Mediterranean Sea. Each of these routes would require seaworthy boats, however, even during those repeated intervals when the great continental ice sheets sucked water from the world ocean and sea level dropped by 140 meters (460 feet) or more. There is no unequivocal evidence for such boats until after 60,000 years ago, when modern humans must have used them to cross the sea from southeastern Asia to Australia.

The first people to leave Africa crossed the border between what is now Egypt and Israel. It is not surprising therefore that Israel contains the oldest firmly documented archeological site outside of Africa. This occurs at 'Ubeidiya in the Jordan Rift Valley, where ancient lake and river deposits have provided nearly eight thousand flaked stones. The tools include hand axes and other pieces that closely resemble early Acheulean artifacts from Olduvai Gorge and other African sites. They have been bracketed in the interval between 1.4 and 1 million years ago by associated mammal fossils, paleomagnetism, and potassium/argon dating of an overlying lava flow.

Most of the mammal species at 'Ubeidiya are Eurasian, but some are African, and this reminds us of just how close Israel is to Africa. During the long time span of human evolution, Israel was repeatedly invaded by African animal species, mainly during the warmer periods between the longer times of great ice sheet expansion. (During the last such warm period, between about 125,000 and 90,000 years ago, the African immigrants included early modern or near-modern humans.) This raises the possibility that 'Ubeidiya marks a slight, transient ecological enlargement of Africa more than a true human dispersal to Eurasia. If we want to demonstrate a genuine dispersal, we have to look further afield.

Eastern Asia with its *Homo erectus* fossils shows that such a dispersal must have occurred by 1 million years ago. Europe may have been occupied equally early, but the oldest widely accepted evidence for human colonization is only about 800,000 years old. The evidence comes from the Gran Dolina, a cave at Atapuerca, near Burgos, Spain, that we discuss in the next chapter. Elsewhere in Europe, there is little or no indication that people were present before about 500,000 years ago, and it was perhaps only then that people gained a permanent foothold. Europeans at 500,000 to 400,000 years ago looked a lot like their African contemporaries, and they made similar Acheulean artifacts. They may thus signal a fresh wave of African immigrants.

Considering only east Asian and European fossils and artifacts, we might conclude that people expanded from Africa (beyond Israel) only about a million years ago or a little before. A spectacular discovery at the site of Dmanisi, Republic of Georgia, has recently shown that that conclusion may be premature. Dmanisi is a ruined medieval fortress that Georgian historical archeologists have excavated for many years. In 1984, they broke through the foundation of a medieval structure into an ancient river deposit with animal bones and flaked stone artifacts. Follow-up excavations have produced more than one thousand artifacts and two thousand bones, and the bones include two partial human skulls (Figure 4.9), two lower jaws, and a bone from the sole of the foot. The skulls closely resemble those of *Homo ergaster* from eastern Africa, but Dmanisi is 1500 kilometers (900 miles) north of 'Ubeidiya, between the Greater and Lesser Caucasus Mountain chains (Figure 4.7). There is thus no question that it marks an early Out-of-Africa dispersal, although there is a question about how early.

Potassium/argon analysis shows that a volcanic basalt at the base of the Dmanisi deposits formed about 1.85 million years ago, If this date is correct, the basalt formed during the Olduvai Normal Paleomagnetic Subchron between 1.95 and 1.77 million years ago (Figure 3.3 on p. 68), and the basalt itself should exhibit normal

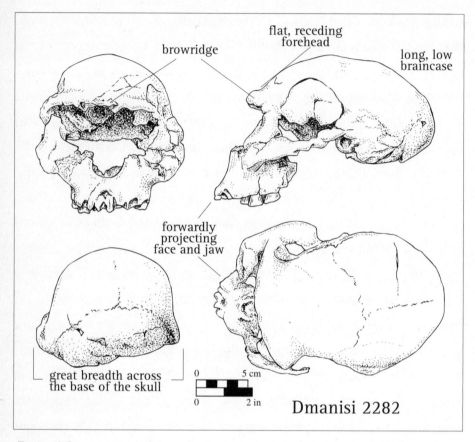

FIGURE 4.9
Skull No. 2282 from Dmanisi, Georgia (drawn by Kathryn Cruz-Uribe from photographs).
(Copyright Kathryn Cruz-Uribe.)

polarity. It does, and so do the overlying river deposits, which contain the fossils and artifacts. Since the surface of the basalt is fresh, the river deposits probably covered it shortly after it cooled, and they probably also date to the Olduvai Subchron, before 1.77 million years ago. With this in mind, the Dmanisi *ergaster* fossils could be as old as any in Africa. There is a catch, however. The human fossils and those of other animals occur in large hollows eroded within the normally magnetized river deposits, and the hollows are filled with deposits that exhibit reversed magnetism. The fossils must then be younger than 1.77 million years, and based on paleomagnetism alone, they could date from anytime between 1.77 million and 780,000 years ago, the last time when Earth's magnetic field was reversed. The Dmanisi mammals are said to imply an age closer to 1.77 million years ago, but they represent a unique mix of species, some of which would be the youngest known records of their occurrence, while others would be the oldest. Continued fieldwork may show that two separate species assemblages have been inadvertently mixed, and if so, additional work will be necessary to show which assemblage includes *Homo ergaster.*

The Dmanisi artifacts include only flakes and flaked pebbles. There are no hand axes, and this could mean that the site formed before Africans invented hand axes roughly 1.7 to 1.6 million years ago. However, even long after this time, not all sites in Africa and Europe contain hand axes, and the reason is obscure. The 800,000-year-old layers at the Gran Dolina, Spain, are an example, and others occur after 500,000 years ago in the same parts of southern and western Europe that hand axe makers had widely settled. In short, the absence of hand axes at Dmanisi need not mean that the people were pre-Acheuleans, and the Dmanisi artifacts require more detailed description to determine whether they differed from Acheulean artifacts in other respects. There is the further problem that different publications on Dmanisi present inconsistent descriptions of the stratigraphic relationship between the artifacts and fossils.

The antiquity of human presence at Dmanisi thus remains an open question. If future research demonstrates that the human bones and artifacts date to 1.77 million years ago, *Homo ergaster* must have left

Africa almost as soon as it appeared, and we will be forced to speculate on how people could expand so far northwards and not manage to reach Europe for perhaps another million years. If the age of Dmanisi is closer to 1 million years, the gap before the initial occupation of Europe would be much smaller, and the Dmanisi skulls would imply that *ergaster* remained essentially unchanged for hundreds of thousands of years.

Excepting the Dmanisi skulls, there are only two others between 1.5 million and 600,000 years old that bear on the question of evolutionary change within *ergaster*. These are a partial skull from Olduvai Gorge which is thought to be roughly 1.2 million years old, and a nearly complete skull from Buia, near the Red Sea coast in Eritrea, eastern Africa, which is about 1 million years old. The Olduvai skullcap is like those of *erectus* in its massive browridge and thick walls, but in other, more detailed characteristics it is *ergaster*-like. The Buia skull differs from earlier *ergaster* skulls only in its somewhat thicker browridge, and it presents a clearer case for long-term anatomical continuity.

♛ ♛ ♛

By 600,000 to 500,000 years ago, people with larger, more modern-looking braincases had appeared in Africa, and for the moment, based in part on our reading of the artifactual record, we hypothesize that these people evolved abruptly from *ergaster*. They closely resembled Europeans of 500,000 to 400,000 years ago, and the Africans and Europeans together have sometimes been assigned to the species *Homo heidelbergensis*, named for a lower jaw found in 1907 in a sand quarry at Mauer near Heidelberg, Germany. It may have been *heidelbergensis* expanding from Africa about 500,000 years ago that brought the Acheulean tradition to Europe.

In the next chapter, we suggest that *Homo heidelbergensis* represents the last shared ancestor of the Neanderthals, who evolved in Europe after 500,000 years ago, and of modern humans, who evolved in Africa over the same interval (Figure 4.3). And in future chapters we stress fossil and archeological evidence that modern humans expanded from Africa after 50,000 years ago to swamp or replace the Neanderthals in Europe. But what then of *Homo erectus,* who was firmly established in eastern Asia long before the Neanderthal and modern human lines diverged? The issue is difficult to address, because relevant east Asian fossils and artifacts are sparser than European ones, and they are more poorly dated. Still, the available fossil and archeological evidence indicates that *erectus* continued on its own divergent evolutionary trajectory after 500,000 years ago, when Neanderthals and modern humans had separated in the west. This suggests that it eventually suffered the same fate as the Neanderthals.

The most telling late *erectus* fossils come from the site of Ngandong on the Solo River near Trinil in central Java. Here, between 1931 and 1933, excavations in ancient river deposits by the Dutch Geological Survey in Java recovered more than 25,000 fossil bones, including twelve partially complete human skulls and two incomplete human shin bones. Between 1976 and 1980, researchers from Gadjah Mada University in Yogyakarta expanded the excavations at Ngandong and unearthed 1200 additional bones, including two incomplete human skulls and some human pelvis fragments. Previously, in 1973, the same research team had recovered a similar skull and a human shin bone from like-aged river deposits near Sambungmacan, between Trinil and Sangiran. The Ngandong and Sambungmacan skulls are somewhat larger than those of classic Indonesian *erectus*, but they exhibit the same basic characteristics, including a massive, shelf-like browridge, a flat, receding forehead, thick skull bone, a tendency for the skull walls to slope inwards from a broad base, and substantial angularity at the rear (Figure 4.10). Based on these features, the Ngandong and Sambungmacan people are commonly assigned to an evolved variant of *erectus*.

Associated mammal species indicate that the Ngandong and Sambungmacan human fossils are less than 300,000 years old, and they may be much younger. In 1996, the same Berkeley Geochronology Laboratory that provided the 1.81- to 1.65-million-year ages for *erectus* at Mojokerto and Sangiran, announced that fossil water buffalo teeth associated with the Ngandong and Sambungmacan skulls were between 53,000 and 27,000 years old. This estimate was based on the Electron Spin Resonance method, commonly abbreviated as ESR. ESR depends on the observation that flaws in the crystalline structure of dental enamel accumulate electrons in direct proportion to radioactivity in the burial environment. The principal sources of radioactivity are tiny but nearly ubiquitous amounts of naturally occurring uranium, thorium, and radioactive potassium. ESR is essentially a laboratory technique for measuring the number of trapped electrons. The yearly rate of irradiation, or "annual radiation dose," can be measured in the field, and if we assume that it has remained constant through time, the number of trapped electrons directly reflects the number of years since burial.

In practice, ESR faces many hurdles, of which the most serious is the possibility that teeth at any given site have experienced a

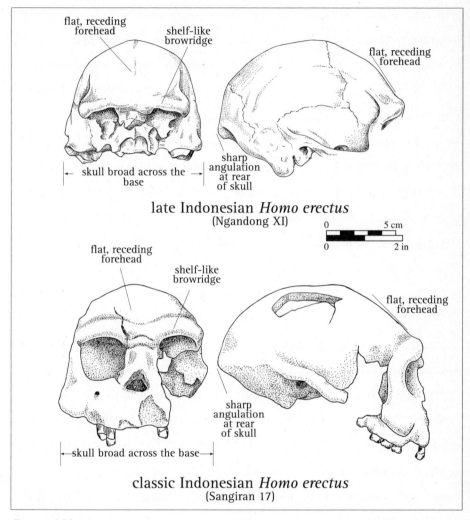

FIGURE 4.10
Skulls of late and classic *Homo erectus* from Indonesia (top redrawn by Kathryn Cruz-Uribe mainly after originals by Janis Cirulis in W. W. Howells 1967, *Mankind in the Making.* New York: Doubleday, pp. 160; bottom redrawn by Kathryn Cruz-Uribe from photographs).

complex history of uranium exchange with the burial environment. Exchange almost always involves uranium uptake from ground water, but it may also involve loss, and the precise pattern of uptake and loss will manifestly affect the annual radiation dose to which a tooth has been subjected. The possibility that this dose changed significantly through time often leaves ESR results open to question, and the dates from Ngandong and Sambungmacan are no exception. If they are valid, they provide strong circumstantial support for the survival of southeast Asian *erectus* until it was swamped or replaced by modern human invaders after 60,000 years ago. But even if the Ngandong and Sambungmacan skulls are actually closer to 300,000 years old, they still show that southeast Asian populations were on a different evolutionary track than their European and African contemporaries.

♕ ♕ ♕

There is an equally important set of *Homo erectus* fossils from China, and they tell basically the same story. The discovery of *erectus* in China stems from the age-old Chinese custom of pulverizing fossils for medicinal use. In 1899, a European doctor found a probable human tooth among fossils in a Beijing (then Peking) drugstore, and the search for its origin led paleontologists to a rich complex of fossil-bearing limestone caves and fissures on the slope of Longghu-shan ("Dragon Bone Hill"), about 40 kilometers (24 miles) southwest of Beijing, near the village of Zhoukoudian. In 1921, the Swedish geologist J. G. Andersson began excavating in a collapsed cave at Zhoukoudian that was particularly intriguing not only for its fossils, but also for quartz fragments that prehistoric people must have introduced. The site was called Locality 1 to distinguish it from other fossil-bearing caves nearby.

Andersson's excavations produced two human teeth which came to the attention of Davidson Black, a Canadian anatomist who was teaching at the Peking Union Medical School. Black secured a grant from the Rockefeller Foundation, and in 1927, excavation began again at Locality 1. Black died in 1933, and in 1935, he was succeeded by Franz Weidenreich, an eminent German anatomist who had been teaching at the University of Chicago. Excavations continued until 1937, and they eventually produced five more or less complete human braincases, nine large braincase fragments, six facial fragments, fourteen partial lower jaws, 147 isolated teeth, and eleven limb bones. The specimens represented more than forty individuals of both sexes and various ages.

Black assigned the Locality 1 fossils to a new species, *Sinanthropus pekinensis* ("Peking Chinese Man"). Later, in 1939, Weidenreich and G. H. R. von Koenigswald compared the *Sinanthropus* fossils to those of Javan *Pithecanthropus,* and they concluded that the skulls were very similar in their shelf-like browridges, receding foreheads, low-domed braincases, thick, inwardly sloping skull walls, and other features (Figure 4.8). For the sake of convenience, Weidenreich continued to call them *Sinanthropus pekinensis* and *Pithecanthropus erectus,* but he noted that they could be regarded as variants of a single primitive human species, *Homo erectus.* This anticipated a professional consensus that crystallized in the 1960s and that continues to the present day.

The Locality 1 fossils were lost at the beginning of World War II, but Weidenreich had described them in detailed monographs and he had prepared an excellent set of plaster replicas, now housed at the American Museum of Natural History. Excavations at Locality 1 produced a few additional fragmentary *erectus* fossils between 1949 and 1966, but following the original Locality 1 excavations, the most diagnostic *erectus* fossils have come from other sites scattered across east-central China (Figure 4.7). The specimens include a lower jaw from Chenjiawo and a skull from Gongwangling, both in Lantian County; a partial skull and a fragmentary mandible from Lontandong Cave in Hexian County; a fragmentary skullcap from a fissure deposit on Qizianshan Hill in Yiyuan County, two badly crushed, partial skulls from a river deposits at Quyuankekou in Yunxian County, and two skulls unearthed in a cave near Tangshan in Nanjing County. Chinese anthropologists often use county names rather than site names when they refer to the fossils.

The Chinese *erectus* fossils have been dated to between 800,000 and 400,000 years ago, mainly by paleomagnetism, by associated mammal species, and by the climatic shifts recorded in the surrounding deposits. "Climate dating" depends on the assumption that local shifts can be accurately correlated with the dated sequence of global shifts recorded on the deep sea floor. The sum of the evidence suggests that the oldest Chinese *erectus* fossil is probably the Gongwangling (Lantian) skull, dated to about 800,000 to 750,000 years ago. The youngest fossils come from Zhoukoudian Locality 1 and Hexian, where at least some specimens accumulated after 500,000 years ago. The dating provides nothing to suggest that *erectus* arrived in eastern Asia long before 1 million years ago, and it indicates that it persisted after other kinds of people had emerged on the west. The Chinese *erectus* fossils differ from the Indonesian ones in some details, and the differences appear to grow with time. This may mean that the Chinese and Indonesian specimens represent two divergent Far Eastern evolutionary lineages, but the basic point remains the same—*erectus* or its variants followed a separate evolutionary trajectory from like-aged populations in Africa and Europe.

♕ ♕ ♕

China adds a dimension to the *erectus* story that Java lacks, for unlike Java, China has provided numerous stone artifacts that local *erectus* populations produced. At most sites, the artifacts are attributed to *erectus* based on similar geologic antiquity, but artifacts are directly associated with *erectus* fossils at the Lantian sites and especially at Zhoukoudian Locality 1. The oldest known artifacts come from sites in the Nihewan Basin, about 150 kilometers (90 miles) west of Beijing. Paleomagnetic analysis of enclosing sediments places their age between 1.3 and 1.1 million years ago.

Some of the Chinese artifacts are as finely trimmed or shaped as like-aged Acheulean artifacts from Africa and Europe, but the Chinese assemblages consistently lack hand axes. Harvard archeologist Hallam L. Movius first stressed the contrast in the 1940s, and he pointed out that hand axes had not been found anywhere in Asia east of northern India. The distinction does not depend on excavation, since in Europe and especially Africa, hand axes are often found on the surface, either because they have been eroded from their burial places or because they were never buried to begin with.

Movius proposed that a rough line through northern India separated the expansive Acheulean Tradition of Africa, Europe, and western Asia on the west from the non-Acheulean tradition in eastern and southeastern Asia (Figure 4.7). His boundary has stood the test of time, and it sends the same message as the fossils—from the moment that people first arrived in eastern Asia, they followed a different evolutionary track than their African and European contemporaries. If the Mojokerto and Sangiran dates that we discussed earlier mean that people had colonized eastern Asia by 1.8 to 1.6 million years ago, then hand axes might be absent because the colonists left Africa before hand axes were invented. However, Indiana University archeologists Nicholas Toth and Kathy Schick have suggested an alternative. If the colonists left after hand axes appeared, they may have passed through a kind of "technological bottleneck," perhaps a large region that lacked suitable raw material for hand axe manufacture, and by the time they emerged, they could have lost the hand axe habit. It was clearly not essential to their continued success, and thereafter isolation by distance could have prevented its reintroduction. Such isolation probably explains why a strong artifactual contrast persisted between east and west, even after 250,000 years ago, when people in the west had given up hand axe manufacture.

♛ ♛ ♛

The difference between east and west in anatomy and artifacts might suggest that there was a telling difference in behavior or ecology, but so far there is no evidence for this. With regard to ecology, for example, we can say only that people everywhere subsisted partly on large mammals. Zhoukoudian Locality 1 is the most informative Chinese site, and it was literally filled with bones from a wide variety of species. Two extinct kinds of deer were particularly abundant, and this might mean that local *erectus* people were skilled deer stalkers. Against this, though, we note that the Locality 1 deposits also provided numerous fossilized hyena feces or coprolites and that many of the animal bones were damaged by hyena teeth. The conspicuous evidence for hyena activity means not only that hyenas could have introduced many of the animal bones, but it also suggests that hyenas successfully competed with *erectus* for living space. Based just on the Locality 1 evidence, we might conclude that as a predator or scavenger on other large mammals, *erectus* was less effective than hyenas.

Animal bones from broadly contemporaneous sites in Africa and Europe suggest that *Homo heidelbergensis* and its immediate successors were equally ineffective hunters. This is true even though *heidelbergensis* and *erectus* produced very different stone artifacts, and the ecological similarity serves to remind us that differences in stone artifacts between regions may say little about key aspects of underlying behavior. More important to this book, the apparent ecological similarity between *heidelbergensis* and *erectus* implies that they remained behaviorally alike even after they had diverged in anatomy. We will show now that Europe and Africa illustrate the same fundamental point—archeological (behavioral) residues remained strikingly similar on both continents, even as Europeans evolved into Neanderthals and Africans evolved towards modern humans. The pattern was broken only about 50,000 years ago, when the Africans developed the modern capacity for culture and then rapidly exported both their anatomy and their behavior to the rest of the world.

5
HUMANITY BRANCHES OUT

By 1 million years ago humans had spread to the northern and southern coasts of Africa and they had also colonized southern Asia as far east as China and Java. But what about Europe? The Dmanisi site puts people on the southern flank of the Caucasus Mountains, at the "Gates of Europe," by 1 million years ago (Figure 5.1). Yet, despite searches that began in the 1830s and that industrial activity has long aided, Europe has yet to produce a single site that is indisputably older than 800,000 years, and it has provided only one or two that are clearly older than 500,000 years. Enthusiasts have repeatedly proposed other sites that antedate 500,000 years or even 1 million years, but Leiden University archeologist Wil Roebroeks and his colleagues have shown that most such sites are dubiously dated or that their artifacts could be geofacts, that is, rocks that were naturally fractured by geologic processes.

FIGURE 5.1
The approximate locations of European sites mentioned in the text.

The contrast with Africa and southern Asia is stark, and it implies that Europe posed special obstacles to early human settlement, particularly during glacial intervals. The first permanent occupants of Europe were late Acheulean hand axe makers, who spread from Spain and Italy on the south to southern England on the north about 500,000 years ago. Occasional human fossils like those from Petralona, Greece, and Arago, France, suggest that the hand axe makers resembled their African contemporaries, and the Europeans probably descended from an expanding African population that brought the late Acheulean Tradition to Europe. For the sake of convenience, we assign this population and its first African and European descendants to the species *Homo heidelbergensis*. We introduced *heidelbergensis* in the last chapter, where we pointed out that the "type" specimen is a massive lower jaw found in 1907 at the Mauer sand quarry near Heidelberg, Germany. Associated animal species indicate that the jaw is about 500,000 years old.

Homo heidelbergensis shared many primitive features with *Homo ergaster* and *Homo erectus,* including a large, forwardly project-ing face, a massive, chinless lower jaw with big teeth, large browridges, a low, flattened frontal bone (forehead), great breadth across the skull base, and thick skull walls (Figure 5.2). At the same time, it departed from both *ergaster* and *erectus* in its much enlarged brain, which aver-aged over 1200 cubic centimeters (cc) (compared to about 900 cc for *ergaster* and 1000 cc for classic *erectus*), in its more arched (versus more shelf-like) browridges, and in the shape of its braincase, which was broader across the front, more filled out at the sides, and less angular in the back. Like *erectus, heidelbergensis* probably evolved from

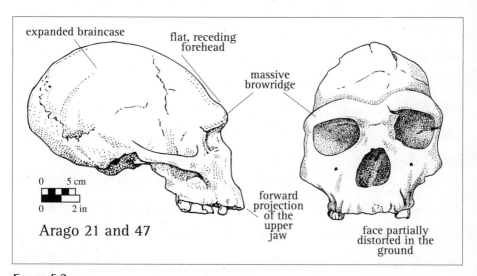

FIGURE 5.2

A partially reconstructed skull from Arago, France, assigned here to *Homo heidelbergensis* (drawn by Kathryn Cruz-Uribe from photographs). (Copyright Kathryn Cruz-Uribe.)

ergaster, and in its anatomy and its geographic distribution, it is a plausible common ancestor for the Neanderthals (*Homo neanderthalensis*) who appeared subsequently in Europe and for modern humans (*Homo sapiens*) who evolved later in Africa.

☷ ☷ ☷

Heidelbergensis may have been the first human species to gain a permanent foothold in Europe, but it was not the first to try. Cave deposits in the Sierra de Atapuerca near Burgos, northern Spain, reveal an earlier, if fleeting attempt, and ancient lake deposits at Ceprano near Rome, central Italy, may record another.

Despite its name, the Sierra de Atapuerca is not a mountain range, but a large limestone hill that is literally honeycombed with caves. Two of these—the Sima de los Huesos ("Pit of the Bones") and the Gran Dolina ("Large Depression")—are so remarkable that the prestigious *Journal of Human Evolution* devoted a thick special issue to each, in 1997 and 1999 respectively. The Gran Dolina stands out, because it has provided the most compelling evidence for human presence in Europe before 500,000 years ago. The Sima is famous for a mass of human fossils that document the local, European evolution of the Neanderthals from *heidelbergensis.*

The Gran Dolina contains 18 meters (60 feet) of sandy, rocky deposits first exposed in a now-abandoned railway trench at the turn of the twentieth century. Excavations that began in 1976 and then accelerated after 1993 show that artifacts and fragmentary animal bones are concentrated in six discrete layers. The layer that interests us here is the second from the bottom, known as TD6, which has provided more than ninety fragmentary human fossils and 200 flaked stone artifacts. An horizon that lies roughly 1 meter (3 feet) higher records the shift in global magnetic polarity from the last (Matuyama) reversed chron to the present (Brunhes) normal chron (Figure 3.3 on p. 68). This means that TD6 must be older than 780,000 years. The Electron Spin Resonance dating method brackets the TD6 fossils and artifacts between 857,000 and 780,000 years ago, and bones of long-extinct rodent species support an equally great age. With admitted uncertainties in mind, the excavators conservatively place TD6 at about 800,000 years ago.

The TD6 human fossils include eighteen skull fragments, four partial jaws, fourteen isolated teeth, sixteen vertebrae, sixteen ribs, twenty bones of the hands and feet, two bones of the wrist, three collar bones, two lower arm bones (radiuses), a thigh bone (femur), two knee caps, and other fragments from a minimum of six individuals. The people were between 3 and 18 years of age when they died. The skull and jaw fragments are too incomplete for detailed diagnosis, but the jaws clearly represent people whose faces were less massive and in some respects more modern-looking than those of *heidelbergensis.* The excavators have assigned them to a new species, *Homo antecessor,* from the Latin word for "pioneer" or "explorer." The relationship of *antecessor* to other human species is debatable, but it seems an unlikely ancestor for *heidelbergensis,* and it may have been an offshoot of *ergaster* that disappeared after a failed attempt to colonize southern Europe. Its doom may have been sealed by an inability to cope with one of the harsh glacial episodes that gripped Europe between 800,000 and 600,000 years ago.

The TD6 people made artifacts on pebbles and cobbles of flint, quartzite, sandstone, quartz, and limestone, all of which they found within a few kilometers of the cave. Their tools were mainly small flakes, some of which they modified by striking tiny flakes or chips from along one or more edges. Archeologists call such modification "retouch," and ancient people did it to alter the shape of an edge, to give it greater stability, or to resharpen it after it had been dulled by use. In addition to flakes, TD6 has provided some hammerstones and a few cores from which the flakes were struck. Hand axes are totally absent, although they are commonplace in like-aged sites in Africa and south-western Asia, and they occur in a higher-lying Gran Dolina layer that formed after 500,000 years ago. Their lack may mean that like *Homo erectus* in eastern Asia, the ancestors of the TD6 people lost the hand axe habit on their trek from Africa. Alternatively, it is just possible that a hand axe will turn up when the small artifact sample is increased. So far, the excavators have exposed only 7 square meters (76 square feet) of TD6, and to enlarge this area, they must first remove a great thick-ness of overlying deposit. At their current pace, they estimate that they will reach TD6 again only in 2008.

TD6 would be exciting if all it had provided were human remains and artifacts, but it has also produced 1056 fragmentary animal bones that the people often cut, chopped, or scraped to obtain flesh and marrow. The bones come mainly from pigs, deer, horses, and bison, but there are also some from carnivores and from rhinoceros and elephant. Compared to the larger species, the smallest ones are represented by a wider range of skeletal parts, suggesting that smaller carcasses more often reached the site intact. A similar contrast in skeletal parts between smaller and larger species characterizes prehistoric campsites of all ages, and it was thus predictable.

The surprise at TD6 is that the human remains resemble those of the smaller animal species not only in the wide range of skeletal parts represented, but also in the abundance and positioning of damage marks from stone tools. Twenty-five percent of the human bones show one or more forms of humanly caused damage. This includes chop and cut marks where large muscles were severed or stripped away; roughened surfaces with parallel groves or a fibrous texture that reflects "peeling," when a bone was partially broken by a blow and then bent across the break to separate the pieces; and percussion marks made when a bone was splintered for marrow extraction. Summing up, Atapuerca team leader and paleoanthropologist Juan-Luis Arsuaga says, "There is no doubt that the bodies were accumulated by other humans that ate them and left the human remains, along with the faunal remains and even the implements they used."

The extent and positioning of damage marks suggest that the TD6 people butchered other people for food and not for ritualistic purposes, and it is tempting to draw a parallel with the situation on Easter Island when Europeans first arrived in the eighteenth century A.D. The Easter Islanders had severely degraded their environment, and their once-thriving population had shrunk by eighty percent. In desperation, the survivors had adopted a wide range of bizarre behaviors, including dietary cannibalism. In the short run, this helped some to carry on, but in the long term, it could only have hastened the slide towards population extinction. If cannibalism at TD6 reflects similar nutritional stress, it could explain why *antecessor* was ultimately unsuccessful.

The Neanderthals also seem to have practiced cannibalism, but only on occasion, and if the custom led to extinction, it affected only local populations. Still, as far as we know, the great apes do not turn to cannibalism when food is short, and the records from TD6, the Neanderthals, Easter Island, and late prehistoric sites in Europe and the

American Southwest suggest that dietary cannibalism may be a specialized human tendency that *antecessor, neanderthalensis,* and *sapiens* inherited from their last shared ancestor.

Unlike TD6, the Italian site of Ceprano has provided only a single human fossil and no artifacts, but the fossil is important for its proposed age and for its form. It comprises most of a human skullcap that was shattered when a bulldozer struck it during highway construction in 1994. Potassium/argon analysis of volcanic layers at possibly younger and older localities nearby suggest that the skullcap is 900,000 to 800,000 years old. As reconstructed (Figure 5.3), it shares

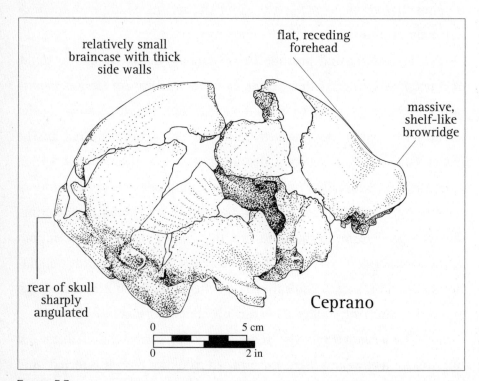

FIGURE 5.3
The human skullcap from Ceprano, Italy (drawn by Kathryn Cruz-Uribe from a photograph). (Copyright Kathryn Cruz-Uribe.)

many features with skullcaps of *Homo erectus*, including a massive, shelf-like browridge, extremely thick skull walls, a sharply angled rear when viewed from the side, and a small internal volume (estimated at 1057 cc). If the Ceprano skull had been found in Java, it might have been assigned to *erectus,* and if its dating is correct, the anatomical contrast with *antecessor* implies a second, early, failed attempt to colonize Europe.

♛ ♛ ♛

Beginning roughly 500,000 years ago, late Acheulean hand axe makers not only demonstrated their ability to hang on in Europe through thick and thin (or warm and cold), they also expanded into more northerly regions that *antecessor* or other earlier Europeans apparently could not reach. The reason was probably that late Acheulean Europeans benefited from technological advances that occurred somewhat before 500,000 years ago in the African source land. The reader will recall that the Acheulean (hand axe) Tradition began in Africa more than 1.6 million years ago and that it persisted in Africa, Europe, and the west Asian bridge between them until about 250,000 years ago.

Most African Acheulean sites are only weakly dated, but we have previously suggested that they may be divided between two stages—an earlier one before 600,000 years ago when the hand axes tended to be relatively thick, weakly trimmed, and asymmetric, and a later one after 600,000 years ago when they were commonly much thinner, more extensively trimmed, and more symmetric, both in plan form and in

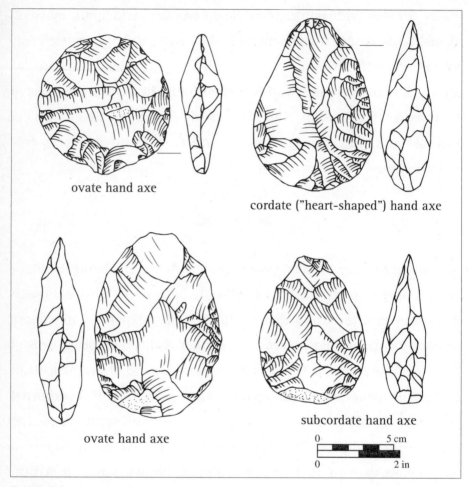

ovate hand axe

cordate ("heart-shaped") hand axe

subcordate hand axe

ovate hand axe

0   5 cm

0   2 in

FIGURE 5.4
Late Acheulean hand axes from southern England (redrawn after J. J. Wymer 1968, *Lower Palaeolithic Archaeology in Britain*. London: John Baker, p. 147).

edge view (Figure 5.4). Later Acheulean people also produced more refined flake tools that are indistinguishable from those of their successors. The greater technological sophistication of later Acheulean people may have been crucial to their successful colonization of Europe.

University of Colorado archeologist Thomas Wynn has stressed that early Acheulean ability to impose even crude, two-dimensional symmetry on a hand axe probably signals a cognitive advance over pre-ceding Oldowan tool-makers. If so, then the wonderful three-dimen-sional symmetry of many late Acheulean hand axes may mark an equally important advance that now allowed the people to rotate the final tool in their minds while it was still encased in the raw rock. The nature and timing of the shift from the early to the late Acheulean remain to be firmly established, but if the transition turns out to have occurred abruptly about 600,000 years ago, it could have coincided closely with a rapid expansion in brain size that biological anthropolo-gists Chris Ruff, Erik Trinkaus, and Trent Holliday have detected. Their analysis suggests that between 1.8 million and 600,000 years ago, brain size remained remarkably stable at roughly sixty-five percent of the modern average, but not long afterwards it increased to about ninety percent of the modern value. If a spurt in brain size and associated changes in skull form sparked the appearance of *heidelbergensis,* its emergence 600,000 years ago would signal a punctuational event like the one that we previously proposed for *ergaster* more than a million years earlier. The analogy would be especially apt if future research confirms a link between *heidelbergensis* and late Acheulean technology to parallel the one that we have postulated between *ergaster* and the ori-gin of the Acheulean Tradition.

☙ ☙ ☙

More research is required to demonstrate that the brain enlarged abruptly in steps as we have suggested, but no one questions that brain size increased roughly threefold over the 5- to 7-million-year span of human evolution. Body size also increased over the same interval, but to a much smaller degree, and the result is not only that living people have large brains, but also that they are highly encephalized, that is, they have brains that are exceptionally large for their body mass. Mammals are generally more encephalized than other kinds of animals, and even the earliest mammals had brains that were about four times larger than those of like-sized reptiles. Much of the difference in size came from the development of the cerebral cortex, the folded mantle of gray matter that we think of first when we visualize a human brain.

The original mammals were probably mainly nocturnal, and their enlarged brains may have functioned to process information from multiple senses—smell, touch, and hearing, as well as sight—as they sought food and safety. Mammalian brains continued to evolve, but in most groups, encephalization—the ratio of brain size to body mass—plateaued early on. The most conspicuous exception to this generalization concerns the Primates, which have routinely spawned more encephalized forms during their entire history, spanning the last 65 million years or so. People are of course Primates, and in this light, their extraordinary encephalization can be seen as the culmination of a long-standing evolutionary trend.

UCLA neuroscientist Harry Jerison notes that the human brain is roughly six times larger than we would predict from the relationship between brain size and body size in other mammals. Even if we restrict the survey to monkeys and apes and scale them to human body size, human brains are about three times larger than we would expect. The fossil record suggests that whenever encephalization has occurred, it occurred rapidly, and the human brain illustrates the point especially well. It may actually have been the most rapidly evolving organ in the history of the vertebrates.

The benefits of a larger brain are obvious, but there are also costs. In modern humans, the brain accounts for only about two percent of body weight, but it consumes roughly twenty percent of the body's metabolic resources. In addition, large brains and the constraints imposed on the birth canal by bipedalism vastly complicate birthing. A survey of other mammals suggests that human brains should be even larger at birth, or more precisely, that the human gestation period should be perhaps three months longer. Restricting it to nine months increases the likelihood that the fetus will make it out, but it also means that newborn human infants are more helpless than those of apes and other mammal species, and this imposes a further cost, mostly on mothers. Obviously the brain got bigger anyway, so the pros must have outweighed the cons, and Jerison proposes that the most general benefit was the ability to accumulate novel behaviors, such as those we detect through time in the archeological record. Jerison also notes that a major function of the brain, and more particularly of the cerebral cortex, is to build a mental image or model of the "real world," which in his words is "the brain's way of handling an otherwise impossible load of information and is the biological basis for mind." Brain expansion after 600,000 years ago presumably increased the amount of data that the human brain could process, and this in turn allowed the development of more sophisticated mental models. "Brains are, after all, information-processing organs," notes Jerison, "and [natural] selection for brain size must have been selection for increased or improved information-processing capacity."

Humans before 600,000 years ago surely had sophisticated mental models of their world, but rapid brain expansion about this time may have enhanced their ability to communicate these models to others, that is, it may mark a major step in the development of human language. No topic is more intriguing and more difficult to address concretely than the evolution of language, but as Jerison points out, language is almost a kind of sixth sense, since it allows people to supplement their five primary senses with information drawn from the primary senses of others. Seen in this light, language becomes a kind of "knowledge sense" that promotes the construction of extraordinarily complex mental models, and language alone may have provided sufficient benefit to override the costs of brain expansion.

We suggest below that the development of fully modern behavior about 50,000 years ago—"the dawn of human culture" to which the title of this book refers—may mark the development of fully modern language and that this development may have been rooted in yet another neurological shift. We emphasize the "may," because the human brain reached its nearly modern size not long after 600,000 years ago, and if a neurological change occurred 50,000 years ago, it was confined to brain structure. Unfortunately, fossil skulls, even ones that are much differently shaped than our own, reveal little about brain structure, and arguments for neurologically driven behavioral change after 600,000 years ago cannot be tested independently of the behavioral (archeological) evidence that suggests them.

♛ ♛ ♛

We turn now to a subject that depends more on evidence and less on speculation. This is the European fossil record after 500,000 years ago, and it is critical to our story because it shows that the Neanderthals were a European phenomenon, evolving in Europe over the same interval that modern humans were evolving in Africa. Occasional proto-Neanderthal fossils have long been known from sites like Swanscombe, England, and Steinheim, Germany, that are between 400,000 and 200,000 years old, but the certainty with which we can now reconstruct Neanderthal roots stems mainly from one site—the extraordinary Sima de los Huesos at Atapuerca, often abbreviated for simplicity as the "Sima" (or "Pit").

Unlike its sister site, the Gran Dolina, the Sima was never exposed by a railway trench or any other commercial activity, and its original entrance long ago collapsed. It is a tiny chamber with a floor area of about 17 square meters (185 square feet) that can be reached today only via a 13-meter (43-foot) vertical shaft located about one-half kilometer (one third of a mile) from the entrance to the cave system. The chamber would probably be unknown to science if young men from nearby Burgos had not long been interested in exploring underground cave systems with torches and ropes. Graffiti show that they had entered the Sima system by the late thirteenth century A.D., and in the mid-1970s an exploratory group told a paleontology student that the Sima abounded in bear bones. The bones were so striking and abundant that the Sima was named for them.

The first human fossil—a lower jaw—turned up in 1976 in a jumble of bear bones and rocks on the cave floor. The jaw intrigued Spanish paleoanthropologists, but the Sima seemed like such a miserable place to work that they directed their attention to other nearby caves. In 1982, they returned for another brief look. "We didn't expect to find any other human fossils," recalls Juan-Luis Arsuaga. "We thought we were lucky with the discovery of the mandible." But after minimal searching, the team found two human teeth and they decided to see what other treasures the Sima might hold. Since 1984, a handful of excavators have descended a ladder into the cave for about a month each summer to work hunched over in tight quarters with limited oxygen. To begin with, the lack of oxygen limited work time to half-hour stretches. Rubble littered the floor of the cave, and the human bones came from deposits below a layer packed with cave bear bones. It took the team five years to remove the rubble and cave bear bones, one backpack at a time. Only then could they begin the interesting work of excavating fossil human bones.

In 1989, lights were installed and a ventilation hole was punched from the surface into an adjacent chamber. The excavators could now stay in the cave for three hours at a time. They lay atop wooden planks, and they used spatulas to carve layers of wet clay away from individual human bones, behaving more like sculptors than fossil hunters. Arsuaga likens the site to an operating room, since the surface is now entirely covered in plastic, except for the small area under excavation. The analogy goes further, for the fossils are very fragile until they have been removed and allowed to dry in the open air. Hands must move with surgical precision to avoid destroying precious specimens. "Every season, we excavate only about 1 square meter (11 square feet) to a depth of just 20 centimeters (8 inches)," says Arsuaga, "but we find two or three hundred human fossils in that small space."

It still took a few years of cold and cramped work to demonstrate the Sima's potential to the paleoanthropological community. Early on, the team recovered tiny bones from the finger tips, and Arsuaga says, "We knew there were complete skeletons in the Sima de los Huesos, but nobody believed us. Now the scientific community is interested, but in the 80s nobody was interested in that damn site." 1992 provided the turning point, for in that year, Arsuaga and his colleagues uncovered the first human skulls.

They first exposed a portion of forehead with a prominent browridge. Patient follow-up showed that the browridge was connected to a braincase. The excavators were elated, and they paused from their work to sip champagne in a roomier, adjacent chamber. Continuing, they turned up a large upper canine tooth and then a second braincase. Returning to the cave for a final time before closing up for a year, crew member Ignacio Martínez insisted on digging a little more. Within half an hour, the team had recovered a face that fit onto the second braincase. A year later, they found a matching lower jaw, and the fossil skull became one of the most complete on record. In the same season, they excavated yet another skull, for a total of three.

Attempts to date the Sima are ongoing, but the best available estimates place the layer with human fossils near 300,000 years ago, about halfway between *heidelbergensis* as we define it here and the full-blown Neanderthals whom we discuss in the next chapter. The Sima people were also intermediate between *heidelbergensis* and the Neanderthals in key anatomical respects. Neanderthal skulls were remarkably large, with an average internal skull volume, or endocranial capacity, of about 1520 cc. This compares to perhaps 1400 cc in living humans. Two of the Sima skulls are relatively small, with endocranial capacities of 1125 and 1220 cc, but the third has a capacity of 1390 cc, which is comfortably within the Neanderthal range. It is in fact the largest skull yet recovered from any site older than 150,000 years. Even more striking, the Sima skulls combine widely shared primitive skull characters with ones that are distinctively Neanderthal (Figure 5.5). Thus, like virtually everyone but the Neanderthals, they had large mastoid processes (a downward facing bony bump behind and below the ear), while unlike everyone but the Neanderthals, they had faces that

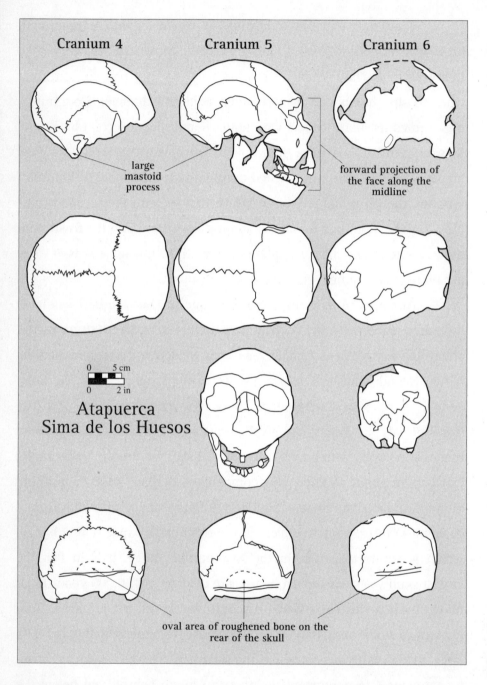

Cranium 4   Cranium 5   Cranium 6

large mastoid process

forward projection of the face along the midline

0   5 cm
0   2 in

Atapuerca
Sima de los Huesos

oval area of roughened bone on the rear of the skull

FIGURE 5.5
Outlines of the three human skulls from the Sima de los Huesos, Atapuerca, Spain.

projected far forwards along the midline (the line that bisects the face from top to bottom) and a conspicuous oval area of roughened or porous bone just above the upper limit for the neck muscles on the rear of the skull. In their retention of primitive skull features, the Sima people were not Neanderthals, but they were clearly on or near the line that produced them.

The Sima fossils have powerfully illuminated the broad pattern of later human evolution, but they have also raised a puzzle all their own—how did they get into the Sima? The layer in which they occur contains only fragmented human bones, and the bones are tightly packed. There are no artifacts, fireplaces, or anything else to suggest that people lived in the cave. The excavated bone sample has grown to more than 2000 individual specimens, including the three skulls, large fragments of six others, numerous smaller skull or facial fragments, forty-one complete or partial lower jaws, many isolated teeth, and hundreds of postcranial bones, that is, bones from parts of the body other than the head.

At least 32 people are represented by bones in the Sima, and measurements on jaws and teeth indicate that they divide about equally between males and females. Tooth eruption and wear shows that seventeen of the thirty-two people were adolescents between 11 and 19 years or age and ten were young adults, between 10 and 25 years old. Only three individuals were younger than 10 and none were older than 35. Children may be rare, because their relatively soft bones were more likely to disappear in the ground, and older adults may be absent, because, like the Neanderthals, the Sima people rarely lived beyond 35 years. Still, the age distribution is puzzling, for if it resulted from normal, everyday mortality events like accidents and endemic disease, we would expect older, weaker people to be much more abundant relative to teenagers and young adults. The implication may be that the Sima people did not die from everyday events, but from a catastrophe that affected everyone equally. One possibility is an epidemic disease, but we would still have to explain how the bodies ended up in the Sima. Another possibility that would cover both death and body disposal would be a devastating attack by a neighboring group. In this instance, however, the Sima bones should show wounds from spears or clubs, and there are none. Also, unlike the bones from the Gran Dolina, the Sima bones exhibit no stone-tool marks, and cannibalism can be ruled out. The only damage is from the teeth of foxes or other small carnivores, who were probably attracted to the chamber by decomposing human remains.

Since the Sima sample includes virtually all parts of the skele-ton, even the tiniest, the excavators believe that whole bodies reached the cave. The bones are mostly broken, and the broken edges are some-times smoothed, perhaps by sediment flow or by occasional cave bear trampling that would have disarticulated the bones and spread them across the cave floor. If we accept that whole bodies were introduced, the mystery boils down to how it happened. At the moment, a plausi-ble explanation is that other people dropped them down the shaft, and we must then ask if the practice was ceremonial or simply hygienic. Ritual or ceremony can never be categorically rejected, but the deposit contains no special artifacts, once-fleshy animal bones, or other items that we can interpret as ritual offerings or grave goods. An under-standable desire to dispose of bodies away from a nearby living site thus becomes a credible alternative. If the Sima people were simply practicing hygienic disposal, they may have anticipated the Neanderthals, who buried their dead, at least on occasion, but who dug the shallowest possible graves into which they inserted bodies also without grave goods. Much more elaborate graves with unequivocal ideological or religious implications show up only after 50,000 years ago, and they are then an important part of what we mean when we talk about the dawn of human culture.

♛   ♛   ♛

The Sima people almost certainly belonged to the late Acheulean tradition that was widespread in Europe, western Asia, and Africa at the time. Most Acheulean sites have produced nothing that could be mistaken for art, but as always in archeology, there are apparent exceptions. The most compelling one comes from the site of Berekhat Ram on the Golan Heights in Syrian territory presently controlled by Israel. Berekhat Ram is a typical late Acheulean site, which has provided eight small hand axes, numerous Levallois flakes, and carefully retouched flake tools like those of the people who succeeded the Acheuleans after 250,000 years ago. Potassium/argon dating of underlying and overlying lavas brackets the artifact layer between 470,000 and 233,000 years ago, and the excavation leader, Hebrew University archeologist Na'ama Goren-Inbar, and her colleagues believe it formed between 280,000 and 250,000 years ago.

Along with flaked stone artifacts, Berekhat Ram has produced a small lava pebble, about 35 millimeters (1.4 inches) long, that arguably resembles a crude human figurine (Figure 5.6). A deep groove that encircles the narrower, more rounded end of the pebble may set off a head and neck, while two shallow, curved grooves that run down the sides could delineate arms.

The most obvious question to begin with is whether the grooves could be natural. To investigate this, archeologists Francesco d'Errico

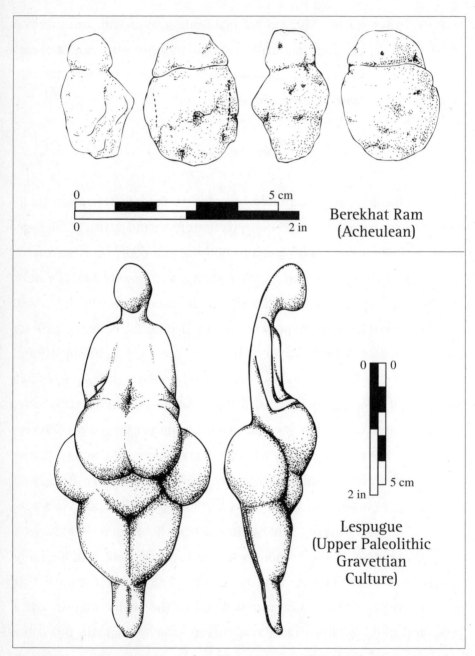

0   5 cm

0   2 in

Berekhat Ram (Acheulean)

0   0

2 in   5 cm

Lespugue (Upper Paleolithic Gravettian Culture)

FIGURE 5.6
The proposed human figurine from the Acheulean site of Berekhat Ram, Golan Heights, and an Upper Paleolithic "Venus" figurine from Lespugue, France (Drawn by Kathryn Cruz-Uribe from a photograph [top] and from a cast [bottom]).

and April Nowell experimentally incised similar pebbles with sharp-edged flint tools, and they compared their results with the grooves on the putative figurine. Their experimental grooves differed conspicuously from natural ones in several features, including, for example, the smoother texture of the bottom and sides, where small rock specks had been gouged out and then ground back in by the motion of a sharp edge. Under a microscope, the groove that defined the figurine's neck closely resembled the experimental ones, and d'Errico and Nowell conclude that it was humanly produced. More tentatively, their comparisons also imply that the arm grooves are artificial.

D'Errico and Nowell are careful to point out, however, that they have not proven that the modified pebble was a figurine. It only dimly recalls the carefully crafted, aesthetically appealing human figurines that mark the dawn of human culture in Europe after 40,000 years ago, and even if it were more persuasively artistic, it is of course unique. It fails to establish a pattern of creative expression not only for the Acheulean, but even for Berekhat Ram, and like other occasional, supposed art objects from before 50,000 years ago, it does nothing to alter the impression of a creative explosion afterwards.

♛　♛　♛

Late Acheulean people may have lacked art, but they were far advanced over earlier people in their ability to flake stone, and we will see below that they were also dedicated hunters. The sum might suggest that they were also distinctively human in another vital respect—a mastery over fire. Archeologists like Alison Brooks of George Washington University and Avraham Ronen of Haifa University have frequently argued that fire must have played a central role in human evolution. Brooks told *Discovering Archaeology* magazine, "It is really the beginning of humans. When you have fire, you have people sitting around the campfire together. You have people changing the environment." And Ronen has written that "Beyond being a tool, fire is a symbol . . . the only substance which humans can kill and revive at will. . . . If there had been a trigger to arouse self consciousness and the ultimate sense of 'otherness', it was fire." So it is only natural to ask when people first tamed fire. The answer must be equivocal.

Logic alone suggests that human expansion throughout Africa and to Eurasia by 1 million years ago required fire for bodily warmth, predator protection, and food preparation. Nonetheless, to demonstrate fire use beyond a shadow of a doubt, most archeologists would require fossil fireplaces, that is, circular or oval lenses of ash and charcoal, surrounded by stone artifacts and broken-up animal bones. This requirement is unfortunate, because most early human sites formed on ancient land surfaces in relatively dry tropical or subtropical environments where charcoal and ash do not last long. Caves provide better preservation conditions, but most caves older than 150,000 to 200,000 years have either collapsed or been flushed of their original deposits, so we have no option but to concentrate on "open-air" sites. Patches of burned earth at two such sites in eastern Africa may indicate human mastery of fire by 1.4 million years ago, but in each case, the burning might simply mark a tree stump or patch of vegetation that smoldered after a brush fire. Occasional charred bones that accompany 1.5-million-year-old artifacts at Swartkrans Cave, South Africa, present the same dilemma. The charring is indisputable, but the bones originated outside the cave, where they might have been naturally burned.

If in fact, we insist on well-defined fossil hearths, the oldest firm evidence for human mastery of fire comes only from African and Eurasian cave sites that are younger than 250,000 years. This puts fire control solidly before the dawn of human culture, but only after *heidelbergensis* and the late Acheulean culture.

Still, we accept the logical argument that people must have tamed fire much earlier, and with our bias laid bare, we suggest relaxing the evidentiary requirement to include an unusually high proportion of burned bones, diffuse spreads of mineral ash, patches of burned earth, possible fire-pits, or some combination of these features. We can then argue for fire use between 500,000 and 300,000 years ago at the famous "Peking Man" cave (Zhoukoudian) in north China, at Montagu Cave and the aptly named Cave of Hearths in South Africa, and at a handful of European sites, including Vértesszöllös in Hungary, Terra Amata and Menez-Dregan in France, and Bilzingsleben and Schöningen in Germany. The logical argument seems particularly strong for north Chinese *erectus* and European *heidelbergensis,* both of whom occupied environments where fire would have been far more than a luxury.

♛　♛　♛

Human stomachs are poorly equipped to digest raw muscle fiber, and without fire people before 250,000 years ago might have had little incentive to hunt. Yet, it is difficult to imagine that people could have colonized Europe 500,000 years ago if they were not active hunters, and excavations at Schöningen, Germany, have now provided incontrovertible proof. It is perhaps no coincidence that Schöningen is

prominent on the list of sites that contain ancient, if admittedly tentative, evidence for fire.

Schöningen is an active, open-cast, brown-coal mine that just
happens to contain one of the most informative early archeological
occurrences in Europe. In October 1994, less than two weeks remained
before the mining company's giant rotor digger was scheduled to oblit-
erate the site. German government archeologist Hartmut Thieme and a
colleague were working to recover the maximum possible number of
stone artifacts and animal bones, when they unearthed a short wooden
stick that had been artificially pointed at both ends. The Schöningen
deposits are dense and waterlogged, meaning that they are relatively
airtight, and it was this unusual circumstance that preserved wood.
Ancient wooden artifacts are the archeological equivalent of hen's teeth,
and the discovery bought Thieme another excavation season. The following year, in a layer dated between 400,000 and 350,000 years ago,
he uncovered three unmistakable wooden spears, each between 2 and 3
meters (6.5 and 10 feet) long and carved from the heartwood of a mature
spruce tree (Figure 5.7). Nearby, he found bones from at least ten wild
horses, many of which showed fractures and cut marks from butchery.
Thieme concluded that stone-age hunters, lurking near the margin of a
former lake, had ambushed the horses, driven them into the water, and
then quickly dispatched them with the spears.

He published his discovery in a February 1997 issue of *Nature*
magazine that also included a startling report on the cloning of Dolly
the sheep. The public was captivated by the cloning, but archeologists
took note of the spears. Before Schöningen, only two other sites had
provided comparable objects. One was Clacton in England, where
deposits that were probably about the same age as those at Schöningen

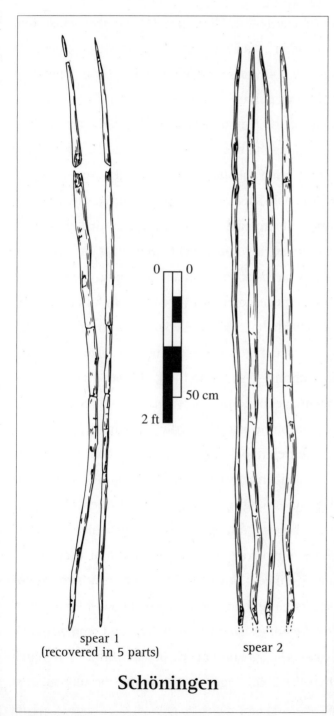

0   0

50 cm

2 ft

spear 1
(recovered in 5 parts)

spear 2

Schöningen

FIGURE 5.7
Wooden spears from
Schöningen, Germany
(redrawn after H. Thieme
1996, *Archäologisches
Korrespondenzblatt* 26,
fig. 9).

had produced a 30-centimeter (1-foot) long pointed wooden object that could be a spear tip. The other was Lehringen, Germany, where deposits that are probably about 125,000 years old had provided a complete spear from among the ribs of an elephant.

In his description of the Schöningen spears, Thieme emphasized that they were heavier towards the business end and tapered towards the back, like modern javelins. From this he argued that they were designed for throwing. Archeologist John Shea of Stony Brook University, who has investigated the evolution of projectile weapons, agrees that they were more aerodynamic than the much younger Lehringen spear, on which the center of gravity was too far back to facilitate throwing. However, he doubts that the Schöningen spears could have been thrown far or that they would have been especially lethal. "Picture yourself with an oversized toothpick trying to subdue an enraged wild bull," he says. "These weapons may have been used for hunting—it's hard to think of other uses for something like the Schöningen javelins—but they weren't very effective."

Another expert on stone-age projectile technology, biological anthropologist Steven Churchill of Duke University, doubts that the Schöningen people ever deliberately let their spears go. Churchill has scoured journals and early ethnographic reports for evidence of spear use by historic hunter-gatherers. Among 96 groups for which he found details on hunting, many employed thrusting spears, and they sometimes threw them short distances. However, he found only two groups who regularly threw spears more than a few meters. These were the aboriginal inhabitants of Melville Island, Australia, and some native Tasmanians. In both cases, the spears that the people threw were much thinner and lighter than the Schöningen javelins, and the targets were much smaller than horses.

Some historic groups, including Australian aborigines and the Aztecs of central Mexico, had spears that could injure a large animal from a distance, but for this purpose, the spears had to be supplemented by the "spear-thrower" or atlatl. This is a wooden or bone rod that is hooked at one end to accommodate a dimple or notch in the dull end of a spear. The spear shaft is laid along the rod and the rod is extended from the hand to lengthen the arm. The resulting mechanical advantage allows the spear to be thrown much harder and farther than it could be otherwise. The Schöningen spears are too large and inappropriately shaped to be atlatl darts, and atlatls are known only from much younger sites, after 20,000 years ago.

♛ ♛ ♛

The broken and cut-marked horse bones found at Schöningen demonstrate that the people obtained large animals, even if their spears were relatively ineffective. Cut-marked or bashed bones permit the same conclusion at other 500,000- to 400,000-year-old sites, including Torralba and Ambrona in north-central Spain, Boxgrove in southern England, and Elandsfontein in the Western Cape Province of South Africa. Still, by themselves, the tool-marked bones don't reveal how often the people obtained animals, that is, how successful they were. To address this, we must consider not just the tool-marked bones, but also their abundance relative to bones that lack tool marks or to bones that were damaged by carnivore teeth. Such observations are available from only a handful of sites, but where they exist, they suggest that late Acheulean people did not obtain large mammals very often. This point is illustrated from the site of Duinefontein 2, on the Atlantic coast of South Africa, about 50 kilometers (30 miles) north of Cape Town.

Like so many other buried sites, Duinefontein 2 owes its discovery mainly to commercial activity. The Electricity Supply Commission of South Africa owns the land, and in 1973, they were planning to build a nuclear power plant nearby. They brought in a bulldozer for subsoil testing, and by luck, a few days later one of the authors of this book (Klein) was hiking nearby with friends. They encountered a bulldozer trench, and on the spoil heap at one end, they saw numerous animal bones, including a broken elephant tusk. When they entered the trench, they noticed a line of bones and stone artifacts protruding from the walls about 60 centimeters (2 feet) below the surface. Two days later, a small test excavation showed that the objects lay on an ancient land surface. The excavation was enlarged in 1975, but power plant construction then made the site inaccessible for more than a decade. The contractors carefully marked the location on their maps, and in the mid-1990s, the author and his colleagues established that the site was still intact. In five seasons between 1997 and 2001, they then exposed the ancient surface over more than 490 square meters (5340 square feet), and they carefully plotted the position of every artifact and bone they uncovered.

The large excavation showed that the bones tend to occur in clusters that probably mark individual carcasses. The most common species are wildebeest, kudu, and a large extinct relative of the African buffalo. Occasional bones of hippopotamus, reedbuck, and other water-dependent creatures show that a marsh or large pond stood nearby. The artifacts include whole and broken Acheulean hand axes, well-made flake tools, and the cores from which they were struck. Tools and bones often occur immediately alongside one another, and their contemporaneity is not in doubt (Figure 5.8). There is no way to estimate how

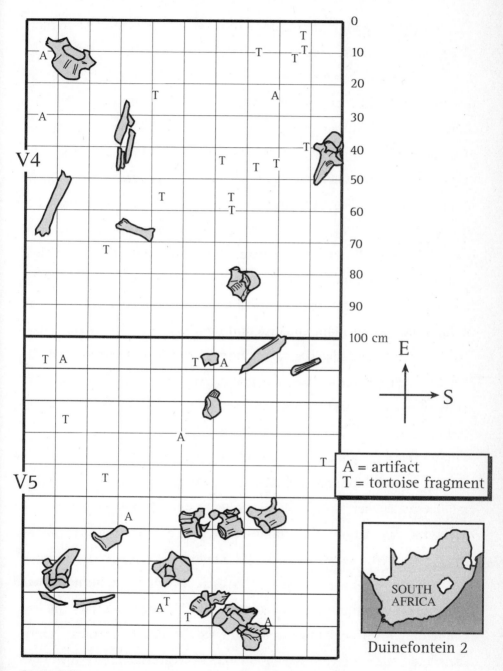

FIGURE 5.8
Artifacts, buffalo vertebrae and other bones, and fragments of tortoise carapace scattered across the surface of excavation squares V4 and V5 at Duinefontein 2.

long the accumulation took to form, but decades or centuries are more likely than months or years.

The Duinefontein deposits are dune sands that can be dated by luminescence, a cousin of the Electron Spin Resonance method. The luminescence technique employs heat or light to release electrons that are trapped in crystal flaws within individual sand grains. As the electrons are released, the sand grains glow and the intensity of the glow (luminescence) is directly proportional to the number of released electrons. Sunlight will also empty the traps, which means that the released electrons must all have accumulated since the sand grains were last exposed at the surface, that is, just before they were buried. The rate of accumulation is directly proportional to natural, low-level, background radioactivity in the soil, and this can be measured in the field today. Measurements conducted over a year at Duinefontein provided the local annual radiation dose, and reassuringly, they suggested nothing unusual, such as leakage from the power plant. In practice, luminescence dating often faces some daunting challenges, including the possibility that the annual radiation dose has varied through time as ground water circulation added or subtracted uranium or other radioactive elements. If potential problems can be overcome or placed aside, the calculation of a luminescence date can be visualized as the number that results when the total number or released electrons is divided by the assumed yearly rate at which they accumulated. Application of luminescence dating at the level of the ancient Duinefontein surface indicates that the sands—and the associated artifacts and bones—were buried about 300,000 years ago. Since the bones mostly lack the superficial cracking that comes from exposure to the elements, it is unlikely that they lay on the surface long before burial, and 300,000 years must closely approximate their geologic age. The site thus formed near the end of the Acheulean era.

So far, Duinefontein 2 has provided no human remains, but if it had produced a skull, this would probably resemble one found at the Florisbad spring site in the South African interior. The Florisbad skull has been tentatively dated by Electron Spin Resonance to about 260,000 years ago, and it is nicely intermediate between the skulls of *Homo heidelbergensis* of 500,000 years ago and those of near-modern Africans after 130,000 years ago. Thus, like *heidelbergensis*, it had thick walls and a broad, massive face, but like much later people, it had a relatively steep and convex forehead and a flat, non-projecting face. It anticipates modern skulls in broadly the same way and to about the same degree that the skulls from the Sima de los Huesos anticipate those of the Neanderthals, and it thus provides direct proof that the modern human and Neanderthal lines had diverged by at least 250,000 years ago.

Archeologist Richard Milo of Chicago State University has carefully scrutinized every Duinefontein 2 animal bone for damage, and he has found stone tool marks like those at Schöningen. However, his research also shows that tool marks are far rarer than carnivore tooth marks and that the tooth marks are about as common as they are on bones at the Langebaanweg paleontological site, 60 kilometers (36 miles) north of Duinefontein. At Langebaanweg, the bones also occur in clusters that represent carcasses scattered on an ancient land surface, and they come from broadly the same range of animals as at Duinefontein 2. However, Langebaanweg dates from about 5.5 million years ago, 3 million years before the oldest stone tools, and it understandably lacks artifacts and tool-marked bones. Duinefontein 2 provides nothing to determine whether people 300,000 years ago mainly hunted or scavenged, but the similarity in bone damage to Langebaanweg implies that whatever they did, their impact on other large mammals was negligible, and they obtained few carcasses overall. The rarity of tool-marked bones at Ambrona, Torralba, Elandsfontein, and a handful of other like-aged sites provisionally supports the same conclusion.

Why then are bones and artifacts so numerous and so closely associated at each site? The answer is probably that each occurred near a water source that attracted both people and animals over a long interval. The people may have only rarely interacted with other animals when they came to drink, and they might not even have seen many of the bones, which could have been previously trampled into the subsoil or obscured by vegetation. From our perspective, 300,000 or more years later, it may appear that the bones and artifacts were deposited at the same time, and in a geologic sense they were. However, they could easily have arrived weeks, months, or even years apart, and we would have no way of knowing.

If we are correct that Acheulean people rarely obtained large animals, the reason was probably their limited technology, and a key consequence was small human population size. Duinefontein 2 provides a way to test this independently, using bones of the angulate tortoise which occur abundantly on the ancient land surface. Tortoise collection requires no special knowledge or technology, and local stone age people have engaged in it for tens of thousands of years. Almost certainly, they always took the largest specimens first, since these are the most visible and the most meaty, and when the number of collectors increased, average tortoise size declined. The Duinefontein 2 tortoises represent natural deaths on the ancient land surface, but their average size must still reflect the intensity of contemporaneous human collection, and on average, they were about as big as angulate tortoises can get. Tortoises at sites associated with early anatomically modern humans, dated between 130,000 and 60,000 to 50,000 years ago, average significantly smaller, and those from sites that postdate 50,000 years ago are smaller yet. The implication is that human populations were especially small in late Acheulean times, that they increased later on, and that they reached historic levels only after the dawn of human culture.

♛ ♛ ♛

Like other African late Acheulean sites, Duinefontein 2 differs from its European counterparts in the species of animals represented, in the kinds of stone used to make tools, and in other details. In addition, the Africans and Europeans surely belonged to different evolutionary lineages. Yet, there is nothing at the various sites to suggest a significant behavioral difference, and on each continent, behavior appears to have been equally primitive by modern standards. Africans and Europeans remained behaviorally similar—and still primitive—until about 50,000 years ago, when the Africans added modern behavior to modern anatomy. For a brief period, Africans and Europeans then differed sharply in behavior, but the modern behavioral mode gave the Africans a competitive advantage, and they soon spread it throughout Eurasia. By 30,000 years ago, people everywhere were modern in appearance and they were once again similar in behavior.

♛ ♛ ♛

6
NEANDERTHALS OUT ON A LIMB

On its way to the Rhine, Germany's Düssel River flows through the verdant Neander Valley, named for a local seventeenth-century vicar and composer. The bedrock is limestone, and the valley walls were once pocked with caves. By 1856, quarrying had destroyed all but two, and in August of that year, quarry workers set out to remove the stone around the cave known as the Feldhofer Grotto. They enlarged the entrance by blasting, and as they cleared away the rubble inside, someone's pickaxe clanged against a dark brown skullcap (Figure 6.1). Other bones—maybe even an entire skeleton—occurred nearby, but the workers retrieved only the skullcap, some arm bones, a pair of thigh bones, a partial pelvis, and some ribs. The quarry owner thought they came from a bear, but he set them aside for a local schoolteacher and natural historian, Johann Fuhlrott. Fuhlrott recognized immediately that they were human but not from anyone like he knew. He was particularly struck by the long, low, flat form of the skullcap, by the

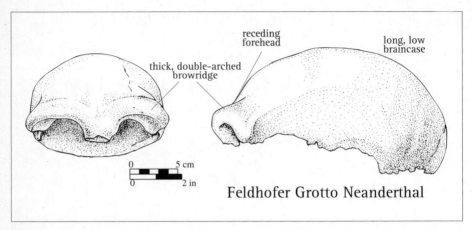

receding forehead

long, low braincase

thick, double-arched browridge

0   5 cm

0   2 in

Feldhofer Grotto Neanderthal

FIGURE 6.1

The fossil human skullcap found in the Feldhofer Grotto, Germany, in 1856 (drawn by Kathryn Cruz-Uribe from photographs) (Copyright Kathryn Cruz-Uribe).

beetling browridge over its eye sockets, and by the thickness of the limb bones. He guessed that the remains represented someone whose body had been washed into the cave during Noah's Flood.

Fuhlrott transferred the bones to Hermann Schaffhausen, an eminent professor of anatomy at the University of Bonn. Schaffhausen carefully compared them to a range of modern human specimens, and in 1857, he concluded that they represented a "barbarous and savage race" that had inhabited northern Europe before the Germans and the Celts. It was left to Thomas Huxley, Darwin's most eminent early disciple, to take the next logical step. In 1863, after a careful study of the skullcap, he concluded that it probably represented an extinct kind of human. In 1864, the Irish anatomist, William King, assigned the Feldhofer fossils to a new species, for which he coined the name *Homo neanderthalensis,* from the German Neanderthal, meaning Neander Valley. In modern German, Thal has become Tal, and some specialists prefer the vernacular term Neandertal to Neanderthal. Either alternative is acceptable, but for those like us who incline to King's original diagnosis, the technical name must remain *neanderthalensis*.

Few authorities followed Huxley or King to begin with, and the problem was only partly opposition to the idea of human evolution. There was also no evidence that the Feldhofer bones were very ancient. Proof came only in 1886, when archeologists excavated two anatomically similar skeletons at Spy Cave, Belgium (Figure 6.2). Associated stone tools and bones of mammoth, rhinoceros, reindeer, and other animals indicated that the Spy skeletons were very ancient. By 1910, archeologists could point to similar associations from France on the west to Croatia on the east (Figure 6.3), and French archeologists had worked out the basic succession of European stone tool cultures. They

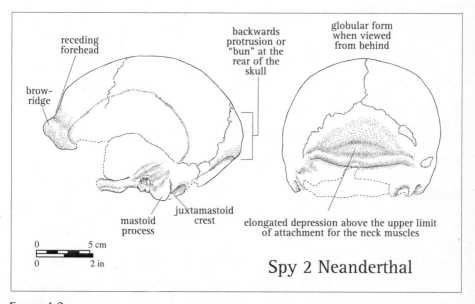

FIGURE 6.2
One of two Neanderthal skulls found at Spy Cave, Belgium, in 1886 (redrawn after A. P. Santa Luca 1978, *Journal of Human Evolution* 7, p. 623).

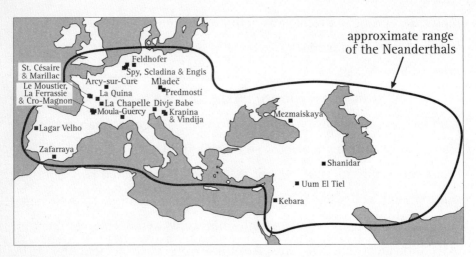

FIGURE 6.3
The European and west Asian range of the Neanderthals showing the approximate locations of the sites mentioned in this chapter.

knew that when Neanderthals and fully modern humans left their tools in the same site, the kinds of tools that Neanderthals made always occurred in deeper layers. It followed that the Neanderthals had been in Europe first, and the stage was set for a controversy that has continued to the present day: did the Neanderthals evolve into modern humans or were they extinguished when modern humans arrived from elsewhere? To us, the issue has now been settled in favor of extinction, and our purpose in this chapter is to explain why we think so.

♛ ♛ ♛

The Neanderthals have sometimes been called primitive or archaic humans and in a sense that is correct. It is more accurate, though, to say that they were not so much primitive as different, and in many features of anatomy, they were actually more specialized than living humans, that is, that they had changed more from the last shared ancestor. We have suggested that this ancestor was *Homo heidelbergensis,* which occupied both Africa and Europe 500,000 to 400,000 years ago. Genetic comparisons that we discuss farther on underscore the likelihood that Neanderthal and modern human lines separated about this time.

In the last chapter, we also stressed that the Neanderthals exhibited some unique features of the face and skull. In combination, these features are unknown in any other human group, and even as isolated traits, they have been found only in the people who lived in Europe just before the Neanderthals. The 300,000-year-old Sima de los Huesos fossils are the prime examples, and it is because the Sima people anticipated the Neanderthals in key respects that we call them Neanderthal ancestors. The absence of Neanderthal specializations in contemporaneous African and Asian populations demonstrates that they were on separate evolutionary tracks.

The Neanderthal face was unique in its extraordinary forward projection along the midline, that is, the line that divides the face equally between right and left halves. If a living human had totally plastic features, he or she could achieve a roughly similar appearance by placing fingers on opposite sides of the nose and pulling forwards about two inches. The cheekbones and everything else along the midline would then sweep sharply backwards. The tooth rows would be pulled forwards, and a large gap would open up between the rear edge of the lower wisdom tooth (the third molar) and the fore edge of the ascending branch of the lower jaw, the part that rises to articulate with the base of the skull (Figure 6.4). Anatomists call such a gap a "retromolar space," and it is known only in Neanderthals and their

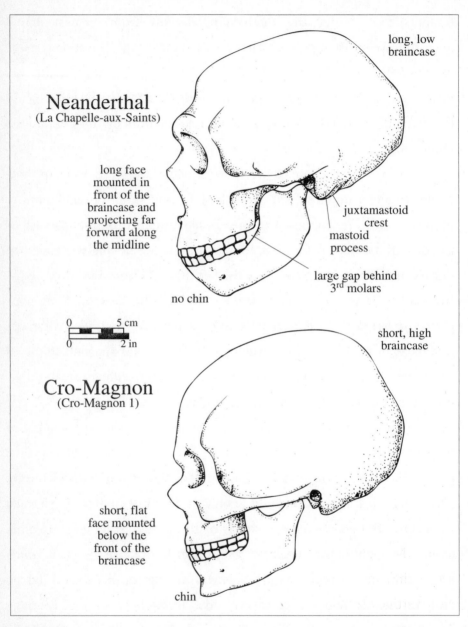

Neanderthal
(La Chapelle-aux-Saints)

long, low braincase

long face mounted in front of the braincase and projecting far forward along the midline

juxtamastoid crest

mastoid process

large gap behind 3rd molars

no chin

0 ___ 5 cm
0 ___ 2 in

Cro-Magnon
(Cro-Magnon 1)

short, high braincase

short, flat face mounted below the front of the braincase

chin

FIGURE 6.4
Reconstructed skulls of a classic Neanderthal and a classic Cro-Magnon (drawn by Kathryn Cruz-Uribe from casts). The term Cro-Magnon is commonly extended to all early modern, Upper Paleolithic Europeans.

immediate ancestors. The Neanderthal face was further unusual, if not unique, in other aspects, including its extraordinary length from top to bottom, the large size of the nasal opening, the great round orbits (eye sockets), and the strong, double-arched browridge just above the orbits.

The braincase was exceptional in its tendency to bulge outwards at the sides, so that it resembled a globe when viewed from behind (Figure 6.2). It was further singular in a depressed area of roughened bone on the back (occiput) just above a bar of bone to which the neck muscles attached and in a peculiar array of bumps and crannies in the vicinity of the mastoid process below and behind the ear. One of these bumps, known as the juxtamastoid crest, lay just inside the mastoid process and usually exceeded the mastoid process in size (Figure 6.4). In other features, such as the long, low outline of the braincase in profile and the tendency for the rear of the skull to bulge backwards like a bun, the Neanderthals were less sharply differentiated from some other fossil people, though when these traits are united with others that are peculiar to the Neanderthals, they serve to emphasize just how distinctive these people were. Recall also that Neanderthal braincases were very large. Internal (endocranial) volume ranged from 1245 to 1750 cubic centimeters (cc), with an average near 1520 cc, or roughly 120 cc beyond the average in living people.

Neanderthal bodies were also remarkable, although in this case, the distinctions were more quantitative than qualitative. They place the Neanderthals on a continuum with living humans, though a bit outside the historic human range. Thus, the Neanderthals had broad trunks and short limbs like the Inuit (or Eskimo), but in both features, they were more extreme. The so-called distal portions of their limbs, meaning the forearm bones between the elbow and the wrist and the shin bone (or tibia) between the knee and the ankle, were especially short (Figure 6.5). And their limb bones tended to be extremely thick-walled with large articular ends, bowed shafts, and strong muscle markings. The bottom line is that their distinctive heads rested on fireplug-like bodies, and in the buff, Neanderthals would garner stares in any modern health club. It has sometimes been said that if they were properly dressed, they would go unnoticed on the New York subway, but even this is doubtful, unless their fellow riders were also Neanderthals, or unless, like many New Yorkers, they made a point of minding their own business.

Anthropological attempts to explain Neanderthal distinctions have focused mainly on possible functions. Thus, chips, scratches, microfractures, and peculiar wear show that the Neanderthals often used their front teeth as clamps or vises, and the long, forwardly projecting face may have enhanced the ability to clamp down hard. Some of the bumps and crannies in the mastoid region might be related, if they provided insertions for muscles that stabilized the lower jaw and head during firm clamping. A functional explanation like this cannot be dismissed, but it faces at least two challenges. First, traditional Inuit often used their front teeth as clamps for processing skins, and the teeth often show similar, if less extensive, chips, fractures, and so forth. Yet the Inuit did this with none of the specializations that distinguish Neanderthal skulls. Second, and more forceful, the fossils from the Sima de los Huesos and other European "pre-Neanderthal" sites exhibit some Neanderthal specializations, but not all, and the ones they exhibit vary from site to site (or from skull to skull). This suggests that the specializations did not evolve as an integrated, functional complex. The most plausible alternative is that they resulted from genetic drift—chance genetic change—in small isolated populations. Chance change

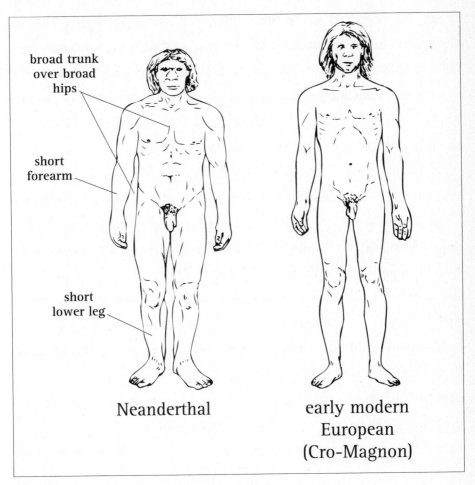

broad trunk
over broad
hips

short
forearm

short
lower leg

Neanderthal

early modern
European
(Cro-Magnon)

FIGURE 6.5
The reconstructed physiques of a Neanderthal and of a Cro-Magnon or Upper Paleolithic European (redrawn after J.-T. Hublin 1999, *Pour la Science* 255, p. 115).

might have been accelerated by sexual selection—the tendency for people to seek mates based on arbitrary, locally defined beauty standards.

The Neanderthal body is easier to explain. Both sexes were heavily muscled, and there is no mystery as to how they got that way—they exercised a lot, and they probably had to, if only to obtain food under challenging circumstances. Despite the great thickness of their bones, Neanderthals often broke them, and anthropologists Thomas Berger and Erik Trinkaus have shown that they suffered head-and-neck trauma about as often as modern rodeo riders. Neanderthals obviously did not ride bucking broncos or Brahma bulls, but they probably found hunting the wild equivalents about equally traumatic, particularly if their weaponry was as limited as we suggest further on.

Climatic adaptation probably explains why the Neanderthals had such broad, barrel-like chests and short limbs. Over the 400,000 years or so when the Neanderthals were evolving in Europe, global climate periodically alternated between cold glacial and warm interglacial periods. On average, glacial episodes were much longer, and times when temperatures approximated historic ones were especially rare and short. This means that the Neanderthals existed mainly under cold-to-very-cold conditions, and we know that living humans who live in cold climates tend to have much larger trunks and shorter limbs than people who live in hot, tropical climates. One need only compare the stocky appearance of an Inuit person with the slender build of a Nilotic African. We explored the reason for the difference when we explained the lanky build of the Turkana Boy and other early true humans. The essential point is that as trunk volume increases, skin area increases much more slowly, and a larger trunk is thus better at conserving heat. Short limbs similarly reduce heat loss. Near the Equator, the problem is to keep cool, and slender trunks and long limbs help to dissipate heat. The bottom line is that Neanderthal body proportions were predictable from the cold conditions under which they evolved.

The story does not end there, however, because the Neanderthals had even broader trunks and shorter limbs than the Inuit, yet even during glacial periods, mid-latitude Europe, where the Neanderthals evolved, was milder than the high arctic where the Inuit lived historically. The Inuit of course adapted more by culture than by body form, and they are famous for their ingenious, well-heated homes and their carefully tailored fur clothing. Archeology reveals neither trait until the appearance of the fully modern humans who succeeded the Neanderthals in Europe. These people arrived with long, linear, tropical body proportions, as if to signal their recent Equatorial origin, and they never developed an "arctic" body shape, even though they soon faced peak glacial cold. They also managed to colonize the harshest, most continental parts of northeastern Europe and northern Asia, where no one, Neanderthals included, had lived before. Their success illustrates what a difference a little culture can make, and their advanced cultural capabilities help to explain how they were able to replace the Neanderthals so quickly and completely.

There remains the need to account for the Neanderthals' large brain. In part, the explanation must be the generic one, in which a larger brain promoted new, highly adaptive behaviors, including an unsurpassed ability to flake stone. However, in living humans, average brain size tends to be greatest in populations that are heavily muscled or that inhabit especially cold environments, and the Inuit top the list, with an average brain size that approaches or equals that of the Neanderthals. The earliest fully modern Europeans had even larger brains, and they were also heavily muscled and surrounded by glacial cold. In short, if we assume that Neanderthals obeyed the same basic physiological principles as living humans, their brains were probably large in part for reasons that had nothing to do with intelligence or behavioral potential. If we consider encephalization—the ratio of brain mass to body mass—the Neanderthals were actually somewhat less encephalized than modern humans. This includes all living humans, none of whom equaled the Neanderthals in body mass, even though some, like the Inuit, approached them in brain size. By itself, a lower degree of encephalization need not mean that Neanderthals were less intelligent than modern humans, but it certainly suggests they could have been. This is especially true because the archeological record suggests that they were behaviorally far less innovative.

♕ ♕ ♕

The Neanderthals manufactured a relatively small range of recognizable stone tool types, and they probably used a single type for multiple tasks like butchering, wood working, or hide processing. In contrast, their fully modern successors generally made a much wider variety of discrete types, and they probably designed each type for a relatively narrow purpose. The difference may mean that Neanderthal tool use was less efficient, in the same way that modern house construction would be if the carpenters had to use their hammers not just for hammering but also for inserting screws or for sawing. The earliest modern Europeans were also less heavily muscled than the Neanderthals, and there is little or no evidence that they used their teeth as tools. With these facts in mind, some authorities have proposed that if the Neanderthals had been handed a more sophisticated tool kit, they might have quickly morphed into modern humans. An implicit assumption is that Neanderthal anatomical distinctions developed mainly as individuals grew up and that the characteristics had little or no genetic basis.

This idea is appealing, but it is almost surely wrong. To begin with, we have skulls and other bones of very young Neanderthals, including infants, and these already exhibit classic Neanderthal facial and skull specializations. Since the very youngest individuals had probably never used tools, their Neanderthal features must have been hardwired. Second, and even more compelling, we now have Neanderthal genes, and they confirm that Neanderthals diverged genetically from living humans long before living human groups diverged from each other.

Until recently, the recovery of genetic material from Neanderthal bones seemed like the biological equivalent of squeezing blood from a stone. The problem is that after an organism dies, its DNA immediately begins to degrade from exposure to microorganisms and to the elements. Bones offer some shelter, but even thick bones will not protect DNA indefinitely. Experts put the upper time limit at about 100,000 years, and to reach that, a relatively cool burial environment is probably required. Among sites that could have provided a suitable context, the Feldhofer Grotto looked likely, and in the early 1990s, a team led by Svante Pääbo and Matthias Krings, now at the Max Planck Institute for Evolutionary Anthropology in Leipzig, began a search for surviving DNA in a 3.5-gram chunk from the right upper arm bone of the original Feldhofer Neanderthal.

The bones of living creatures are rich in proteins, which are composed of amino acids. As a first step in their analysis, Pääbo's team sought to determine whether the Feldhofer bone retained different amino acids in the same proportions in which they occur in proteins and whether their physical state had been strongly altered during burial. When both indicators suggested a promising degree of protein survival, the investigators concentrated on retrieving mitochondrial DNA, routinely abbreviated as mtDNA. Unlike nuclear DNA, which by definition is confined to the nucleus of each cell, mtDNA resides outside the nucleus, in hundreds of organelles or mitochondria that supply the cell with energy. The sheer abundance of mtDNA (versus nuclear DNA) copies in a live person increased the likelihood that some would survive in the Feldhofer bone. Compared to nuclear DNA, mtDNA has two strong additional advantages for reconstructing evolutionary history: it evolves about ten times faster, and it is inherited entirely through females. The faster rate of change (mutation) means that mtDNA is much more likely to reveal recent population splits. Inheritance only through females facilitates the tracing of individual evolutionary lineages. Nuclear DNA lines are harder to trace backwards, because nuclear DNA comes half from the female parent and half from the male, and it is reshuffled at conception, blurring its specific parental origin. For a rough understanding of the problem this presents and why mtDNA offers an advantage, consider how much more difficult it would be to reconstruct a person's genealogy if children could arbitrarily mix portions of their father's and mother's premarital last names to formulate their own.

In 1987, University of California geneticists Rebecca Cann, Mark Stoneking, and Alan Wilson introduced many paleoanthropologists to mtDNA when they published a landmark study of mtDNA variation in living humans. They showed that mtDNA diversity is greater in Africa than anywhere else, that diversity elsewhere is essentially a subset of diversity in Africa, and that the oldest (deepest) mtDNA lineages reside in Africa. From the way the diversity was patterned, they reasoned that the last shared mtDNA ancestor of living humans must have lived in Africa, and from the presumed rate of mtDNA divergence, they suggested that she—and by definition it had to be a she—existed there within the last 200,000 years. In a mix of scientific and biblical metaphors, this "one lucky mother" soon became known popularly as "African (or mitochondrial) Eve." Subsequent studies of mtDNA variation in living humans, including an especially thorough analysis that Pääbo's team published in December 2000, have repeatedly corroborated the original University of California result. The bottom line is that even as Pääbo's group began their quest for Neanderthal mtDNA, there was already good reason to suppose that no ancient Eurasian group—neither the Neanderthals nor east Asian *Homo erectus*—could have contributed many genes to living human populations. Studies of nuclear DNA, cleverly designed to circumvent the problem of biparental inheritance and recombination at fertilization, support the same conclusion, and recent analyses of the Y chromosome confirm it even more strongly. Loosely speaking, the Y chromosome is the male equivalent of mtDNA, since it is inherited only through males. Its pattern of diversity in living humans reveals that mitochondrial Eve had a male counterpart—"African Adam"—who existed in Africa sometime between 200,000 and perhaps 50,000 years ago.

Structurally, DNA comprises strings of four chemical building blocks called nucleotides (or bases, individually abbreviated as A, T, C, and G), and to reconstruct evolutionary history, geneticists now routinely compare nucleotide sequences. If two individuals share similar sequences, they are presumed to share a relatively recent ancestor; if their sequences are more divergent, the individuals are assumed to be more distantly related. The mtDNA genome in living humans comprises about 16,500 nucleotides, but Pääbo and his team never expected to find a complete sequence in the Feldhofer Neanderthal, and they were delighted when the arm bone provided small fragments. They amplified the fragments using the now famous polymerase chain reaction (PCR), which lies at the heart of most modern molecular genetic research. Their first task was to determine whether the fragments might originate from shed skin cells or ill-timed sneezes by some of the people who had handled the Feldhofer bones since their discovery 140 years earlier. Ten percent of the fragments exhibited sequences that suggested they were modern contaminants, but the remaining ninety percent were readily distinguishable from their counterparts in living humans, and it was on these that Pääbo's team concentrated.

They sequenced a reconstructed fragment 379 nucleotides long from the so-called mitochondrial control region, and they compared the result to sequences at the same position in the control regions of 994 living humans drawn from all over the globe. On average, the modern sequences differed from each other at eight nucleotide positions, while the Neanderthal sequence differed from the modern ones at twenty-seven positions. Using a rate of sequence divergence inferred from a chimpanzee/human split 4 to 5 million years ago, Pääbo and his colleagues estimated that the last shared mtDNA ancestor of Neanderthals and modern humans lived between 690,000 and 550,000 years ago. When they applied the same procedure to the modern human sequences in their analysis, they estimated that the last shared mtDNA ancestor of living people existed much later, between 150,000 and 120,000 years ago. Since the actual time when the Neanderthal and modern human lines split must postdate the age of their last shared mtDNA ancestor, the estimated age for the ancestor is completely compatible with a population split following the spread of

Homo heidelbergensis and late Acheulean artifacts from Africa to Europe about 500,000 years ago.

To provide maximum credibility for their finding, Pääbo's group sent a sample of the Feldhofer arm bone to the Anthropological Genetics Laboratory at Pennsylvania State University, and when the second lab independently extracted mtDNA with the same sequence, the two labs published the result jointly. Their report appeared in the July 1997 issue of the journal *Cell,* accompanied by a commentary that called it "a tour-de-force investigation of ancient DNA."

Pääbo's team subsequently sequenced a somewhat longer fragment of mtDNA from the same Feldhofer bone, and this confirmed that Neanderthal and living human mtDNA differed from each other in about three times as many positions as modern human sequences differ from each other. There was still the problem that the Feldhofer Neanderthal comprised a sample of one, but in March 2000, a University of Glasgow team led by William Goodwin published a very similar result from the rib of a Neanderthal child excavated at Mezmaiskaya Cave in southern Russia, and in October 2000, Pääbo's team reported a third, confirmatory sequence from a piece of Neanderthal bone recovered at Vindija Cave in Croatia. There could now be no doubt that even Neanderthals widely dispersed throughout Europe were much more closely related to each other than they were to any living humans, European or otherwise. In the words of Pääbo's team, the fossil DNA sequences demonstrated that "Neanderthals did not end up contributing mtDNA to the contemporary [that is, historic] human gene pool."

It doesn't follow that Neanderthals and modern humans couldn't interbreed or that they never did, but the DNA results strongly support fossil and archeological findings that if interbreeding occurred, it was rare, and it will be very difficult to detect. To us, this inference, together with fossil evidence that Neanderthals and modern humans had long been on separate evolutionary tracks, justifies their assignment to the separate species *Homo neanderthalensis* and *Homo sapiens* respectively.

♕ ♕ ♕

When we place Neanderthals and modern humans in separate species, we are implying that the Neanderthals are extinct, for only modern humans survive. But what then happened to the Neanderthals? How could a group that had been successful in Europe for hundreds of thousands of years fail to survive to the present, or, as archaeology shows, even beyond 30,000 years ago? We believe the answer is clear: they disappeared because they could not compete effectively with modern humans of African origin, who appeared on their doorstep beginning about 40,000 years ago. The proof is in the archeological record.

Archeologists assign the artifact assemblages that the Neanderthals made to the Mousterian Tradition or Culture, named for the Le Moustier rock shelters in southwestern France where archeologists excavated such artifacts beginning in the 1860s. The Mousterian is known alternatively as the Middle Paleolithic, and it succeeds the Lower Paleolithic, whose primary manifestation in Europe is the Acheulean (hand axe) Tradition. The Mousterian is distinguished from the Acheulean primarily by the absence of large hand axes and other large "core" tools. The reason that Mousterian people stopped making large hand axes remains obscure, but the most plausible speculation is that they had discovered a way to haft stone flakes on wooden handles, and the new tools performed the same functions as hand axes but were easier to make or to carry around.

The timing of the shift from the Acheulean to the Mousterian is not yet firmly established, and it need not have been exactly the same everywhere. Current evidence suggests that the last Acheulean people lived in Europe between 250,000 and 200,000 years ago. The Mousterian then persisted until after 50,000 years ago, when it was replaced by the Upper Paleolithic. In general, the Upper Paleolithic was distinguished from the Mousterian by the presence of numerous especially long flakes or "blades," often struck from specially prepared cores, and by an abundance of chisel-ended tools known as burins (Figure 6.6). The term burin is taken from the French for a modern metal engraving tool, and Upper Paleolithic people probably often used stone burins to engrave or incise in bone, ivory, or antler. They manufactured many different kinds of burins and a wide variety of other, readily recognizable stone and bone artifact types. Particular types are often restricted to certain times and places, which has allowed archeologists to define multiple Upper Paleolithic cultures. Among the most famous are the Aurignacian Culture, which stretched from Bulgaria to Spain between about 37,000 and 29,000 years ago, the Gravettian Culture, which extended from Portugal across southern and central Europe to European Russia between roughly 28,000 and 21,000 years ago, the Solutrean Culture which existed in France and Spain between about 21,000 and 16,500 years ago, and the Magdalenian Culture, which occupied France, northern Spain, Switzerland, Germany, Belgium, and southern Britain between about 16,500 and

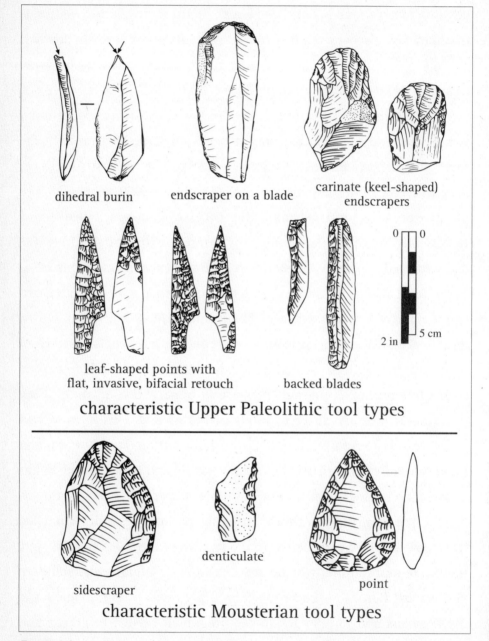

dihedral burin

endscraper on a blade

carinate (keel-shaped) endscrapers

leaf-shaped points with flat, invasive, bifacial retouch

backed blades

0
0
5 cm
2 in

characteristic Upper Paleolithic tool types

sidescraper

denticulate

point

characteristic Mousterian tool types

FIGURE 6.6

Characteristic Mousterian and Upper Paleolithic stone artifact types. Upper Paleolithic people manufactured a much wider range of readily recognizable stone tool types, and the types varied much more through time and space.

11,000 years ago. The Upper Paleolithic is ordinarily said to terminate about 11,000 years ago, but it was replaced by cultures that differed from it not so much in artifacts as in their adaptation to milder interglacial climatic conditions beginning between 12,000 and 10,000 years ago.

Determining exactly when the Upper Paleolithic first appeared is important to us here, because the people who made Upper Paleolithic artifacts were anatomically modern. They are often known popularly as the Cro-Magnons, from a rock shelter in southwestern France where their bones were found with early Upper Paleolithic (Aurignacian) artifacts in 1868 (Figure 6.4). Artifacts far outnumber human bones in ancient sites, and tracking the appearance of the earliest Upper Paleolithic artifacts across Europe can thus tell us how quickly the Mousterians (Neanderthals) succumbed. For simplicity, in this chapter, we equate Neanderthal with Mousterian and Cro-Magnon with Upper Paleolithic, although we will see that the equation is imperfect, since some late Neanderthals apparently produced Upper Paleolithic artifacts, and the African contemporaries of the Neanderthals made Mousterian-like artifacts, even though the Africans were more Cro-Magnon-like in their anatomy.

Neanderthals and Cro-Magnons shared many advanced behavioral traits including a refined ability to flake stone, burial of the dead, at least on occasion, full control over fire (implied by the abundance of hearths in their sites), and a heavy dependence on meat probably obtained mainly through hunting. In addition, both Neanderthal and Cro-Magnon skeletal remains sometimes reveal debilitating disabilities that imply that the people cared for their old and their sick. There could be no more compelling indication of shared humanity.

Still, there are many behavioral (archeological) respects in which the Neanderthals appear to have been significantly more primitive than the Cro-Magnons. First and foremost, with one intriguing exception that we address below, the Neanderthals left no compelling evidence for art or jewelry, and perhaps in keeping with this, their graves contain nothing to suggest burial ritual or ceremony. We could even surmise that they dug graves simply to remove an unpleasant inconvenience from needed living space. Neanderthal stone flaking techniques may have been extraordinarily refined, but compared to the Cro-Magnons, Neanderthals nonetheless produced a very small range of readily distinguishable stone tool types. They also rarely if ever crafted artifacts from plastic substances like bone, ivory, shell, or antler. Perhaps because Neanderthals produced such a small range of stone artifact types and virtually no bone tools, their artifact assemblages are remarkably homogeneous over vast areas and many millennia. The advent of the Upper Paleolithic witnessed a sharp acceleration in assemblage variability through time and space, which is reflected in the multiplicity of distinct Upper Paleolithic cultures to which we have already referred. Most of these can be further subdivided into smaller, spatially and chronologically circumscribed units that probably mark identity-conscious, ethnic groups in the modern sense. Neither the Mousterian nor anything that precedes it has provided comparably compelling material evidence for ethnicity.

Both Neanderthals and Cro-Magnons frequently sheltered in caves, and the stratification of Mousterian layers below Upper Paleolithic ones provided the first evidence that Neanderthals preceded the Cro-Magnons in Europe. Artifact densities tend to be low in Neanderthal layers, however, and throughout Europe, Neanderthals often ceded their caves to bears, hyenas, or wolves. In contrast, artifact densities tend to be higher in Cro-Magnon layers, and the people had the caves pretty much to themselves. This implies that Cro-Magnon populations were larger and that the people competed more effectively with other potential cave dwellers. They may in fact have driven the cave bear to extinction, for the last known cave bear fossils date from the very beginning of the Upper Paleolithic. Finally, when Neanderthals occupied sites outside caves, they left no persuasive evidence for substantial "houses," even though the people often faced extraordinarily cool conditions. Cro-Magnon sites are the oldest to provide indisputable "ruins," and the well-heated homes they imply help to explain why the Cro-Magnons were the first to expand into the harshest, most continental parts of northeastern Europe where no one had lived before.

To some archeologists, cataloguing the behavioral differences between Neanderthals and Cro-Magnons smacks of Neanderthal-bashing, a kind of paleo-racism that all caring people should resist. Yet, our point is precisely that skeletal remains and genes imply that Neanderthals were not analogous to a modern "race," however that is defined. Modern "races" all originated very recently, mostly within the past 10,000 years, and we don't need genetics to tell us that they routinely interbreed. We also have abundant evidence that a member of any modern "race" can become a fully functional member of any modern culture. If we accept the idea of human evolution, we must also accept that some ancient human populations differed from modern humans not only in appearance, but also in their behavioral potential, and to us, the Neanderthals fill the bill, despite their large brains, their patent humanity, and their relatively recent existence. In sum, we suggest that they disappeared not simply because they didn't behave in a fully modern way, but because they couldn't. Unfortunately, the one piece of evidence that could confirm this completely—a structural analysis of the Neanderthal brain—is not available and probably never will be.

♛ ♛ ♛

A reader who has just seen us deny Neanderthal art and burial ritual may wonder about contrary observations in the popular press. These observations receive such wide attention precisely because they are so rare, and this alone suggests a qualitative difference from the Upper Paleolithic where new evidence for art or ritual is hardly newsworthy in itself. Moreover, given that nature is bound to mimic art every once in a while, that Upper Paleolithic objects may occasionally filter down undetected into Mousterian layers, and that archeologists have now excavated scores of Mousterian sites, it would be remarkable if such sites did not occasionally produce an apparent Mousterian art object or ritual item. Some may even be genuine, but we present two cases here that we think illustrate a common problem—the probability or at least strong possibility that most such items originated naturally.

The first and probably most famous case comes from Shanidar Cave in northern Iraq. To this point, we have emphasized the European origin of the Neanderthals, but 80,000 to 70,000 years ago when global climate turned sharply cooler, the Neanderthals expanded their range to western Asia. At this time, they actually seem to have displaced anatomically modern or near-modern humans who had expanded to the southwest Asian margin of Africa during the especially warm early part of the last interglacial episode, between roughly 125,000 and 90,000 years ago.

Between 1957 and 1961, archeologist Ralph Solecki of Columbia University uncovered a thick sequence of Upper Paleolithic layers overlying an even thicker series of Mousterian layers at Shanidar Cave. The Mousterian layers provided the remains of nine Neanderthals, mainly if not entirely from graves. In the course of the excavation, Solecki routinely sampled the sediments to determine if they preserved fossil pollen that could illuminate the ancient vegetation, and he collected several samples from the vicinity of an adult male Neanderthal skeleton known as Shanidar IV. Two of these samples turned out to contain numerous, large clumps of flower pollen from eight different species. Historically, local people used seven of the eight as herbs or medicines, and since flower pollen was lacking in sediment samples from other graves, Solecki speculated that the Shanidar IV male was a Neanderthal medicine-man or shaman who was laid to rest on a bed of flowers. He concluded that "The association of flowers with Neanderthals [sic] adds a whole new dimension to our knowledge of his humanness, indicating that he had a 'soul'."

Solecki's beguiling conclusion cannot be simply dismissed, but paleoanthropologists generally agree that a cultural (behavioral) explanation should be accepted only if an equally plausible natural explanation can be ruled out. In this instance, a small burrowing rodent, the gerbil-like Persian jird, provides a plausible natural alternative. Burrows of jirds or other small rodents riddled the sediments near each Shanidar burial, and Solecki's team often used their number and angle to home in on possible graves. Since jirds are known to store large numbers of seeds and flowers at points within their burrows, they could easily have deposited the flower pollen near Shanidar IV. The jird explanation is less exciting than the human one, but it is in keeping

with the total lack of evidence for ritual with other Neanderthal buri-
als, including the others at Shanidar Cave.

Our second example comes from Divje Babe Cave 1 in the alpine
foothills of Slovenia. Divje Babe 1 is a prime instance of what we had
in mind when we said that bears occupied many Mousterian caves as
often as people. Excavations at Divje Babe 1 directed by Ivan Turk of
the Slovenian Institute of Archeology have uncovered a few dozen
Mousterian artifacts and some fossil fireplaces, but ninety-nine percent
of the bones come from cave bears who appear to have died on the spot.
In 1995, Turk's team excavated a new Mousterian fireplace and nearby
they found what they believed was a flute made on the shaft of a young
cave bear thigh bone (femur). The specimen was about 11 centimeters
(4.3 inches) long and it exhibited four evenly spaced, circular holes on
one surface (Figure 6.7). Two of the holes were complete and the other
two were only partially preserved on the broken ends of the shaft.

Like the overwhelming majority of cave bear bones from Divje
Babe 1, the supposed flute bears no detectable stone tool marks, and
the key question is whether another agency could have produced the
holes. Francesco d'Errico, who also studied the Berekhat Ram figurine,
has joined colleagues to examine bones from cave bear dens where
artifacts and fireplaces are totally lacking and bears were probably the
sole occupants. d'Errico's group found that between four and five percent of the bear bones had punctures like those on the putative flute,
and biting by cave bears or perhaps another large carnivore is the most
economic explanation. They conclude that the flute was actually a
fluke, an accidental product of cave bear or other carnivore feeding.

If the Divje Babe flute is placed aside, the oldest unequivocal
musical instruments are bird bone flutes from 30,000- to 32,000-year-

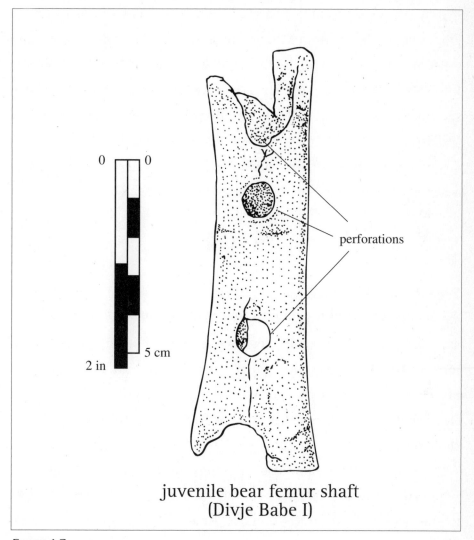

0   0

perforations

5 cm

2 in

juvenile bear femur shaft
(Divje Babe I)

FIGURE 6.7
The putative bone flute from Divje Babe 1, Slovenia (drawn by Kathryn Cruz-Uribe from a photograph).

old Aurignacian layers at Geissenklösterle Cave in southern Germany and Isturitz Cave in the French Pyrenees. Both sites have also provided indisputable, even spectacular, art objects, and the contrast with the Mousterian could not be more stark.

We could expand our discussion here to include perhaps fifteen proposed art objects from Mousterian sites scattered across Europe and western Asia, and not all can be as easily dismissed as the Divje Babe flute. Still, none are as convincingly artistic as many Upper Paleolithic specimens, and in the words of Cambridge University archeologist Paul Mellars, we conclude that "the sheer scarcity and isolation of these objects . . . makes it difficult to see this kind of symbolic expression as a real and significant component of Neandertal behavior."

♛ ♛ ♛

Neanderthal sites often contain fragmented bones of medium-sized mammals like deer, bison, and horses, and two lines of evidence indicate that the Neanderthals were active hunters. First, polishes that formed from friction with wood or encircling thongs show that Mousterians mounted triangular stone flakes on the ends of wooden spear shafts. Second, traces of proteins retained in Neanderthal bones show that the people were highly carnivorous.

Archeologist John Shea of Stony Brook University on Long Island has made a special study of the triangular (Levallois) points from the Mousterian layers at Kebara Cave, Israel, and other southwest Asian sites, and he has often observed chipped tips or other fractures that occurred during impact. Either strong jabbing or throwing could produce such damage, but Shea argues that the spears tipped with triangular flakes were too heavy and unwieldy for throwing, and they were probably used close up, as thrusting weapons. They would have been far more effective for this purpose than the 400,000-year-old all-wooden spears from Schöningen, but the need to get up close would still have exposed the hunter to great risk. This could explain why Neanderthal bones so often exhibit healed fractures. Biological anthropologist Steven Churchill of Duke University also notes that repeated use of the body to thrust spears could largely explain why Neanderthals were so heavily muscled. Archeologists excavating the Mousterian site of Umm el Tlel in Syria recovered a neck vertebra of a wild ass that shows just how hard a Neanderthal could jab. Embedded in the vertebra was a 1-centimeter (0.3-inch) long fragment of a triangular, Levallois point that snapped off when the animal was killed. The location of the point was probably not accidental, since its entry would have severed the spinal cord and left the animal totally unable to defend itself. Still, closing in on a large animal was dangerous, and the Neanderthals' principal coping strategy may have been to hunt in groups that could essentially surround a target. Shea imaginatively thinks of them as "wolves with knives."

We have already noted that ancient bones sometimes retain traces of protein (collagen) and that geneticists seek such traces before attempting the more difficult task of extracting DNA. The protein traces are valuable in themselves, for they can be used to reveal ancient diet. Species like wolves or lions that are highly carnivorous tend to have proteins that are enriched in the variant (isotope) of nitrogen known as ^{15}N. ^{15}N composition has been determined in Neanderthal bones from caves at Marillac, France, Scladina, Engis, and Spy, Belgium, and Vindija, Croatia, and in each case, the results indicate an extremely carnivorous diet. The degree of meat-eating is certainly too great to result mainly from scavenging, and like stone-tipped spears, it thus implies active hunting.

The Cro-Magnon successors to the Neanderthals focused mainly on the same species of medium-sized mammals, and from the animal bones alone, it is difficult to argue that Neanderthals and Cro-Magnons hunted very differently. Nevertheless, two circumstantial observations imply that Cro-Magnons were more successful. First, Cro-Magnon sites are more numerous per unit of time and they tend to contain greater quantities of cultural debris. This suggests that Cro-Magnon populations were larger, even though environmental conditions remained roughly the same. Second, the Cro-Magnons were almost certainly better armed, and their stone and bone artifacts include pieces that were probably parts of projectile weapons—perhaps throwing spears or darts to begin with and arrows later on. Better armament could explain why the Cro-Magnons, though heavily muscled, were less so than the Neanderthals and also why they apparently broke their bones less often. Reduced musculature would also mean that the average Cro-Magnon required fewer calories per day, and Cro-Magnons could thus have been more numerous, even if they obtained only the same number of animals and other resources as the Neanderthals.

Finally, while we're on the subject of food, we should say something about Neanderthal cannibalism. Recall that the earliest inhabitants of Europe—the people who occupied the Gran Dolina cave 800,000 years ago—were cannibals, and that we attributed their practice to dietary stress. We suggested that such stress could explain similar cases of cannibalism among late prehistoric and historic modern humans. So far, no Cro-Magnon site has provided compelling evidence for dietary cannibalism, but one or two Neanderthal sites have. The evidence is slim, but Neanderthal sites are rarer, and the implication might be that Neanderthals engaged in cannibalism more often, perhaps because they faced severe hunger more often. The two most relevant Neanderthal sites are Krapina Rockshelter in Croatia and Moula-Guercy Shelter in southeastern France.

The Croatian paleoanthropologist Dragutin Gorjanovic-Kramberger recovered roughly nine hundred Neanderthal bones at Krapina between 1899 and 1905. His excavation methods were crude by modern standards, but they helped to establish the great antiquity and wide geographic distribution of the Neanderthals within Europe. They also showed that Krapina did not contain graves or articulated skeletons. Nearly all parts of the skeleton were present, but they were scattered through the deposit, and most were broken. Subsequent studies have shown that at least twenty individuals are represented, and most were either teenagers or young adults. Preservatives now coat the bone surfaces, which impedes any attempt to estimate the extent of damage from stone tools or carnivore teeth. This is unfortunate, because the accompanying animal bones come partly from bears, hyenas, or wolves that might have played a role in the bone accumulation. Human occupation doesn't seem to have been intense, since Mousterian artifacts only slightly outnumber the Neanderthal bones. Still, cannibalism remains a plausible explanation for the sheer quantity of human bones and for their high degree of fragmentation. The age bias towards individuals who are the least likely to die of natural causes may imply the intentional destruction of one Neanderthal group by another.

The evidence from the Moula-Guercy shelter is more compelling. In 1991, archeologist Alban Defleur of the French National Center for Scientific Research recovered twelve fragmentary Neanderthal bones from Mousterian layer XV, and he noticed that several had stone tool cutmarks. Metal excavation tools can sometimes mimic stone tool cutmarks, so in his continuing work, Defleur instructed his team to use bamboo tools instead. He also avoided the application of any preservative that might obscure bone surfaces. The Moula-Guercy bones are extremely well preserved to begin with, and their surfaces are almost pristine.

In 1999, Defleur and his team published a report on a significantly enlarged sample of seventy-eight Neanderthal bones from the same Mousterian layer, and they compared the human fragments with about three hundred bones of red deer (elk to Americans), which dominated the animal bone assemblage. Both the human and the deer bones came from virtually every region of the body. The human bones represent at least six individuals ranging in age from 6 or 7 years to mature adult at time of death, while the deer represent at least five individuals, from newborn or even fetal to adult. Both sets of bones were extensively damaged by stone tools, and the damage tended to occur in the same anatomical positions regardless of species, showing that the butchers had used their tools first to disarticulate bodies and cut away flesh and then to open the skull and the long bones for brains and marrow. When they were done, the butchers scattered the human and deer bones equally across the surface of the site.

Like the Gran Dolina people 700,000 years before, the Moula-Guercy Neanderthals thus fed on people in the same way that they fed on other animals. Other Mousterian sites have provided occasional cut-marked Neanderthal bones, but most have not, and among those that have not are other layers at Moula-Guercy. From the perspective of a species competing with others, cannibalism is obviously a zero-sum game (or worse), and like modern humans, Neanderthals probably did not eat each other routinely.

♛ ♛ ♛

Strictly speaking, Neanderthals and modern humans should be placed in separate species only if they could not interbreed to produce fertile offspring. Biologists have often compromised on this criterion, however, and most place dogs and wolves in separate species even though dog/wolf crosses are well known and the crosses are usually fertile. The key point is that free-ranging wolves and dogs do not interbreed very much and they have developed behavioral or anatomical specializations that limit the possibilities. Ancient and modern genes suggest that if modern humans and Neanderthals interbred, they didn't do it very often, and we have proposed that behavioral differences provided the isolating mechanism. Not everyone agrees, and as counterevidence, they can point to the recently discovered Lagar Velho Upper Paleolithic skeleton, which its describers believe represents a hybrid between Neanderthals and Cro-Magnons.

In November 1998 João Maurício and Pedro Souto from the Torrejana Speleological and Archeological Society in Torres Novas, Portugal, were surveying rock art in the narrow limestone Lapedo Valley of west-central Portugal. They passed the Lagar Velho rock shelter whose fill had been largely bulldozed away during road construction six years earlier. A rabbit had dug a burrow into the remaining deposit, and when Maurício reached in, he pulled out the left forearm and hand bones of a child. Inspection showed that the rest of the skeleton was mostly still buried, although the bulldozer had broken and scattered the skull and some other parts. Archeologist João Zilhão of the Portuguese Institute of Archeology and his physical anthropologist colleague, Cidália Duarte, immediately mounted an excavation to recover what was left.

Zilhão and Duarte were intrigued, because the skeleton appeared to date from the Upper Paleolithic, based partly on its estimated 2-meter (6.5-foot) depth from the original surface of the deposit and partly on a mass of red-coloring matter that surrounded it. Both Neanderthals and Cro-Magnons sought out naturally occurring red ocher (iron oxide), and some archeologists have speculated that Neanderthals used it to paint their bodies. The most widely accepted alternatives are that they employed it to tan skins or to treat the surfaces of wooden artifacts. In contrast, Cro-Magnons commonly pulverized ocher to make pigment for wall painting, and unlike the Neanderthals, they often scattered large amounts in graves. At Lagar Velho, the tight concentration of pigment around the skeleton suggested that the body had been buried in a wrap. It had been laid out on its back, with the trunk and head slightly turned towards the wall of the rock shelter. The legs were extended, and the feet were crossed. The only artifact found in the rescue excavation was a pierced sea shell pendant, but careful screening of the deposits redistributed by the bulldozer produced three perforated red deer canines along with some additional skeletal fragments.

The layout of the body, the red-staining, and the pierced shell and teeth suggested to Zilhão that the child belonged to the Upper Paleolithic Gravettian culture, which we previously noted was spread across Europe between about 28,000 and 22,000 years ago. Subsequent radiocarbon dating of associated charcoal and animal bone showed the skeleton was about 24,500 years old, confirming Zilhão's suspicion.

Duarte and her colleagues invited human paleontologist Erik Trinkaus of Washington University to analyze the skeleton with them. The state of the dentition indicated that the child was about 4 years old when it died, and in virtually all respects, the bones closely resembled those of a modern 4-year-old. There was no surprise in that, given the

Gravettian dating. However, Trinkaus and the Portuguese scientists also detected what they believe are two Neanderthal traits: the backwards slope of the bone below the incisor teeth at the front of the lower jaw and, especially, the shortness of the shin bone (tibia) relative to the thigh bone (femur). Recall that short shin bones are a typical Neanderthal feature and they are an important part of the reason why Neanderthals are thought to have been physiologically adapted to cold. In June 1999, Duarte, Trinkaus, and their colleagues published their findings in the *Proceedings of the National Academy of Sciences,* and they concluded that the Lagar Velho child demonstrated that Neanderthals and modern humans interbred.

In an accompanying commentary, anthropologists Ian Tattersall of the American Museum of Natural History and Jeffrey Schwartz of the University of Pittsburgh were skeptical. They pointed out that the child's anatomy was overwhelmingly modern and that the skeleton showed no features that are unique to the Neanderthals. In addition, they argued that only a first- or second-generation hybrid would likely show a clear mix of discrete modern and Neanderthal traits, while the Lagar Velho child had lived and died at least 200 generations after the last Neanderthals in Portugal or Spain. They concluded that the proposed hybrid was "simply a chunky Gravettian child, a descendant of the modern invaders who had evicted the Neanderthals from Iberia several millennia earlier." No one has formally polled anthropologists on the question, but most would probably accept this conclusion. DNA might provide further insight if it could be extracted from the child's bones, but the prospects appear poor, because the bones do not preserve remnants of original protein.

Other evidence for hybridization is even more dubious, but the earliest Cro-Magnons were often remarkably robust, and in that sense, they sometimes recall the Neanderthals. The Aurignacian people who lived near Mladeč in the Czech Republic are prime examples, but Günter Bräuer of the University of Hamburg and his colleague Helmut Broeg recently scrutinized their skulls and failed to detect a single Neanderthal specialization. Nor did they find any in some slightly younger Czech skulls. Excepting perhaps Lagar Velho then, like the genes of living humans, early Upper Paleolithic skeletal remains suggest that if Cro-Magnons and Neanderthals interbred, it was probably on a very small scale.

♛ ♛ ♛

Of course, even if early Cro-Magnons and Neanderthals did not exchange genes, they surely saw each other, and some contact would have been inevitable. Across Europe, artifacts far outnumber human fossils, and we might reasonably ask if these ever suggest interaction. The answer is mainly no. At most sites that contain both Mousterian and Upper Paleolithic layers, the Upper Paleolithic layers overlie the Mousterian ones with no evidence for either population contact or a substantial gap in time. The sum suggests that Cro-Magnons replaced Neanderthals in a geologic eye blink, and we think that in most regions that's exactly what happened. There are, however, occasional exceptions—those unusual sites with a mix of Mousterian and Upper Paleolithic artifacts that cannot be explained simply by poor excavation. Such sites unquestionably exist, and they are a major thorn in the side of the claim that Neanderthals were biologically precluded from behaving in a modern human fashion.

The principal sites occur in a restricted area of northern Spain and western and central France (west of the Rhône River), where archeologists assign them to the Châtelperronian Industry or Culture (Figure

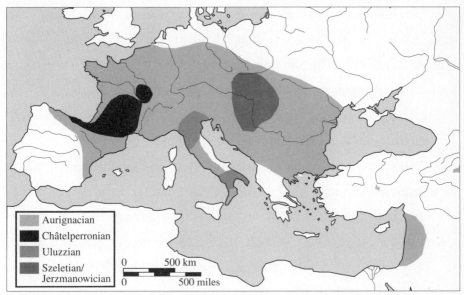

FIGURE 6.8.

The geographic distribution of the early Upper Paleolithic Aurignacian Culture and of the preceding Châtelperronian, Uluzzian, and Szeletian/Jerzmanowician cultures (redrawn after P. A. Mellars 1993, in *The Origin of Modern Humans and the Impact of Chronometric Dating*, Princeton University Press: Princeton, NJ, fig. 1).

6.8). In deeply stratified deposits, Châtelperronian layers directly overlie Mousterian layers, and they are covered in turn by layers with artifacts from the early Upper Paleolithic Aurignacian culture. All known Aurignacian human fossils, including, for example, those from the Mladeč site, represent fully modern Cro-Magnons, and even the earliest Aurignacian artifact assemblages contain indisputable, often spectacular art objects and well-made bone implements. Radiocarbon dating of charcoal incorporated in pigment has now shown that Aurignacian people also painted on cave walls. Dates on the Châtelperronian and the early Aurignacian overlap significantly, and the time difference between the two may have been too brief to measure with current methods. At the moment, a reasonable inference is that the Châtelperronian began about 45,000 years ago and that it persisted until perhaps 36,000 years ago, when the Aurignacian had already appeared nearby. Human remains from caves at Saint-Césaire and Arcy-sur-Cure, France, show that Châtelperronian people were Neanderthals. At both sites, the Châtelperronian occupations are among the latest known, and the people were probably among the last Neanderthals.

If only stone artifacts were involved, the Châtelperronian might be considered simply a kind of final Mousterian, and the earlier part of the Châtelperronian, before 37,000 to 38,000 years ago, may have been no more than that. At Arcy-sur-Cure, however, Châtelperronian people not only produced a mix of Mousterian and Upper Paleolithic stone artifact types, they also manufactured quintessential Upper Paleolithic bone tools and personal ornaments (Figure 6.9). The Châtelperronian layers provided 142 bone implements, including some that appear to have been decorated, and 36 animal teeth and pieces of ivory, bone, or shell that were pierced or grooved for hanging as beads or pendants. Nearly identical pierced teeth have also been found in the Châtelperronian layers of Quinçay Cave, France. Francesco d'Errico has shown that the Arcy Châtelperronians manufactured their bone artifacts and ornaments on the spot and that they employed their own distinctive techniques.

At Arcy, the Châtelperronians also modified their living space to an extent that is common only in the Upper Paleolithic. The Châtelperronian layers contain traces of several "hut emplacements,"

FIGURE 6.9

Châtelperronian artifacts from the Grotte du Renne ("Reindeer Cave") at Arcy-sur-Cure, France. In general, only Upper Paleolithic Cro-Magnons manufactured well-formed burins, bone artifacts, and pendants, yet the people who left such artifacts in the Châtelperronian layers of the Grotte du Renne appear to have been Neanderthals.

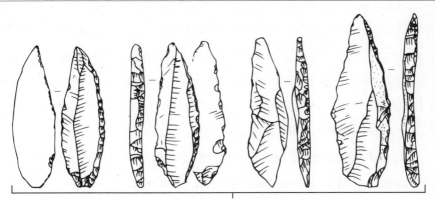

Châtelperronian points (backed knives)

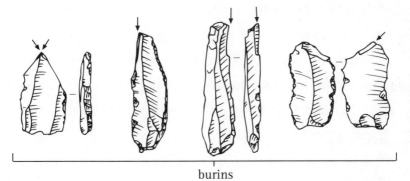

burins

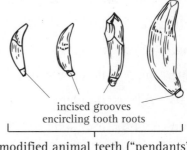

incised grooves
encircling tooth roots

modified animal teeth ("pendants")

| 0 | | | 5 cm |
| 0 | | | 2 in |

Grotte du Renne,
Arcy-sur-Cure

bone artifacts

of which the best preserved is a rough circle of eleven postholes enclosing an area 3 to 4 meters (10 to 13 feet) across that was partially paved with limestone plaques. Pollen recovered from the Arcy deposits indicates that wood was rare nearby, and the postholes probably supported mammoth tusks, which are more numerous in the Arcy site than in any other Paleolithic cave.

João Zilhão and Francesco d'Errico have argued that the Neanderthals independently invented the Châtelperronian, but the most persuasive Upper Paleolithic elements appear only near its very end. This suggests to us and others that the Châtelperronians borrowed the underlying concepts from early Aurignacian Cro-Magnon neighbors. Zilhão's and d'Errico's careful analysis of all the available dates indicates that the Aurignacian Culture penetrated central and western Europe 36,000 to 37,000 years ago, when the late Châtelperronian flowered. The late Châtelperronian didn't last long, and by 35,000 years ago, only the Aurignacian survived.

Archeologists in Italy and Central Europe have proposed cultures called the Uluzzian and Szeletian/Jerzmanowician that they think may also reflect early Upper Paleolithic influence on Neanderthals (Figure 6.8), and future research may show that one or both are as compelling as the Châtelperronian. Still, even if the Châtelperronian remains unique, it presents us with a problem, for if Neanderthals could imitate Upper Paleolithic culture, they were not biologically precluded from behaving in an Upper Paleolithic way. And if, as we believe, Upper Paleolithic culture was superior (meaning minimally that it promoted larger human populations), Neanderthals should have acculturated more widely, and we would expect their anatomical traits and their genes to be more obvious in later populations. In sum, we see the Châtelperronian as the biggest obstacle to our ideas about how and why the Neanderthals disappeared.

♛ ♛ ♛

In Chapter 1, we noted that a key modern behavioral marker—art in the form of jewelry—appeared in eastern Africa before 40,000 years ago, and we have just noted that art and other modern behavioral markers appeared in central and western Europe only about 37,000 to 36,000 years ago. This is, of course, an expected difference if anatomically modern Africans had to develop modern behavior before they could expand to Europe. However, we may still ask how quickly modern human invaders replaced the Neanderthals. Did the Neanderthals manage to hold on longer in some places than in others and might this imply that we have underestimated their behavioral capabilities? If Neanderthals and modern humans overlapped for a long time in some regions, wouldn't that increase the likelihood that they interbred, or at least that they exchanged culture? The issue of timing might seem straightforward, but it's actually quite complex. The core problem is the difficulty of obtaining reliable dates between 60,000 and 30,000 years ago. Virtually everyone agrees that before 60,000 years ago, the Neanderthals were alone in Europe and that after 30,000 years ago they were gone.

The famous radiocarbon method has long been and still is the principal available technique for dating the demise of the Neanderthals. Chemist Willard Libby and his colleagues developed the method at the University of Chicago in the late 1940s, and it is no exaggeration to say that its widespread application afterwards revolutionized archeology. In recognition of his achievement, Libby himself was awarded a Nobel Prize. The reasoning behind the method is elegant and clear-cut. The abundant element carbon (C) occurs naturally in three varieties or isotopes—^{12}C, ^{13}C, and ^{14}C. For present purposes we can ignore ^{13}C and concentrate on ^{12}C, which is by far the most abundant of the three isotopes, and on ^{14}C, which is much rarer. Unlike ^{12}C, ^{14}C is radioactive, and it decays with a half-life of about 5730 years, which means that after 5730 years, any given amount will be reduced by half (through decay to Nitrogen 14 or ^{14}N). This half-life may seem long, but it is very short by comparison to that of many other radioactive isotopes, including, for example, radiopotassium or ^{40}K, whose half-life is approximately 1.3 billion years. The potassium/argon dating technique depends on ^{40}K, and its slow decay rate explains why potassium/argon is useful for dating ancient volcanic rocks like those at the east African australopith sites that are millions of years old. ^{14}C would be useless for the same purpose, because even if suitable material were available, ^{14}C's short half-life means that after just a few tens of thousands of years—perhaps 100,000 at the outside—it will be too meagerly represented for accurate measurement.

^{14}C would essentially disappear from the planet, except that the interaction between cosmic rays and ^{14}N constantly creates a new supply in the upper atmosphere. In general, plants obtain their carbon directly from the atmosphere (from carbon dioxide), and animals obtain theirs from ingesting plants or other animals. Plants and animals ordinarily do not discriminate between ^{14}C and ^{12}C when they build their tissues, which means that the $^{14}C/^{12}C$ ratio in live creatures approximates the ratio in the atmosphere. When an organism dies, however, it ceases to assimilate carbon, and the ratio of ^{14}C to ^{12}C decreases at a rate that is directly proportional to the half-life of ^{14}C. This means that the $^{14}C/^{12}C$ ratio in ancient organic matter, such as a piece of charcoal or the degraded protein (collagen) extracted from bone, can be used to estimate when the organism—tree or animal—died.

In practice, the radiocarbon method confronts numerous complications, including well-documented variation in the atmospheric content of ^{14}C through time, probably caused mainly by fluctuations in cosmic ray intensity. In the context of dating the last Neanderthals, the biggest challenge stems from ^{14}C's short half-life and the possibility that an ancient piece of organic matter acquired some of its carbon in the ground, after burial. Humic acids (decayed plant matter) percolating down from the surface are probably the most frequent source of such "contamination," and their impact will be especially great on objects that are older than 20,000 to 25,000 years. Such objects will retain very little of their original ^{14}C, and the addition of even a small amount of more recent carbon will increase their ^{14}C content significantly, producing an apparent radiocarbon age that is much too young. It can be shown mathematically that just a one percent increment of modern carbon to a sample that is actually 67,000 years old will make the sample appear to be only 37,000 years old, and no laboratory can guarantee to remove such tiny amounts of contaminant. Contamination is particularly likely to affect degraded bone protein, and it is less likely to affect charcoal. Unfortunately, charcoal is relatively rare in sites older than 25,000 years ago, and bone dates predominate heavily. The bottom line is that on radiocarbon alone, it can rarely be said that a site dated to 30,000 years ago is not actually 5000, 10,000, or even 20,000 years older. And it is here that we confront the problem of dating the last Neanderthals.

The radiocarbon method has been applied directly to Neanderthal bones at Mezmaiskaya Cave (Russia) and Vindija (Croatia), both of which we have already cited for their provision of Neanderthal DNA. At Mezmaiskaya, the radiocarbon result implies that a

Neanderthal infant died about 29,000 years ago, while at Vindija, it suggests that Neanderthals persisted locally until 29,000 to 28,000 years ago. If the Mezmaiskaya and Vindija dates are taken at face value, Neanderthals co-existed with early Upper Paleolithic people in each region for at least 6000 to 7000 years, and we might conclude that Neanderthals often held their own against Cro-Magnon invaders. On the other hand, if the bones at both sites were only minutely contaminated by much more recent carbon, they could easily be 8000 to 10,000 years older, and we wouldn't need to infer any overlap with Cro-Magnons. Given the ever-present potential for contamination, particularly in bone protein, many specialists routinely regard radiocarbon dates older than 25,000 or 30,000 years as only minimum ages, meaning that the dated specimens could be the stated age or much older. When potential contamination is taken into account, a useful rule of thumb is that where dates depart from stratigraphic order within a site (that is, when dates from the same layer differ or when they fail to become older with depth), the oldest dates probably most closely approximate the true age. Mezmaiskaya Cave illustrates the point, for it has provided a radiocarbon date of 32,000 years on wood charcoal from an Upper Paleolithic layer that is stratified above the layer with the Neanderthal infant. The implication is that the infant must actually be older than 32,000 years, and Mezmaiskaya does not show that Neanderthals and modern people overlapped for thousands of years in southern Russia.

Given the ever present problem of contamination, it follows that the best estimate for when the Neanderthals succumbed will come not from the youngest Mousterian (or Neanderthal) dates but from the oldest Upper Paleolithic ones. The comprehensive analysis by João Zilhão and Francesco d'Errico indicates that the early Upper Paleolithic Aurignacian Culture intruded into western and central Europe about 37,000 to 36,000 years ago. And in most places, site stratigraphies indicate that whatever the date, early Upper Paleolithic Cro-Magnons quickly replaced Mousterian Neanderthals, probably within centuries or a millennium. We stress "most places," because there is one well-publicized, putative exception.

The exception to quick replacement involves the Iberian cul-de-sac, meaning Spain and Portugal south of the Ebro and Tagus Rivers. Three Spanish sites north of the Ebro have provided early Aurignacian dates near 40,000 years ago, but Zilhão and d'Errico believe that in each case the dated material was actually associated with older Mousterian or perhaps Châtelperronian artifacts, and they place the earliest local Aurignacian closer to 37,000 years ago. Even then, however, it would be 7000 to 8000 years older than any dated Upper Paleolithic south of the Ebro and Tagus. Equally important, some southern Spanish and Portuguese Mousterian sites have produced radiocarbon dates ranging up to 30,000 years ago. The most striking dates are from Zafarraya Cave, where they were obtained directly on Neanderthal bones. To Zilhão, d'Errico, and others, the sum means that Neanderthals found refuge on the Iberian Peninsula long after modern humans had displaced them elsewhere in Europe. There is an alternative interpretation, however. First, the Iberian late Mousterian/ Neanderthal dates are still few, and as always, it is possible that they are only minimum age estimates. Second, the absence of the Upper Paleolithic before 30,000 years ago may mean only that much of the Iberian Peninsula was sparsely populated or even abandoned from before 37,000 years ago until 30,000 years ago or later. The reason would be adverse climate. Archeological layers that fall unequivocally between 40,000 and 20,000 years ago are rare or absent in northwestern Africa, just across the Straits of Gibraltar, and the reason appears to have been persistent, extreme aridity. The question of how long Neanderthals survived in Iberia differs from the Châtelperronian issue, because it can be resolved by additional research. In the meanwhile, we see no compelling reason to suppose that Neanderthals persisted anywhere in Europe long after modern humans had appeared.

♛ ♛ ♛

The Neanderthals are fascinating because they were so much like us and yet so different. Before we abandon them completely, we want to address one well-known speculation for what could explain the difference. This is the possibility that they possessed only a limited ability to speak, that is, to produce the kind of rapidly spoken, phonemic speech that characterized all historic people. Historic cultures may vary greatly in their complexity, but historic languages do not—they are all equally sophisticated and they can all be translated one from the next, meaning that any one can be used to express any idea, however intricate.

What about Neanderthal language? The truth is that we don't know. We can only imagine that Neanderthals had a system that was far more complex than that of chimpanzees or for that matter than the systems of the australopiths, *Homo ergaster,* and probably even *Homo heidelbergensis.* But does that mean it was as sophisticated as modern language? One clue may come from the position of the voice box (or larynx), which is crucial for the production of the entire range of sounds that all modern languages require. In apes and newborn humans, the voice box is located high in the throat, restricting the range of possible sounds. A major advantage of this position is that it permits apes and human infants to swallow and breathe at the same time, reducing the risk of choking. The voice box begins its descent in humans between the ages of 1½ and 2 years, and since this significantly increases the risk of choking, there must be a countervailing natural selective benefit. The most obvious one is the newly created ability to produce all the sounds that are essential for phonemic speech, and no one doubts the survival benefit of speech. The position of the voice box is related to the shape of the skull base—flat in apes and modern human infants and arched upwards or flexed in modern human adults. On the three Neanderthal skulls that are well enough preserved to show the skull base, it appears to have been flat, and this might mean that Neanderthals could not have produced speech as we know it.

Against this, however, we must consider the tongue bone (or hyoid), which provides hard support for the voice box and which differs significantly in shape between apes and modern humans. Only a single tongue bone is known for the Neanderthals, but it's a dead ringer for its modern human counterpart. And we must also consider the Neanderthals' African contemporaries—the modern or near-modern people, who, unlike the Neanderthals, included our ancestors. They had flexed cranial bases, but we will see that in virtually every detectable archeological respect they were no more modern than the Neanderthals. So, if they could speak in a fully modern way, the ability doesn't seem to have fostered full-blown modern behavior—the dawn of human culture to which the title of this book refers. A newly found capacity for language may still have prompted fully modern behavior, but if so the capacity must have been rooted in a brain change. We argue later that such a brain change is the most economic explanation for why modern human behavior emerged and spread so abruptly.

7
BODY BEFORE BEHAVIOR

Raymond Dart ignited the search for human origins in Africa when he announced the Taung child's skull in 1925, but it was not the first significant human fossil to emerge from Africa. Already in 1921, lead-and-zinc miners had recovered a remarkable skull from a cave at the Broken Hill Mine in Northern Rhodesia. The skull exhibited a flat, receding forehead above a thick browridge and a massive face. Yet it possessed typically human teeth, and its braincase approached modern ones in size. The teeth were remarkable mainly for their advanced decay, associated with infection (abscessing) that penetrated the jaw bone. Spread of the infection before death possibly produced a partially healed puncture on the skull wall.

The mining company transferred the skull to London, and in 1922, the distinguished anatomist Arthur Smith Woodward presented it to a meeting of the Anatomical Society. Dart was present, and he later recalled, "It was a staggering sight to see an undoubtedly human skull with beetling eyebrow ridges thicker than those of Neanderthal Man and a muzzle as massive as that of a gorilla. Yet the teeth were like those of any modern man and the brain quite large (1,280 cc)." The skull has sometimes been likened to those of the Neanderthals, but it differed from Neanderthal skulls in numerous respects, including its great breadth near the base, the relatively large size of its mastoid process, and the absence of an oval depression just above the upper limit for the attachment of the neck muscles (Figure 7.1). Woodward assigned the skull to the species *Homo rhodesiensis,* which the popular press quickly translated as "Rhodesian Man." The specimen is still housed in London, but in 1964, Northern Rhodesia gained independence as Zambia, and Broken Hill became Kabwe (Figure 7.2). The fossil is thus now usually known as the Kabwe skull.

The Kabwe skull exemplifies an all-too-frequent paradox in paleoanthropology—the skull might never have been found without intensive commercial activity, yet the same activity all but erased key stratigraphic information. The miners recovered animal bones and some other less spectacular human remains from the same cave, but we do not know which, if any, were in the same layer as the skull. We also do not know if there were artifacts nearby, although it seems likely that there were. Paleoanthropologists rely on associated artifacts and animal species for many purposes, not the least of which is to gauge the relative age of important human fossils. And it goes without saying that fossils lose much of their value if they cannot be arranged in time. The circumstances of discovery at Kabwe preclude secure dating, but the miners recovered bones of some archaic mammal species, and if we assume that these occurred with the skull, they suggest it is between 700,000 and 400,000

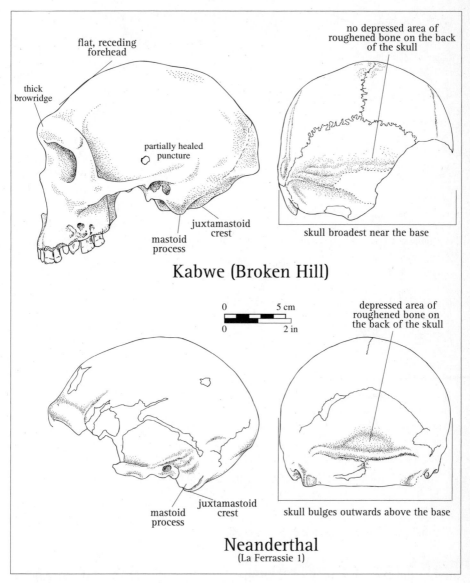

FIGURE 7.1

The fossil human skull from Kabwe, Zambia, compared to the skull of a Neanderthal from La Ferrassie, France (redrawn after A. P. Santa Luca 1978, *Journal of Human Evolution* 7, p. 623 pp. 622, 626).

years old. In this event, it would be roughly contemporaneous with three similar, more recently found African specimens. These come from Bodo in

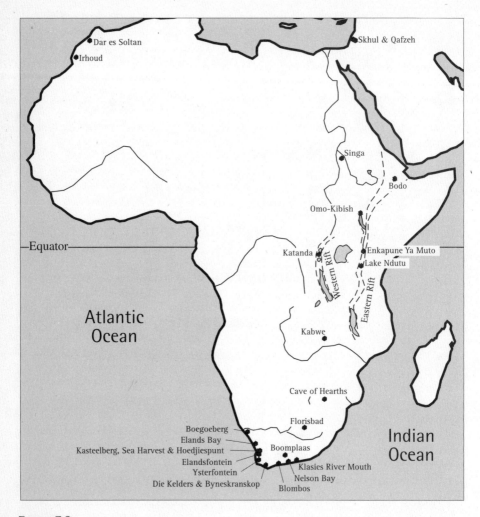

FIGURE 7.2
The locations of the sites mentioned in this chapter.

the Middle Awash Valley of Ethiopia, Lake Ndutu near the western end of the main Olduvai Gorge in northern Tanzania, and Elandsfontein (also known as Hopefield or Saldanha) in the Western Cape Province of South Africa. At each site, the age range has been gauged mainly from associated mammal species, stratigraphic position, or both, and it is confirmed at Bodo by a potassium/argon date of about 600,000 years ago.

The Kabwe skull and its probable contemporaries each combine primitive characters that occur in *Homo ergaster* and *Homo erectus* with advanced characters that typify both the Neanderthals and modern humans. The primitive features include large browridges, a low, flattened forehead, great breadth across the base of the skull, and thick skull walls. The most striking advanced features are the large size of the braincase (averaging more than 1200 cubic centimeters [cc] compared to 1000 cc in classic *erectus*) and a tendency for the braincase to be relatively broad at the front, expanded at the sides, and rounded at the back. At Bodo, Lake Ndutu, and Elandsfontein, the skulls are associated with late Acheulean hand axes, and the people may have been related to those Africans whose descendants brought the Acheulean Tradition to Europe about 500,000 years ago. An Out-of-Africa movement at this time could explain why the African skulls resemble European specimens that are probably about the same age or a bit younger. For the sake of convenience, we have referred the joint African/European population to *Homo heidelbergensis,* and we have suggested that *heidelbergensis* was the last shared ancestor of the Neanderthals and modern humans. The more important point here is that in form and probable geologic age, the Kabwe, Bodo, Lake Ndutu, and Elandsfontein skulls comprise a plausible link between *Homo ergaster* before 600,000 years ago and more modern-looking Africans after 400,000 years ago.

♛ ♛ ♛

A decade after Woodward had added Rhodesian Man to the roll call of ancient humans, zoologist T. F. Dreyer went prospecting for fossils at the Florisbad hot spring about 50 kilometers (30 miles) northwest of

Bloemfontein, South Africa. The spring owner had encountered animal fossils and stone tools when he enlarged baths for a spa, but he feared losing his investment if the baths were temporarily drained. Dreyer thus had to wade and grope for bones. The story goes that he stuck his hand underwater into the spring deposits and pulled out part of a human skull—his fingers lodged in the eye sockets.

The Florisbad skull comprises the right side of the face, most of the forehead, portions of the roof and sidewalls, and an isolated upper right wisdom tooth (third molar) that probably goes with it. It bears tooth marks from a hyena or other large carnivore that may reveal the cause of death. By modern standards, the skull walls are very thick and the face is remarkably broad (Figure 7.3). Nonetheless, despite conspicuous thickening above the eye sockets, there is no true browridge (no interruption or inflection between the region immediately above the sockets and the forehead above), the forehead rises relatively steeply, and the face is short, flat, and tucked in beneath the front of the braincase. In these last important respects, Florisbad differs not only from Kabwe and its allies but also from the Neanderthals, and it approaches the condition in modern humans.

The single tooth associated with the Florisbad skull has been dated to about 260,000 years ago by the Electron Spin Resonance (ESR) method. We noted previously that this method often provides only tentative results, mainly because it depends on site-specific assumptions about the history of uranium uptake and loss in a tooth. Still, even if the Florisbad ESR result is placed aside, geologic context and associated mammal species indicate that the skull is younger than those from Elandsfontein, Lake Ndutu, and Bodo and that it is older than more fully modern fossils known from African sites that postdate 130,000 years ago.

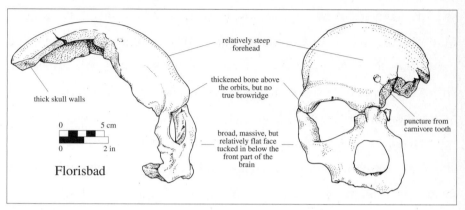

FIGURE 7.3
The partial skull from Florisbad, South Africa (drawn by Kathryn Cruz-Uribe from a photograph) (Copyright Kathryn Cruz-Uribe).

Sites at Singa, Sudan, and Irhoud, Morocco, have provided fossil skulls that probably fall in the same time span as Florisbad, between roughly 300,000 and 130,000 years ago, and the specimens exhibit a similar mix of primitive and essentially modern characters. Collectively then, the Florisbad, Singa, and Irhoud skulls document the transition from more archaic to modern humans in Africa in broadly the same way that the Sima de los Huesos fossils document the transition from more archaic humans to Neanderthals in Europe.

♛ ♛ ♛

At least seventeen sites from Morocco and Libya on the north to the Cape of Good Hope on the south have provided human fossils that probably or possibly date from the same time as the classic Neanderthals, between about 130,000 and 50,000 to 40,000 years ago. Representative sites that are especially well known for the completeness of their fossils, the security of their dating, or both include Dar es Soltan Cave 2 in Atlantic Morocco, the Omo-Kibish river margin locality in southern Ethiopia, and the Klasies River Mouth Cave complex on the southern coast of South Africa (Figure 7.2). To the African sites proper we can also add the famous Skhul and Qafzeh caves in Israel. To explain their inclusion, we stress two facts. First, anyone migrating from Africa to southwestern Asia would encounter Israel first, and it is outside of Africa only by technical, historic geopolitical definition. Second, recall that during the long time span of human evolution, global climate has repeatedly fluctuated between glacial and interglacial intervals. On average, the glacial intervals were not only cooler, they were also drier, while the interglacial intervals tended to be both warmer and moister. The changes in temperature and precipitation often caused redistributions of plants and animals, and zoologist Eitan Tchernov of the Hebrew University in Jerusalem has shown that climatic conditions during past interglacial periods repeatedly enabled African animals to expand into what is now Israel. During the especially warm earlier part of the Last Interglacial, between roughly 125,000 and 90,000 years ago, the African invaders included early modern humans. The Israeli fossils are in fact the most numerous and most complete early modern human specimens yet discovered.

The African fossils from between 130,000 and 50,000 years ago are mostly fragments and isolated teeth, but even these are often adequate to show that the people were not Neanderthals, and they make it abundantly clear that the Neanderthals never penetrated Africa. Where lower jaws are available, they are sometimes large and rugged, but where the appropriate parts are preserved, they uniformly lack retromolar spaces (the gap that Neanderthal jaws have between the third molar and the part of the jaw that rises to articulate with the skull), and they usually have well-defined chins like those of living people. Together with other facial bones, the lower jaws show that unlike the Neanderthals, their African contemporaries generally had short, flat, modern-looking faces. Where skulls are known, they are sometimes ruggedly built, but the braincases tend to be short and high as in living people, rather than long and low as in Neanderthals (Figure 7.4). Where the internal capacity of the braincases can be estimated, it ranges between roughly 1370 cc and 1510 cc, comfortably within the range of both Neanderthals and living humans.

Limb bones show that like the Neanderthals, their African contemporaries were well muscled, but the especially abundant bones from Skhul and Qafzeh caves also show that the Africans lacked the squat body form and short limbs that are a Neanderthal hallmark (Figure 7.5). Instead, the people were long and linear like most historic people living near the Equator. Since both early modern Africans and the Neanderthals were highly mobile hunter-gatherers, the difference in bodily proportions probably does not reflect a significant difference in activity levels, and it reinforces the conclusion that Neanderthal body form was primarily an adaptation to cold climate. This adaptation was extreme by modern standards, probably because it was less strongly mediated by culture or technology.

It is possible to overemphasize the modernity of Africans after 130,000 years ago, and the fossils vary significantly both between and within sites. As a group, the Skhul-Qafzeh skulls, for example, are highly variable in their expression of a chin, in the extent to which their foreheads rise vertically, and even in basic braincase shape. In some respects, such as well-developed browridges, large teeth, and a tendency for the jaws to protrude far forwards, they often recall more

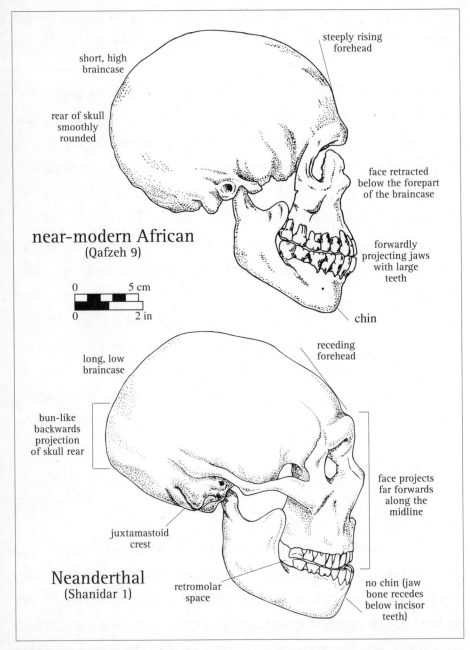

near-modern African
(Qafzeh 9)

short, high
braincase

rear of skull
smoothly
rounded

steeply rising
forehead

face retracted
below the forepart
of the braincase

forwardly
projecting jaws
with large
teeth

chin

0   5 cm

0   2 in

Neanderthal
(Shanidar 1)

long, low
braincase

bun-like
backwards
projection
of skull rear

juxtamastoid
crest

retromolar
space

receding
forehead

face projects
far forwards
along the
midline

no chin (jaw
bone recedes
below incisor
teeth)

FIGURE 7.4
A modern or near-modern skull from Qafzeh Cave, Israel, compared to a Neanderthal skull
from Shanidar Cave, Iraq (drawn by Kathryn Cruz-Uribe from casts and photographs)
(Copyright Kathryn Cruz-Uribe).

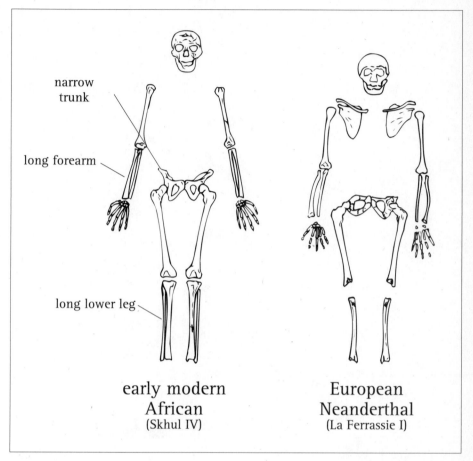

narrow
trunk

long forearm

long lower leg

early modern
African
(Skhul IV)

European
Neanderthal
(La Ferrassie I)

FIGURE 7.5
Contrasting body proportions of an early modern African and a Neanderthal (redrawn after
O. M. Pearson 2000, *Evolutionary Anthropology* 9, p. 241).

archaic humans. The much less numerous and more fragmentary
Klasies River Mouth fossils, which date from basically the same interval between 120,000 and 90,000 years ago, differ from the Skhul-
Qafzeh fossils in detail, and they are also remarkably variable among
themselves. One of the Klasies River Mouth lower jaws is among the
smallest human specimens ever found (Figure 7.6), and some isolated

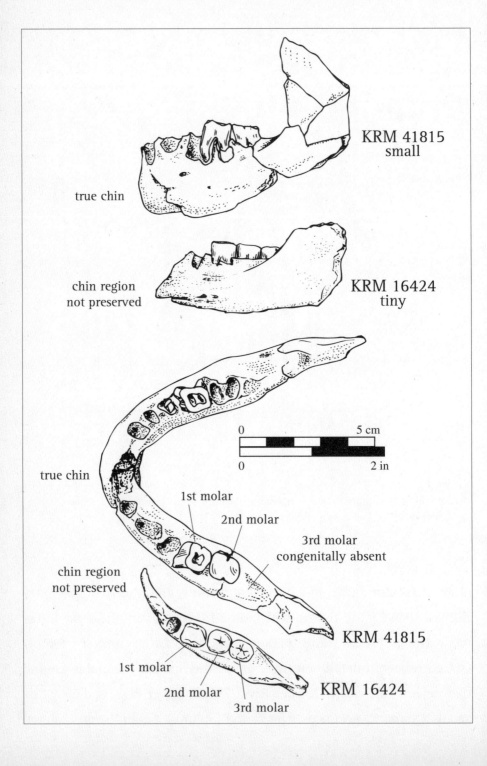

KRM 41815
small

true chin

chin region
not preserved

KRM 16424
tiny

true chin

0   5 cm

0   2 in

1st molar

2nd molar

3rd molar
congenitally absent

chin region
not preserved

KRM 41815

1st molar

2nd molar

3rd molar

KRM 16424

teeth suggest that other jaws were equally tiny. At the same time, the Klasies River Mouth human fossils include jaws and other bones from significantly larger people, and the degree of size variation is striking. It may indicate a level of sexual difference (dimorphism) that has never been documented in any other "modern" human population.

The bottom line is that the Skhul-Qafzeh people and their Klasies River Mouth contemporaries are perhaps best characterized as "near modern." Neither group is likely to have been ancestral to anyone after 50,000 years ago, if only because each probably disappeared long before that. The Skhul-Qafzeh people were apparently replaced by Neanderthals when climate turned cooler after 80,000 years ago, while the Klasies River Mouth people and other near-modern southern Africans experienced a population crash when southern Africa turned mostly very dry in the middle of the last glaciation, about 60,000 years ago. When all the facts are considered, the Skhul-Qafzeh and Klasies River Mouth fossils are significant not because they represent the lineal ancestors of later modern people (they almost certainly do not), but because they pinpoint Africa as the place where modern anatomy evolved. The precise birthplace of the later modern humans is uncertain, but on present evidence, it probably lay in equatorial eastern Africa. Climatic conditions remained favorable there for human occupation throughout the last 130,000 years, and eastern Africa has provided some of the earliest evidence for the behavioral advance that allowed modern Africans to spread to Eurasia.

FIGURE 7.6
Lower jaws from the Klasies River Mouth site, South Africa (drawn by Kathryn Cruz-Uribe from casts). Note the contrast in size. Specimen No. 16424 is among the smallest adult human jaws ever recorded (Copyright Kathryn Cruz-Uribe).

♛ ♛ ♛

We turn now to a curious discrepancy that we identified at the beginning of the book: the people who lived in Africa between 130,000 and 50,000 years ago may have been modern or near-modern in form, but they were behaviorally similar to the Neanderthals. Like the Neanderthals, they commonly struck stone flakes or flake-blades (elongated flakes) from cores they had carefully prepared in advance; they often collected naturally occurring pigments, perhaps because they were attracted by the colors; they apparently built fires at will; they buried their dead, at least on occasion; and they routinely acquired large mammals as food. In these respects and perhaps others, they may have been advanced over their predecessors. Yet, in common with both earlier people and their Neanderthal contemporaries, they manufactured a relatively small range of recognizable stone tool types; their artifact assemblages varied remarkably little through time and space (despite notable environmental variation); they obtained stone raw material mostly from local sources (suggesting relatively small home ranges or very simple social networks); they rarely if ever utilized bone, ivory, or shell to produce formal artifacts; they buried their dead without grave goods or any other compelling evidence for ritual or ceremony; they left little or no evidence for structures or for any other formal modification of their campsites; they were relatively ineffective hunter-gatherers who lacked, for example, the ability to fish; their populations were apparently very sparse, even by historic hunter-gatherer standards; and they left no compelling evidence for art or decoration.

Archeologists usually assign the African artifact assemblages to the Middle Stone Age or MSA. However, the MSA closely resembles the

Mousterian Tradition (or Culture) of Europe and western Asia, and the variation of artifacts is greater within the Mousterian and the MSA than it is between them. The difference in naming mainly reflects geographic distance and separate archeological traditions. The MSA and the Mousterian both differed from the preceding Acheulean Tradition primarily in the absence of hand axes and other large bifacial tools, and they replaced the Acheulean at about the same time, between 250,000 and 200,000 years ago (Figure 7.7). Both were in turn replaced after 50,000 years ago by new culture complexes that differed from the MSA and the Mousterian much more sharply than either did from the preceding Acheulean. In Europe, the new complex was the Upper Paleolithic, which we described in the last chapter. Archeologists call the new complex in Africa the Later Stone Age or LSA.

The LSA diverged from the preceding MSA in Africa in exactly the same fundamental features that distinguish the Upper Paleolithic from the Mousterian in Europe. Thus, LSA people tended to manufacture a wider range of easily recognizable stone artifact types; their artifact assemblages varied much more through time and space; they routinely produced standardized (formal) bone artifacts and art; they dug elaborate graves that unequivocally imply a burial ritual; and they were more effective hunter-gatherers whose population densities approximated those of their historic successors in similar environments. Together, LSA and Upper Paleolithic material residues are the oldest to resemble those of historic hunter-gatherers in every detectable respect, and they are thus the oldest from which we can infer unambiguously that the people were behaviorally modern.

LSA and Upper Paleolithic artifact assemblages differed in specifics from the very beginning, and the blades and burins that are

millions of
years ago

millions of
years ago

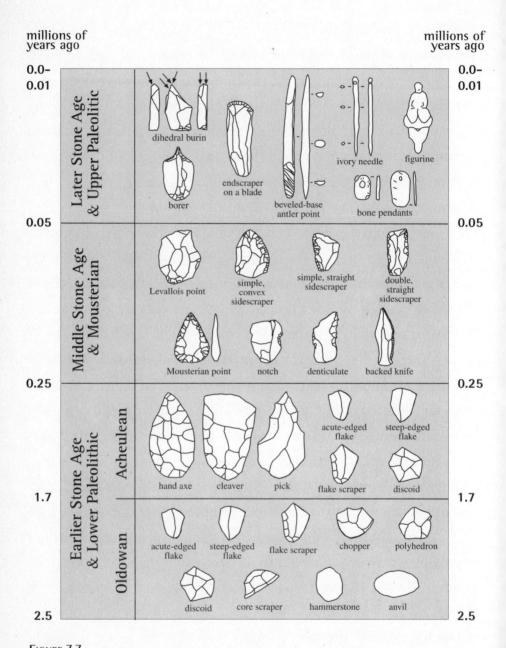

FIGURE 7.7
The principal artifact complexes ("cultures" or "culture-stratigraphic units") discussed in the
text. The individual artifacts are not drawn to scale.

a hallmark of the Upper Paleolithic are much rarer in the LSA. In their place are small stone scrapers and other equally small stone bits that were intentionally dulled ("backed") along one edge, probably to facilitate hafting in wooden or bone handles (Figure 7.8). The detailed differences between the LSA and the Upper Paleolithic contrast sharply with the equally detailed similarities between the preceding MSA and Mousterian, and they serve to underscore the significant increase in geographic variability that followed the appearance of the LSA and Upper Paleolithic. If the greater variety of artifact types, the more complex graves, and especially the art and ornamentation of the LSA and Upper Paleolithic signal the dawn of culture in the fully modern sense, then the great increase in artifactual diversity through time and space provides the oldest concrete indication for ethnographic "cultures" or identity-conscious ethnic groups.

Like the latest Mousterian, the latest MSA is difficult to date, because it lies beyond 25,000 years ago, in an interval when even a minute amount of recent, undetectable carbon contamination can make a radiocarbon-dated sample seem 20,000 to 30,000 years younger than it really is. We have already pointed out that other methods like luminescence and ESR that might be used instead commonly require unverifiable site-specific assumptions, and their accuracy is thus often questionable. The problem of dating the latest MSA is exacerbated in southern Africa, where many sites were abandoned between 60,000 and 30,000 years ago, probably because of extreme aridity in the middle of the last glacial period. For the moment, the most informative dates come from eastern Africa, where they indicate that the LSA probably began between 50,000 and 45,000 years ago. The most important site is Enkapune Ya Muto ("Twilight Cave") in the central Rift Valley of

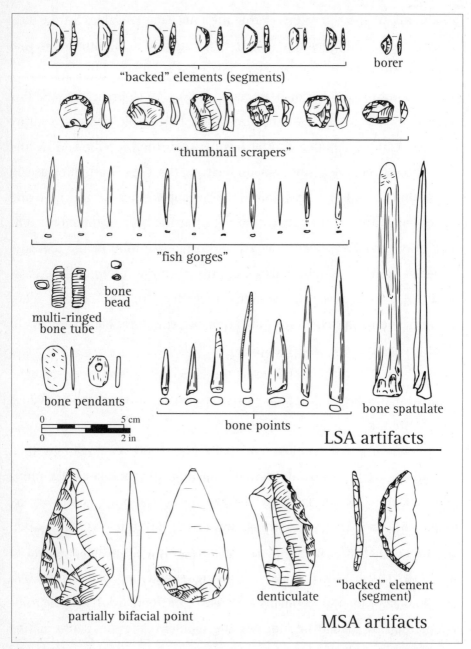

"backed" elements (segments)

borer

"thumbnail scrapers"

"fish gorges"

multi-ringed
bone tube

bone
bead

bone pendants

bone points

bone spatulate

LSA artifacts

partially bifacial point

denticulate

"backed" element
(segment)

MSA artifacts

FIGURE 7.8
Typical MSA and LSA artifacts (top redrawn after J. Deacon, 1984, *British Archaeological Reports* International Series 213, pp. 198, 244; bottom after T. P. Volman 1981, *The Middle Stone Age in the Southern Cape.* Ph.D. Thesis, University of Chicago, pp. 229, 232, and 238).

Kenya excavated by Stanley Ambrose of the University of Illinois. Enkapune Ya Muto has provided ostrich eggshell beads that are among the oldest personal ornaments so far found, and we emphasized their modern behavioral implications in Chapter 1. Here, we stress that Enkapune Ya Muto and other east African sites place the LSA in Africa firmly before the Upper Paleolithic in Europe. The precise origins of the Upper Paleolithic remain unclear, but a small number of dates suggest it appeared in western Asia 45,000 to 43,000 years ago, perhaps only shortly after the LSA had emerged, that it was present in eastern Europe between 40,000 and 38,000 years ago, and that it reached central and western Europe last, roughly 38,000 to 37,000 years ago (Figure 7.9). This is the expected pattern if the populations that spread the Upper Paleolithic ultimately had their roots in Africa.

Labels and precise dates aside, the basic point is that LSA/Upper Paleolithic people are the first for whom we can infer the fully modern capacity for culture, or perhaps more precisely, the fully modern ability to innovate. It was surely this ability that allowed LSA/Upper Paleolithic people to disperse at the expense of their more primitive contemporaries, beginning between 50,000 and 40,000 years ago. Upper Paleolithic innovations included solidly built houses, tailored clothing, more efficient fireplaces, and new hunting technology that not only allowed Upper Paleolithic Cro-Magnons to displace their predecessors but also to colonize the harshest, most continental parts of Eurasia where no one had lived before. By 25,000 years ago, Upper Paleolithic people had spread through central Siberia, and by 14,000 years ago, they had reached its northeastern corner. This was in the waning phase of the Last Glaciation, when sea level was still low because of water locked up in the great continental glaciers and when

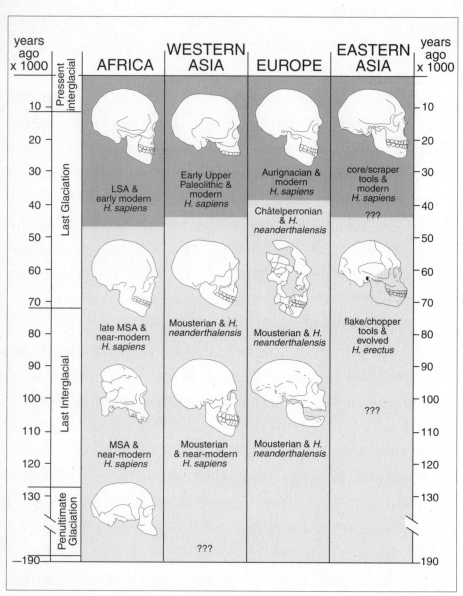

FIGURE 7.9

Approximate chronological arrangement of various cultures and human physical types in Europe, western Asia, eastern Asia, and Africa from 190,000 years ago to the historical present.

a broad land bridge linked northeastern Siberia to Alaska. Sometime between 14,000 and 12,000 years ago, Siberian Upper Paleolithic people made the relatively short trek across. By 11,500 years ago, they had spread southwards through the Americas to become the people known to archeologists as the Paleoindians.

♟ ♟ ♟

One important way in which LSA people differed from their predecessors was in their ability to hunt and gather more effectively. This alone could explain how they (or their Upper Paleolithic descendants) managed to spread so quickly and widely. The evidence for an LSA hunting-and-gathering advance comes mainly from the southern and western coasts of South Africa, where archeologists have been systematically excavating rich MSA and LSA sites for many decades. Some of these sites, like the Klasies River Mouth Main cave complex, Blombos Cave, and Die Kelders Cave 1, contain both MSA and LSA occupation layers. The most persuasive comparisons are between MSA layers dating from the warmer parts of the Last Interglacial period, between roughly 125,000 and 80,000 years ago, and LSA layers dating from the Present Interglacial period or Holocene, between 12,000 years ago and the historic present. This is because climatic conditions were similar during these two time intervals and any observed MSA/LSA contrasts are thus likely to reflect a human behavioral difference as opposed to an environmental one. Analyses of animal remains so far suggest four principal contrasts. We previewed these in Chapter 1, and we summarize them only briefly here.

First, Present Interglacial LSA coastal sites (Elands Bay Cave, Die Kelders Cave 1, Blombos Cave, Nelson Bay Cave, Klasies River

Mouth Main site, and others) contain many more bones of fish and airborne birds than do Last Interglacial MSA sites (Blombos Cave and Klasies River Mouth Main site). Only LSA sites contain "fish gorges" (polished, toothpick size, double-pointed bone splinters), grooved stone net sinkers, and other implements that recall ethnographically recorded fishing and fowling gear. Archeological evidence thus reinforces the conclusion that only LSA people fished and fowled routinely. Greater LSA ability to catch fish and birds would surely have promoted larger LSA populations.

Second, in Present Interglacial LSA sites (Nelson Bay Cave, Byneskranskop Cave 1, and others), buffalo and wild pigs outnumber eland, roughly mirroring the abundance of buffalo and wild pigs in the historic environment. In contrast, in Last Interglacial MSA sites (Klasies River Mouth Main site and Blombos Cave), eland greatly outnumber buffalo and pigs, even though historic observations imply that eland were probably much rarer nearby. Eland continue to dominate in MSA layers that date from the early part of the Last Glaciation (Klasies River Mouth Main site and Die Kelders Cave 1), which increases the probability that eland dominance reflects MSA behavior and not some undetected environmental factor. Since eland are much less dangerous to hunt than buffalo and wild pigs, and since MSA sites lack firm evidence for projectile weapons, an MSA preference for eland may actually reflect MSA reluctance to attack species that were especially likely to injure hunters. LSA people almost certainly had projectile weapons, arguably including the bow and arrow from 20,000 years ago, and they could thus have stalked buffalo and wild pigs at significantly reduced personal risk. If this deduction is correct, and buffalo and pigs were more common than eland on the ground near both MSA and LSA sites,

LSA people would have obtained many more animals overall, even if their hunts were often unsuccessful. Again, a likely result would be larger LSA populations.

Third, the tortoises, shellfish, or both in MSA sites (Klasies River Mouth Main site, Blombos Cave, Die Kelders 1, Ysterfontein, Hoedjies Punt, Sea Harvest, and Boegoeberg 2) tend to be much larger than those in LSA sites (Nelson Bay Cave, Die Kelders Cave 1, Byneskranskop Cave 1, Kasteelberg A and B, Elands Bay Cave, and others) that were occupied under similar environmental conditions. Since tortoises and shellfish can be collected with limited technology and minimal risk, the smaller average tortoise and shellfish size in LSA sites probably reflects more intensive LSA collection that understandably removed the largest individuals first. The most plausible explanation for more intensive collection is that LSA collectors were more numerous, in keeping with their ability to fish, fowl, and hunt more effectively.

Fourth, the ages of fur seals in LSA sites (Elands Bay Cave, Kasteelberg A and B, Die Kelders 1, Nelson Bay Cave, and others) suggest that the people timed their coastal visits to the August-to-October interval when 9- to 10-month-old seals could be harvested on the shore and when resources inland were probably at their poorest. The ages of MSA fur seals suggest that MSA people remained at the coast more or less throughout the year, even when resources were probably more abundant inland. This difference is the most weakly substantiated of the four listed here, since only the Klasies River Mouth Main site has provided a large enough MSA seal sample for numerical comparison to the LSA samples. If fresh MSA samples confirm a likely MSA/LSA contrast in seasonal mobility, a reasonable explanation is that MSA people could not transport water effectively. So far, only LSA sites have provided secure evidence for water containers, in the form of ostrich eggshell canteens.

In sum, the South African sites suggest that LSA technological advances contributed directly to an enhanced ability to hunt and gather and that this in turn promoted larger human populations. Unfortunately, it is not yet possible to show that the hunting-gathering advance occurred abruptly in the earliest LSA, tentatively dated between 50,000 and 40,000 years ago, rather than more gradually afterwards. The issue will ultimately have to be addressed outside the coastal regions of South Africa, since these areas were largely abandoned between 60,000 and 30,000 years ago, probably because of the regional aridity to which we have already referred. Still, pending fresh research elsewhere, the South African evidence is certainly sufficient to argue that MSA animal remains, like MSA artifacts, imply less than fully modern behavior. If we accept that MSA people were anatomically modern or near-modern, then the artifacts and animal remains together suggest that modern anatomy lagged modern behavior by at least 50,000 years and that it was the evolution of modern behavior between 50,000 and 40,000 years ago that allowed anatomically modern people to spread from Africa.

♛ ♛ ♛

Not all archeologists agree with our perspective on the origins of modern human behavior, and some have argued that the behavioral differences between MSA and LSA people have been exaggerated. The strongest proponents of this opposing view are Hilary Deacon of the

University of Stellenbosch, and, writing together, Sally McBrearty of the University of Connecticut and Alison Brooks of George Washington University. In their opinion, the real advance to modern behavior occurred with the appearance of the MSA. This conclusion eliminates the nagging need to explain why modern (LSA) behavior lagged behind modern (MSA) anatomy, since they would have arisen together, 250,000 to 200,000 years ago. It then fails, however, to confront the equally knotty problem of why the modern human diaspora to Eurasia lagged behind modern anatomy by 50,000 years or more.

The idea that MSA people were behaviorally modern is founded mainly on two observations. The first is that MSA and LSA people shared prominent evolved behaviors such as a sophisticated ability to produce and modify sharp stone flakes and blades, regular hunting of large mammals for food, an interest in collecting and modifying naturally occurring lumps of pigment (ocher), and the capacity to construct fireplaces routinely. The second is that MSA people sporadically exhibited some of the same advanced behaviors that LSA people usually did, including especially the manufacture of standardized, ground or polished bone artifacts.

We agree that MSA and LSA populations shared many evolved, uniquely human behaviors, such as the use of naturally occurring pigments and the routine construction of fireplaces. However, Mousterian populations in Europe also possessed these traits, and future research may show that later Acheulean people did too. In this case, Mousterians in Europe and MSA people in Africa could have inherited the behaviors from their last shared ancestor, and the key question is whether they lacked other behaviors that only LSA and Upper Paleolithic people shared with historic hunter-gatherers. If so, it is certainly reasonable to conclude, as we have, that MSA and Mousterian people were behaviorally evolved in the direction of modern humans, but that they were still not fully modern.

The case that MSA people occasionally manufactured sophisticated bone artifacts depends primarily on findings at two localities: the Katanda riverside sites in the Democratic Republic of the Congo and Blombos Cave in South Africa. At Katanda, ESR dates on hippopotamus teeth and luminescence dates on covering sands bracket mammal and fish bones, non-diagnostic stone artifacts that could be either MSA or LSA, eight whole or partial barbed bone points ("harpoons") (Figure 7.10), and four additional formal bone artifacts between 150,000 and 90,000 years ago. At Blombos Cave, luminescence dates on overlying sands indicate that numerous mammal bones and shells, occasional fish bones, classic MSA stone artifacts, two or three whole or fragmentary, symmetrical, polished bone points, and about twenty-five less formal bone artifacts accumulated before 70,000 years ago.

The Katanda and Blombos findings cannot be summarily dismissed, but they require additional substantiation before the MSA is radically reinterpreted. At Katanda, the most important issue that requires clarification is why the bone artifacts appear relatively fresh while the associated mammal bones are heavily abraded and rounded, as if they had been transported in a stream. The implication might be that the artifacts accumulated after the bones and that the age of the artifacts has been significantly overestimated. This possibility might be

FIGURE 7.10
Barbed bone points from Katanda, Democratic Republic of the Congo (redrawn after J. E. Yellen 1998, *African Archaeological Review* 15, p. 189).

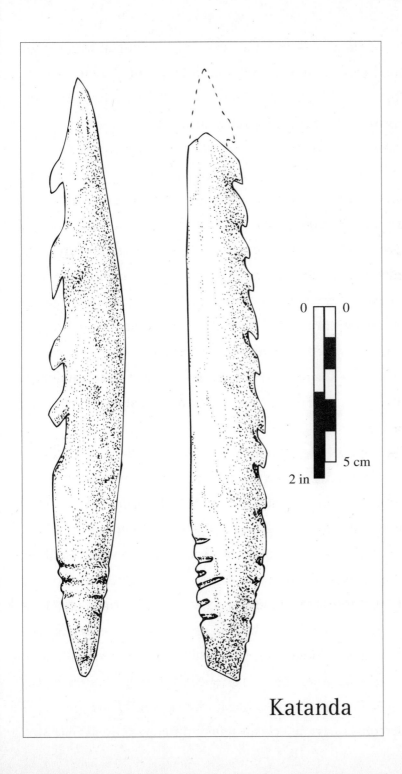

Katanda

0   0

5 cm

2 in

checked by determining if the bone artifacts and animal bones differ in geochemical content or by direct radiocarbon dating of the artifacts. Elsewhere in Africa, radiocarbon dates suggest that similar bone artifacts are mostly younger than 12,000 years.

At Blombos Cave, there is the problem that the polished bone points came from a part of the deposit where radiocarbon dates indicate that MSA and much younger LSA deposits were mixed. In chemical composition, the bone points resemble MSA bones more closely than LSA bones, but bone preservation varies across the surface at Blombos Cave, and the MSA bones for comparison came from the same admixed deposits as the polished points. These deposits also produced fish bones in quantities that are otherwise known only in LSA layers. In contrast, in parts of the Blombos excavation where admixture can be ruled out, the MSA layers contain many fewer fish bones, and these come mainly from large individuals that could represent occasional beach wash-ups.

If the sophisticated Katanda and Blombos bone artifacts are accepted at face value, archeologists must then explain why the advanced behavior they represent remained isolated for tens of thousands of years before becoming commonplace in other LSA locations. This is an especially difficult question to answer, if, as seems likely, such bone artifacts conferred an adaptive advantage, because they were used for purposes that stone tools could not perform or could not perform as well. In this light, it is hard to understand, for example, why the MSA occupants of Blombos Cave would have produced polished or ground bone points when their nearby MSA contemporaries at Die Kelders Cave 1, Boomplaas Cave, Klasies River Mouth, and other sites did not. The contrast is unlikely to reflect differences in sample size, because the other sites have provided many more MSA animal bones than Blombos Cave, while LSA bone assemblages that are smaller than the Blombos assemblage often contain many more formal bone arti- facts. They also contain bone manufacturing waste and incompletely formed intermediate pieces (preforms) that Blombos Cave lacks. The answer may be that the Blombos MSA polished points actually derive from overlying LSA layers.

The Blombos case raises the point that there will always be some evidence for LSA/Upper Paleolithic behavior in MSA/Mousterian contexts, if only because even the most careful excavations may fail to detect occasional LSA/Upper Paleolithic intrusions into MSA/ Mousterian layers. Archeologists must then decide whether sporadic exceptions, ordinarily involving a small number of pieces, truly con- tradict a widespread pattern. Until the exceptions are repeatedly rep- licated to form a pattern of their own, it is surely fair to argue no. For the moment then, we stand behind our view that the LSA/Upper Paleolithic represents a qualitative advance over the MSA/Mousterian, and that this advance explains why LSA/Upper Paleolithic people became so much more successful.

♛ ♛ ♛

At this point, a reader might ask if there are any reasonable observa- tions outside of Africa to contradict our view that the fully modern capacity for culture appeared in Africa only between 50,000 and 40,000 years ago and that it underlay the subsequent expansion of modern Africans to Eurasia. The answer of course depends partly on whom you ask, but as we see it, there is only one set of developing observations that could seriously challenge our position. These come from what may seem to be a particularly unexpected quarter—the island continent of Australia, and they concern the time when the first Australians arrived.

To begin with, we should emphasize that despite its geographic isolation, Australia has often played a central role in discussions of modern human origins. This is mainly because anthropologists like Milford Wolpoff of the University of Michigan and Alan Thorne of the Australian National University have repeatedly argued for an evolutionary link between ancient Indonesian *Homo erectus* and the historic Australian aborigines, based on perceived similarities in skull form. Genetic analyses now show, however, that the perceived similarities do not imply such a link, since after a decade of intensive analysis, no population in eastern Asia or anywhere else outside of Africa has been shown to possess a gene that cannot be traced to a recent African ancestor. The implication is that all living humans shared such an ancestor and that *Homo erectus* and other non-modern Eurasian populations contributed few if any genes to living humans.

A survey of the Y-chromosome published in *Science* magazine in May 2001 is particularly telling. The authors examined Y-chromosomes from 12,127 men representing 163 historic Asian populations, including Australian aborigines, and they showed that Y-chromosome variability can be traced to a single type "which originated in Africa about 35,000 to 89,000 years ago." They go on to say that "the data do not support even a minimal *in situ* hominid contribution in the origin of anatomically modern humans in East Asia." One of the oldest known Australian human fossils—the Mungo 3 skeleton—did possess a kind of mitochondrial DNA (mtDNA) that is unknown anywhere today, but it is only barely outside the living human range. We previously stressed the great difference between the mtDNA recovered from three different Neanderthal individuals and the mtDNA of living people. The mtDNA from the Mungo 3 skeleton resembles that of living people far more closely, and it need represent only a type that became extinct after modern humans spread from Africa.

The history of early Australian colonization raises more difficult questions. During glacial periods when vast amounts of water were locked in the ice caps, sea level fell by 100 meters (330 feet) or more, and New Guinea, Tasmania, and Australia were joined in a land mass christened Greater Australia (or Sahul Land) (Figure 7.11). However, Australia was never connected to southeastern Asia (Sunda Land), and even when sea level was lowest, newcomers to Australia would have had to cross at least 80 kilometers (50 miles) of open water. Arguably, only modern people could have invented sufficiently seaworthy watercraft, and if they spread from Africa only after 50,000 years ago, Australia could not have been colonized before this time.

Until the early 1990s, it appeared that the first Australians were in fact fully modern people who arrived between 40,000 and 30,000 years ago, bringing with them complex burial practices, fishing technology, art, and probably other modern behavioral markers. Now, two sets of dates suggest that people had reached Australia by 60,000 years ago or even before. The first are luminescence determinations between 60,000 and 50,000 years ago on quartz sands that enclose stone artifacts at Malakunanja II and Nauwalabila I in northern Australia. The second are uranium (or U-) series and ESR ages averaging 62,000 years ago on elements of human skeleton number 3 from the Lake Mungo site in southeastern Australia. Bert Roberts of La Trobe University (Melbourne) and his colleagues produced the Malakunanja II and Nauwalabila I ages,

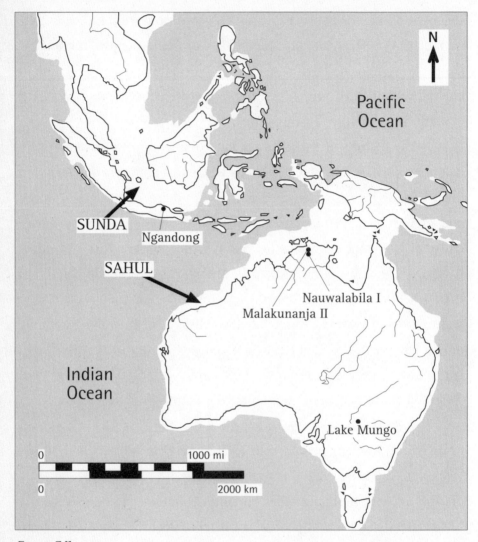

FIGURE 7.11

Australia and southeast Asia, with the archeological sites mentioned in the text. Present-day land-
masses are outlined in black. Additional land that would be exposed by a 200-meter (660-foot) drop
in sea level is shown in white.

while Rainer Grün of the Australian National University (Canberra) and
his colleagues provided the Lake Mungo dates. The Mungo 3 age of
62,000 years is particularly significant, because the skeleton represents

a fully modern person, and it lay in a grave that recalls many European Upper Paleolithic examples in the layout of the body and in the abundance of powdered red ochreous pigment. Upper Paleolithic-like (fully modern) behavior is perhaps also implied by the need to import the ocher from as far as 200 kilometers (120 miles) away.

We have already outlined the principles behind luminescence and ESR dating. The U-series method depends on the observation that uranium occurs naturally in small quantities virtually everywhere and that it is soluble in water, while products of its radioactive decay, thorium and protactinium, are not. Thus, when uranium precipitates from groundwater, as for example in a newly formed stalagmite, the stalagmite will initially contain no daughter products, but these will subsequently accumulate inside at a rate that is directly proportional to the rate at which uranium decays. The ratios between the daughter products and uranium can then be used to estimate the time when the uranium precipitated from groundwater, meaning, in the case of a stalagmite, the time when it formed.

U-series dating is most reliable when it is applied to stalagmites or similar substances that subsequently remained closed to the addition or subtraction of uranium. In theory, it can be applied to fossil bone, since fresh bone contains little or no uranium, and the uranium in a fossil must then have been adsorbed from groundwater after burial. The timing and rate of adsorption, however, are generally unknowable, and adsorption can even alternate with loss (leaching). There is thus usually no way to set the clock to zero to determine when the bone was buried. U-series dates on bones from a single layer often scatter widely, and different dates have even been obtained on parts of the same bone.

The occupation of Australia by modern humans at or before 60,000 years ago would argue not only against a radical behavioral shift between 50,000 and 40,000 years ago, it would also require modifications to the more fundamental hypothesis that modern humans originated in Africa. Minimally, it would call for at least two separate expansions of modern Africans, an earlier one perhaps across the southern end of the Red Sea to southern Asia and then to Australia, and a later one perhaps through the Sinai Desert of Egypt to western Asia and then to Europe. It might also mean that the modern human expansion to Australia some-how bypassed nearby Indonesia, since we pointed out in Chapter 4 that ESR dates on associated animal teeth suggest that the famous Ngandong (or Solo River) human fossils date from 50,000 years ago or later. The Ngandong fossils clearly do not represent modern people, and they have been assigned to an evolved variety of *Homo erectus*.

The early Australian dates are revolutionary if they are correct, but they have encountered serious skepticism. Archeologists Jim O'Connell of the University of Utah and Jim Allen of La Trobe University have questioned the Malakunanja II luminescence dates, because the sands on which they are based lay less than 50 centimeters (20 inches) below a layer dated to 22,000 to 20,000 years ago by radio-carbon. The implication is that the sands accumulated very slowly between about 60,000 and 20,000 years ago, and this raises the possibility that bioturbation (the activity of living organisms in the soil) displaced much younger artifacts downwards. Termites, which are common in the region, are known to produce sufficient downward displacements elsewhere. At Nauwalabila I, stratigraphic inconsistency in the available radiocarbon dates underscores the possibility that bioturbation caused downward movement.

Bert Roberts has challenged the validity of the 62,000 years date for Mungo 3, even though this age would broadly support the Malakunanja II and Nauwalabila I luminescence dates for which he was primarily responsible. The main problem at Lake Mungo is the common one—the possibility or even likelihood that the human bones have experienced a complex history of uranium uptake and loss after burial. This would not only confound U-series dating, it could also mislead ESR, which depends intimately on the same uranium signal. Geomorphologist Jim Bowler of the University of Melbourne, who discovered the Mungo 3 skeleton in 1974, has voiced an even more basic objection. Luminescence and other dates from samples that were carefully selected in the field indicate that Mungo 3 was buried into sediments that accumulated in the interval between 46,000 and 40,000 years ago. The skeleton could then be no older than this.

In sum, human arrival in Australia before 50,000 years ago is far from proven, and pending fresh, more conclusive dates, Australia does not provide a compelling reason to rethink either the time when the LSA appeared or to modify other important aspects of the Out-of-Africa hypothesis.

♛ ♛ ♛

If as we believe, the first Australians descended from Africans who had achieved a fully modern level of hunting-gathering competence, their arrival in Australia might have proven catastrophic for the local fauna. Bert Roberts and his colleagues have in fact recently published dates which suggest that many large Australian marsupials and reptiles disappeared abruptly about 46,000 years ago. They argue that a human cause is more likely than a climatic one, since climate was relatively stable at the time.

The initial arrival of people has also been blamed for a similar wave of large animal extinctions that occurred in the Americas between 12,000 and 10,000 years ago. The American case is more complicated than the Australian one, because the extinctions coincided with the period of rapid climatic change from the Last Glaciation to the Present Interglacial. Still, the extinct species had survived earlier glacial/interglacial transitions, and a human role seems particularly likely given the advanced hunting-gathering skills that the earliest Americans surely brought with them from Asia.

Finally, advanced Upper Paleolithic and LSA hunter-gatherers could have precipitated the demise of a few large mammal species in Eurasia and Africa between 12,000 and 10,000 years ago. As in the Americas, adverse climatic change may have contributed, but the extinct species had survived similar changes earlier on, and the only conspicuous difference 12,000 years ago was the presence of much more sophisticated hunters. Many fewer species became extinct in Eurasia and Africa than in the Americas and Australia, but then the Eurasian and African faunas had evolved with humans, and they were surely much less naïve.

If late Paleolithic people in Australia, the Americas, and Eurasia reduced species diversity in the way the data suggest, then the dawn of human culture represents not only a profound behavioral or sociocultural transition. It also marks the transformation of humanity from a relatively rare and insignificant member of the large mammal fauna to a geologic force with the power to impoverish nature. In short, from early on, the modern human ability to innovate may been both a blessing and a curse.

♛ ♛ ♛

The Australian case is a potent reminder that a comprehensive theory of modern human origins must also embrace the Far East (eastern Asia). Genetics and above all the Y-chromosome study that we previously cited argue strongly that living Far Easterners share a recent African ancestor with all other living humans, but the Far Eastern fossil and archeological records provide less support. The problem is not that they present contrary evidence, but that they present very little evidence at all.

We have already summarized fossils and dates that suggest that *Homo erectus* persisted in Indonesia until perhaps 50,000 years ago. The dates are questionable because they were obtained by the ESR method, but if they are confirmed by future research, they would clearly be consistent with a recent African origin for modern southeast Asians.

The east Asian mainland has provided few fossils that postdate classic *erectus* after 500,000 to 400,000 years ago. The most important specimens include skulls from the Chinese sites of Dali, Yinkou (Jinnuishan), and Maba, all of which have been tentatively dated to between 200,000 and 100,000 years ago. The skulls variably combine massive browridges, low, flat, receding foreheads and other primitive features that mark *erectus* with more rounded braincases, less massive faces, and other advanced features that mark *Homo sapiens* (Figure 7.12). The Chinese skulls differ both from contemporaneous Neanderthal skulls in Europe and from early modern or near-modern skulls in Africa, but in their mix of archaic and derived features, they recall the 600,000- to 400,000-year-old African and European fossils that we previously assigned to *Homo heidelbergensis*. This could imply

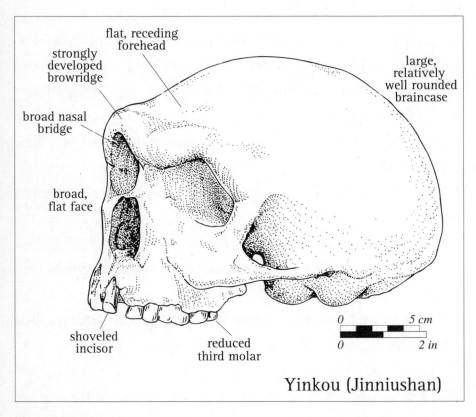

FIGURE 7.12
A human skull from Yinkou (Jinniushan), northeastern China (drawn by Kathryn Cruz-Uribe from a photograph) (Copyright Kathryn Cruz-Uribe).

that *heidelbergensis* extended its range to China after it had disappeared on the west, or it might mean that Chinese *erectus* and African/European *heidelbergensis* evolved similar features independently.

We favor independent (parallel) evolution, if only because the Chinese archeological record reveals no evidence for a population incursion like the one that brought Acheulean hand axes from Africa to Europe. We suggested previously that the hand axes may mark the spread of *heidelbergensis*. In addition, the later Chinese fossils tend to resemble Chinese *erectus* in a handful of features, such as the shortness of the upper jaw, the flatness and horizontal orientation of the cheekbones, the great breadth of the nasal bridge, the shovel-like shape of the upper incisor teeth, and the small size of the third molars. If independent evolution is accepted, then Chinese and Indonesian *erectus* followed separate evolutionary trajectories, and Chinese *erectus* might have to be relegated to a separate species. The more important point here is that the Chinese fossil record by itself is too meager to confirm or reject an African origin for modern east Asians.

The associated Chinese archeological record is even sparser, and the Indonesian record is nonexistent. We predict that when archeological observations become more abundant in eastern Asia, they will reveal the same rupture between 50,000 and 37,000 years ago that we have observed in Africa and Europe, involving the first appearance of art, well-made bone, ivory, and shell artifacts, complex graves, and other modern behavioral traits. In the meanwhile, except again for the genetics, the pattern of modern human origins must be decided almost exclusively on evidence from the Far West. Decades of research have left little doubt about the rupture there, but they have yet to reveal why it occurred.

♛ ♛ ♛

8
NATURE OR NURTURE
BEFORE THE DAWN?

One week before Christmas in 1994, three cave explorers made their way along one of the precipitous gorges cut into a limestone plateau in the Ardèche region of south-central France. Jean-Marie Chauvet, Éliette Brunel Deschamps, and Christian Hillaire had grown up in this dry, rocky region and had spent the past two decades probing its vast, underground mysteries. Sometimes they dug through dirt and rubble and squeezed into cracks only to find nothing. Other times their efforts were rewarded with the sight of luminous cave formations shaped by water, minerals, and the slow passage of time. On this evening, they would become the first people to gaze upon something even more fantastic: images created in the minds of people who lived more than 30,000 years ago.

Following an old mule path to a narrow cliff ledge at the entrance to a maze of gorges, the team noticed an opening in the cliff about 80 centimeters (30 inches) high and 30 centimeters (12 inches) wide. One at a time they slipped into the hole and emerged in a chamber where the rock ceiling was just above their heads. A slight breeze blew towards them, suggesting that a larger opening lay behind a pile of rubble blocking their way. The trio pulled away stones until they had enough room to move forward. Deschamps was in front, and about 3 meters (10 feet) in, the light from her headlamp revealed a drop of ten meters (33 feet) to the floor of a gallery below. The team shouted out and the resonating echoes told them that the cave's innards offered far more to explore. First they needed to hike back to their van and obtain a flexible ladder. Night had fallen and weariness had set in, so the explorers nearly chose to head home and return a week later. But curiosity about what lay deeper inside the cliff overcame their fatigue.

Back in the cave, the team lowered the ladder and then themselves into a dark gallery smelling of wet clay, where sparkling calcite curtains and stalactites hung from the 15-meter (50-foot) high ceiling. A much larger chamber loomed ahead, and at this point the explorers knew the cave was more extensive than any they had seen in the Ardèche gorges. They noticed cave bear bones and teeth scattered about, along with hibernation nests that the bears had scooped into the clay floor. Entering another narrower gallery, Deschamps cried out when her headlamp beam caught two short lines of red ocher on the wall. Then looking up the team spotted a mammoth drawn in red on a rocky spur hanging from the ceiling. More mammals soon materialized on the walls: bears, wild horses, lions, rhinoceroses, reindeer.

The cave was christened Chauvet Cave for Jean-Marie Chauvet, and continued exploration showed that it contained four gallery chambers over a length of about 500 meters (1650 feet). Together, the four chambers contained more than 260 painted and engraved animals, together with dots, geometric patterns, and stenciled hand prints. In most previously known decorated caves, like Lascaux, Les Trois-Frères, and Niaux in southwestern France and Altamira in northern Spain (Figure 8.1), the artists mainly depicted horses, bison, wild cattle, deer, or wild goats (ibex). They rarely portrayed mammoths, rhinoceroses, lions, and bears. Yet the Chauvet artists focused on these species, and they used subtle shading and perspective to portray their subjects in naturalistic poses. France's Inspector General of Decorated Caves,

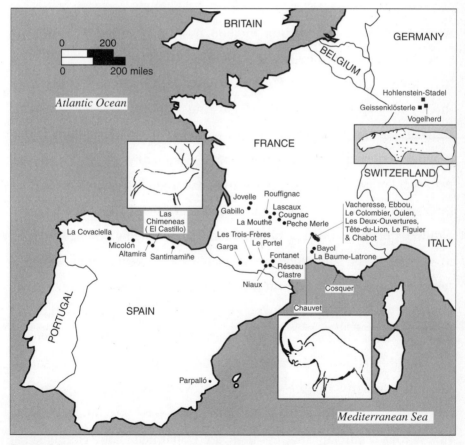

FIGURE 8.1
The main Upper Paleolithic art sites of Western Europe.

archeologist Jean Clottes, who leads the team now studying Chauvet, believes that a single artist, a prehistoric Leonardo, produced most of the charcoal images. The rhinoceroses, of which there are more than forty, often share exaggerated horns and distinctively curled ears as if they were painted by the same skilled hand. The cave's largest single frieze shows a dozen rhinoceroses presented from various angles but in the same singular style.

♛　♛　♛

Advances in the radiocarbon method now make it possible to date charcoal fragments the size of a pinprick (half a milligram), and less than a year after Chauvet Cave was discovered, minute samples from three charcoal images—a pair of jousting rhinoceroses and a bison—showed that the paintings had been created between 32,000 and 31,000 years ago. The artists then must have been early Upper Paleolithic Aurignacian people, whose ancestors had replaced the Neanderthals (Mousterians) in France only a few thousand years before. The Chauvet paintings precede the next-oldest radiocarbon-dated examples by 5000 to 10,000 years, and they are at least 15,000 years older than the famous (Magdalenian) paintings of Lascaux, Niaux, and Altamira. Still, they are not the only examples of spectacular art from the dawn of human culture in Europe. Early Aurignacian layers in the caves at Vogelherd (Stetten), Geissenklösterle, and Hohlenstein-Stadel in south-western Germany (Figure 8.1) have provided seventeen spectacular ivory figurines that are as old or older. They tend to feature the same "dangerous" animal species that were painted and engraved at Chauvet, and one 30-centimeter (12-inch) tall statuette from

Hohlenstein-Stadel depicts a fantastic figure with a lion's head planted unmistakably on a human body (Figure 8.2). At Galgenberg Hill, near Krems, Austria, an Aurignacian artist working 32,000 years ago transformed a small slab of green serpentine rock into a remarkable 7-centimeter (2.75-inch) tall figure of a woman, left hand in the air, bent right arm and hand on the hip, and left breast protruding in profile (Figure 8.3). Finally, some early Aurignacian sites contain numerous personal ornaments, especially ivory beads, each carefully shaped by a meticulous, time-consuming process that we describe below.

The preceding Mousterian has provided nothing to compare to the Aurignacian paintings, engravings, figurines, and beads. Together with an increase in stone-tool diversity and standardization and the first routine manufacture of standardized (formal) artifacts in bone, ivory, and antler, the art and ornaments underscore the great gulf that separated even the earliest Upper Paleolithic people from the preceding Mousterians. The contrast becomes even starker when we consider the remarkable monotony of the Mousterian over thousands or even tens of thousands of years and compare this to the rapid diversification in both utilitarian and non-utilitarian artifact types that occurred from the Aurignacian onwards. In the rate at which material culture changed and diversified, only the Upper Paleolithic recalls later prehistory and recorded history. Like the yet earlier cultural traditions, in its conservatism the Mousterian suggests a system for which we have no historic analog.

We are not the first to emphasize the contrast between the Upper Paleolithic and everything that preceded it, and where we speak of the "dawn of human culture," others refer to a "human revolution," a "creative explosion," "a great leap forward," or a "sociocultural big bang."

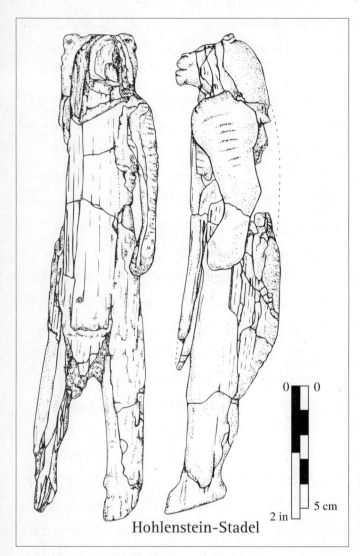

0 0

2 in 5 cm

Hohlenstein-Stadel

FIGURE 8.2
Mammoth ivory "lion-
human" statuette from
an Aurignacian layer at
Hohlenstein-Stadel,
southwestern Germany
(redrawn from an origi-
nal by J. Hahn in J.
Clottes 1996, *Antiquity*
70, p. 280).

Most authorities highlight European findings, but we have stressed even older evidence for the "dawn" in Africa. The African data are less abundant and spectacular, at least in part because the vagaries of preservation have left fewer relevant African sites and there have been fewer archeologists to seek them out. Related to this, archeologists have been

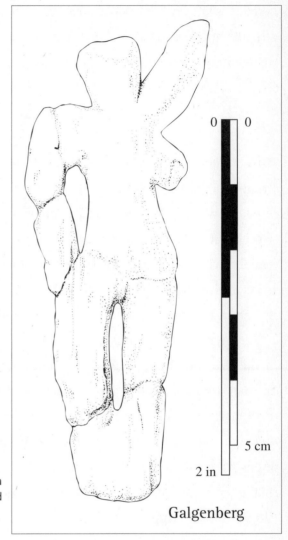

Galgenberg

0   0

5 cm

2 in

FIGURE 8.3
Female figurine in serpentine from an Aurignacian layer at Galgenberg Hill, Austria (drawn and copyrighted by Kathryn Cruz-Uribe from a photograph).

accumulating relevant evidence in Europe since the 1860s, while the key African observations all postdate 1965. Yet, the "dawn" is just as real in Africa, and, equally important, it occurred there first. Spectacular as it is, the European Upper Paleolithic, beginning around 40,000 years ago, was simply an outgrowth of behavioral change that occurred in Africa perhaps 5000 years earlier. That said, we must now proceed to the most difficult question of all: what accounts for the "dawn." The answer as we shall see is contentious, and it may always be that way.

☙ ☙ ☙

Most archeologists who have tried to explain the "dawn" favor a strictly social, technological, or demographic cause. A small minority, of whom we may be the majority, favor a biological one. We'll outline two characteristic social or technological explanations first and then explain why we think our biological explanation is preferable. We stress at the outset that unlike the "dawn" itself, the explanation for it is more a matter of taste or philosophy than it is of evidence.

Archeologist Randall White of New York University specializes in the study of Upper Paleolithic portable art (the kind found in the ground). He believes that ivory beads, perforated shells, pierced animal teeth, and other ornaments or portable art objects are as symbolic as the charcoal rhinoceroses that early Upper Paleolithic Aurignacian artists drew on the walls of Chauvet Cave or the multicolored bison that later Upper Paleolithic Magdalenians painted on the ceiling of Altamira Cave. Upper Paleolithic people often portrayed animals that they hunted and ate, judging by the food debris in their sites, but they also commonly showed species that they rarely obtained and that were probably rare on the landscape. The choice of what to show was thus arbitrary, and it was probably often rooted in local beliefs about how nature was organized or about the relationship between nature and society. White notes that Upper Paleolithic people were equally arbitrary in producing ornaments or portable art objects, and the choice varied widely through time and space. In the early Aurignacian inter-val before 30,000 years ago, for example, people produced ivory beads and animal-tooth pendants mainly in France and Russia, they perfo-rated shells for hanging mostly in Spain, France, and Italy, they crafted three-dimensional animal sculptures mainly in Central Europe, and they engraved limestone blocks only in a small area of southwestern France. Since none of the objects were utilitarian, the choice of what to produce was probably rooted in locally varying beliefs about the natural or social order.

White's research shows that the production of early Aurignacian beads required extraordinary time and effort, which underscores the likelihood that they had symbolic meaning. The man-ufacturing process involved multiple steps: the fashioning of a pencil-like rod in ivory or soft stone; the incision of grooves 1 to 2 centimeters (0.4 to 0.8 inches) apart around the rod; the application of pressure to snap off cylindrical bead blanks or preforms between the grooves; the creation of a hole for hanging, either by gouging each blank inwards from the ends or by rotational drilling; and finally the use of a naturally occurring abrasive to smooth and grind each bead into a standardized shape.

White's experiments show that a single bead usually required one to three person-hours, yet some Upper Paleolithic sites contain scores, hundreds, or even thousands. The most spectacular example is from Sungir', Russia, an open-air site that was occupied about 29,000 years ago. Sungir' lies 210 kilometers (125 miles) northeast of Moscow in a region that was unoccupied before the Upper Paleolithic, and its location alone highlights a newly developed human ability to adapt to especially harsh circumstances. The Sungir' people surely invested a lot

of time in finding food and in keeping warm, yet they managed to produce no less than thirteen thousand beads, three thousand of which
occurred in the grave of an adult male and ten thousand of which were
about equally divided between the bodies of two children buried head
to head in a second, common grave. The beads occur in strands that
were probably fastened to leather clothing, and they are accompanied
by other art objects that suggest a burial ritual and a concern or respect
for the deceased that living humans commonly share. The Sungir'
graves are in fact among the oldest from which such ritual and respect
can be unambiguously inferred, but White goes further. The ten thousand beads in the children's grave took more than ten thousand
person-hours to produce, and their abundance may mean that the children occupied a special position or status in Sungir' society.

In Chapter 1, we described how the exchange of ostrich eggshell
beads fostered social cohesion among historic southern African hunter-
gatherers. With ethnographic observations like this in mind, White
argues that "the rapid emergence of personal ornamentation [in the
Upper Paleolithic] may have marked, not a difference in mental capacities between Cro-Magnons and Neanderthals, but rather the emergence
of new forms of social organization that facilitated and demanded the
communication and recording of complex ideas." In his view, either an
increase in population density or a greater tendency for people to gather
in large groups could have precipitated the underlying social transformation.

Archeologist Ofer Bar-Yosef of Harvard University offers a different, but complementary hypothesis. Bar-Yosef specializes in the
archeology of southwestern Asia (the Near East) and he has investigated both the origin of modern humans and the origin of agriculture,

which occurred about 30,000 years later. He refers to both events as "revolutions," and he believes that they were driven by similar forces.

About 11,000 years ago, hunter-gatherers along the eastern margin of the Mediterranean Sea relied heavily on wild cereals (wheat, barley, and rye) and other plant foods, much as their forebears had in the preceding millennia. Their adaptation was stable, and it even allowed for a degree of sedentary life—permanent or semi-permanent hamlets from which the people could exploit abundant wild plants and an accompanying supply of gazelles and other wild animals. Then, starting about 11,000 years ago, climate turned suddenly and sharply colder and drier, and the downturn persisted for 1300 years, during what paleoclimatologists call the Younger Dryas period. Wild cereals and other key food plants became much scarcer, and Bar-Yosef and other archeologists believe that the people responded by encouraging them to grow in nearby fields. To produce the next crop, they naturally selected seeds from those individual plants that grew best under their care, and in the process they transformed wild species that could grow on their own into domesticates that required human assistance. By 9500 years ago, they had added animals (sheep, goats, cattle, and pigs) to the repertoire of domesticates, and they were full-fledged farmers. The economic transformation encouraged human population growth, and for this reason alone, it also promoted changes in social and economic relations. As population density increased and world climate ameliorated after 9000 years ago, splinter groups broke off to seek new land and they eventually spread the new agricultural way of life westwards to Spain and eastwards to Pakistan.

Bar-Yosef suggests that like the agricultural revolution, the much earlier event we call the "dawn of human culture" involved the invention of new ways to obtain food and that this resulted in population growth and in new modes of social and economic organization. Splinter groups would again have carried the new adaptation from its core area, which in this case was probably eastern Africa.

Like White and Bar-Yosef, other archeologists have proposed models in which the "dawn" followed naturally on a technological advance, a change in social relations, or both. Such explanations are attractive in part because they rely on the same kind of forces that historians and archeologists routinely use to explain much more recent social and cultural change. In regard to the "dawn," however, they share a common shortcoming: they fail to explain why technology or social organization changed so suddenly and fundamentally. Population growth is an inadequate reason, first, because it too would have to be explained, and second, because there is no evidence that population was growing anywhere just prior to the "dawn." We have noted that the Africans who lived just before the "dawn" made MSA (Middle Stone Age) artifacts, while those who lived afterwards produced LSA (Later Stone Age) assemblages. In southern and northern Africa, the interval between 60,000 and 30,000 years ago that encompasses the MSA/LSA transition appears to have been mostly very arid, and human populations were so depressed that they are nearly invisible to archeology. Conditions for human occupation remained more favorable in eastern Africa, but so far, excavations and surveys here also fail to suggest a population increase in the late MSA. Neither the number of sites nor the density of occupation debris they contain increase conspicuously towards the LSA, which began between 50,000 and 40,000 years ago. And in Europe populations grew only after the "dawn" arrived, not in anticipation of it.

Conceivably, the trigger was a climatic event like the Younger Dryas of 11,000 years ago, but the "dawn" occurred during a long interval of fluctuating climate that on present evidence did not include a comparably dramatic episode. Even if one is eventually detected, it will be difficult to explain why it prompted such a far-reaching behavioral response, when yet earlier, equally or even more radical climatic spikes did not. The most notable preceding spike was a millennium-long bout of intense cold that followed the Mt. Toba volcanic supereruption in Sumatra, Indonesia, about 73,500 years ago. The Mt. Toba eruption was the most massive in the last 2 million years and perhaps in the last 450 million years. To provide perspective, Toba ejected roughly four thousand times as much material as Mt. St. Helens (Washington State) in 1981 and about forty times more than Mt. Tambora (Sumbawa Island, Indonesia) in 1815. The Tambora eruption was the largest in historic times, and the aerosols from it reduced sunlight and global temperatures so much that 1816 became known as "the year without a summer" when New England experienced snow in July and August. The far more extensive aerosols from Toba produced a "volcanic winter" akin to the "nuclear winter" that some have hypothesized would follow a new world war, and the effect was accentuated and prolonged by feedback from a global trend toward colder climate in the early part of the last glacial period. Plant and animal populations must have declined sharply almost everywhere, and the impact on human populations was probably catastrophic. Yet, the aftermath of Mt. Toba is notable precisely because it did not provoke a revolutionary cultural response. The lack of a response supports artifactual evidence that people possessed limited ability to innovate before 50,000 years ago.

Finally, there is no evidence that the "dawn" was prompted by a technical innovation comparable to the invention of agriculture.

Archeology not only fails to reveal such an innovation, it suggests that the "dawn" actually marks the beginning of the human ability to produce such remarkable innovations. From an archeological perspective then, the "dawn" is not simply the first in a series of ever more closely spaced "revolutions," starting with agriculture and running through urbanization, industry, computers, and genomics, it was the seminal revolution without which no other could have occurred. This brings us to what we think was the key change that explains it.

♛ ♛ ♛

In our view, the simplest and most economic explanation for the "dawn" is that it stemmed from a fortuitous mutation that promoted the fully modern human brain. Our case relies primarily on three circumstantial observations extracted from our preceding survey of human evolution. The first is that natural selection for more effective brains largely drove the earlier phases of human evolution. The neural basis for modern human behavior was not always there; it evolved, and we are merely using the available behavioral evidence to suggest when.

The second observation is that increases in brain size and probably also changes in brain organization accompanied much earlier behavioral/ecological shifts. These include especially the initial appearance of stone artifacts 2.6 to 2.5 million years ago, the first appearance of hand axes and the simultaneous human expansion into open, largely treeless environments 1.8 to 1.6 million years ago, and possibly also the advent of more sophisticated hand axes and the first permanent occupation of Europe about 600,000 to 500,000 years ago.

Our third and final observation is that the relationship between anatomical and behavioral change shifted abruptly about 50,000 years ago. Before this time, anatomy and behavior appear to have evolved more or less in tandem, very slowly, but after this time anatomy remained relatively stable while behavioral (cultural) change accelerated rapidly. What could explain this better than a neural change that promoted the extraordinary modern human ability to innovate? This is not to say that Neanderthals and their non-modern contemporaries possessed ape-like brains or that they were as biologically and behaviorally primitive as yet earlier humans. It is only to suggest that an acknowledged genetic link between anatomy and behavior in yet earlier people persisted until the emergence of fully modern ones and that the postulated genetic change 50,000 years ago fostered the uniquely modern ability to adapt to a remarkable range of natural and social circumstances with little or no physiological change.

Arguably, the last key neural change promoted the modern capacity for rapidly spoken phonemic language, or for what anthropologists Duane Quiatt and Richard Milo have called "a fully vocal language, phonemicized, syntactical, and infinitely open and productive." In the 4 October 2001 issue of *Nature* magazine, a team of geneticists led by Cecilia Lai of Oxford University indirectly supported this idea when they identified a single gene that is probably "involved in the developmental process that culminates in speech and language." Individuals who possess a defective copy of this gene have great difficulty recognizing basic speech sounds, learning grammatical rules, and understanding sentences. They are not necessarily impaired in other respects, and they often score normally for non-verbal intelligence. In short, the new discovery shows that a single mutation could underlie the fully modern capacity for speech. Still, we stressed earlier that there is no compelling anatomical evidence for the evolution of language, and the suggestion that its final development underlay the "dawn" follows mainly from the intimate bond between language and culture among living humans. Living people use language not only for communication, but also for mental modeling and for posing the kind of "what if" questions that enable the uniquely modern human ability to innovate. And in our view, it is above all a quantum advance in the human ability to innovate that marks the dawn of human culture.

The strongest objection to the neural hypothesis is that it cannot be tested from fossils. The connection between behavioral and neural change earlier in human evolution is inferred from conspicuous increases in brain size, but humans virtually everywhere had achieved modern or near-modern brain size by 200,000 years ago. Any neural change that occurred 50,000 years ago would thus have been strictly organizational, and fossil skulls so far provide only speculative evidence for brain structure. Neanderthal skulls, for example, differ dramatically in shape from modern ones, but they were as large or larger, and on present evidence, it is not clear that the difference in form implies a significant difference in function. There is especially nothing in the skull to show that Neanderthals or their contemporaries lacked the fully modern capacity for language.

♛ ♛ ♛

So we must conclude partly inconclusively. Since the 1910s, fossil and archeological evidence have suggested that fully modern (Cro-Magnon) invaders replaced the Neanderthals in Europe. Fossil and archeological support for an abrupt replacement grew stronger in succeeding decades, but it became particularly compelling after the middle 1980s with the development of three new, crucial lines of evidence. First were new dates which showed that modern or near-modern humans inhabited Africa between 120,000 and 50,000 years ago when only the Neanderthals lived in Europe. Second were new fossils (mainly from the Sima de los Huesos at Atapuerca, Spain) which showed that the Neanderthals evolved in Europe between about 400,000 and 130,000 years ago. And third were increasingly sophisticated genetic analyses which show that the Neanderthals diverged from living humans long before living human groups diverged from one another. Some of the new (and old) evidence is ambiguous, circumstantial, or even contradictory, but this is inevitable in historical science, which has more in common with a criminal trial than it does with a physics experiment.

Our readers sitting as jurors must still reach a verdict, and if we have presented our case capably, they will agree that anatomically modern Africans became behaviorally modern about 50,000 years ago and that this allowed them to spread to Europe where they rapidly replaced the Neanderthals. They will probably also accept the likelihood that modern behavior allowed modern humans of recent African descent to replace non-modern people in the Far East, although in this instance, we as prosecutors would understand if they asked for more evidence. Their only serious reservation, roughly akin to reasonable doubt in the legal system, may concern our argument for what prompted the emergence of modern human behavior about 50,000 years ago. The crux here is logic and parsimony, not evidence, and with the full sweep of human evolution in mind, we would appreciate feedback on just how persuasive our logic is.

APPENDIX
PLACING ANCIENT SITES IN TIME

To lay observers, it may appear as if human fossils and artifacts are the main facts of human evolution, and they are obviously vital to it. However, they would lose much of their value if they could not be arranged in time or "dated." We introduced key dating techniques at relevant points in previous chapters, but given the importance of the topic, we pull them together in this brief appendix. They can be broadly divided between "relative" and "absolute (or numerical)" methods.

Relative methods are ones that allow objects to be arranged from younger to older (or vice versa) without specifying precisely how old any given object is. The most obvious relative dating method is the principle of stratigraphic superposition, which states that all other things equal, the deeper the rock layer in which an object occurs, the older the object is. When this principle is carefully applied in the field, it allows specialists to construct the sequences of animal communities and artifact assemblages that have existed through time within a given region. Animal fossils or artifacts can then be used to determine the antiquity of a site with respect to others, even when the site contains only a single layer. Thus, in Africa, the particular species of elephants, horses (zebras), or pigs that occur in two ancient human fossil or archeological sites often suffice to determine whether one site is older, younger, or perhaps the same age as the other. In eastern Africa, the time ranges of fossil species or species groups have often been determined in years, and this has allowed age estimates in years for significant australopith and other sites in southern Africa where the same species or species groups occurred. The use of fossil species to arrange sites in time, and in some cases to estimate how old they are in years, is often known as "faunal dating," and it is by far the most widely applied relative dating method in paleoanthropology.

Absolute dating methods are ones that provide age estimates in years. Since sites dated in years are automatically arranged in time with respect to others, absolute dating methods may be regarded as especially precise variants of relative dating. In paleoanthropology, the most important absolute methods rely on the decay of naturally occurring radioactive isotopes (varieties of elements). So far, the two most informative and reliable methods are based on the decay of radiocarbon (carbon-14) and radiopotassium (potassium-40). Radiopotassium decays into argon, and the method is thus commonly known as the potassium/argon technique. We introduced the potassium/argon and radiocarbon techniques on pp. 44 and 209 respectively, and Figure A.1 presents the approximate time range that each method covers and the materials to which it is routinely applicable. Application in each case is limited partly by the absence of suitable materials in many sites and

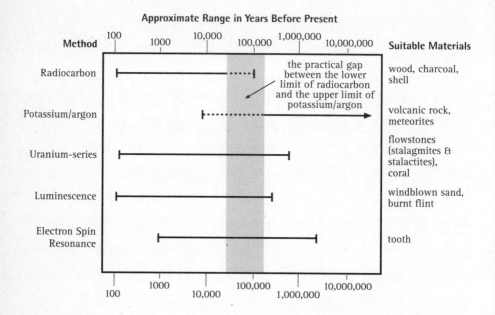

FIGURE A.1
The time ranges covered by the absolute (or numerical) dating methods that are important to paleoanthropology.

partly by the possibility of contamination from older or younger materials that were introduced into a site during or after burial. The absence of volcanic materials, for example, precludes the use of potassium/argon dating at ancient southern African sites, while the possibility that minute amounts of more recent carbon have contaminated many ancient samples makes it difficult to obtain reliable radiocarbon ages beyond 25,000 to 30,000 years ago, even when materials suitable for dating are present.

There is the further problem that except in unusual circumstances, the potassium/argon method cannot produce reliable ages younger than about 200,000 years, while the radiocarbon method is limited to roughly the last 50,000 years. In practice then, there is a gap in time of about 150,000 years that the two methods cannot cover (Figure A.1). The most dependable technique for filling the gap is the uranium (U-) series method that we described on p. 249. This is based on the radioactive decay of uranium and its daughter products Thorium (Th) and Protactinium (Pa), but its applicability is limited by the rarity of suitable target materials in ancient human sites. The Electron Spin Resonance (ESR) and luminescence methods that we introduced on pp. 124 and 164 respectively are more widely applicable, and they have provided many interesting and oft-cited ages. However, in general, the results of each method depend heavily on unverifiable site-specific assumptions about the history of radioactivity in the burial environment or in the dated object, and their reliability in many instances is thus questionable.

Finally, it is sometimes possible to use the known history of past shifts in the direction of Earth's magnetic field to estimate the age of a site in which the deposits record one or more shifts in past direction. We introduced such paleomagnetic dating on pp. 66–67. Similarly, specialists can sometimes provide an age estimate by comparing the sequence of glacial/interglacial alternations that a site records to the dated sequence that has been firmly established from deposits on the deep sea floor. This method works best for sites that formed within the last 700,000 years or so, and it generally requires deposits that accumulated continuously (without major breaks) and that have been partially dated by another method such as potassium/argon or radiocarbon. Such "climatic dating" is particularly effective for determining whether a site formed during the last interglacial period, between roughly 127,000 and 71,000 years ago, or during the last glacial period, between about 71,000 and 12,000 years ago.

Selected Further Reading

General

Johanson, D. & Edgar, B. (1996). *From Lucy to Language.* New York: A Peter N. Nevraumont Book/Simon & Schuster.

Klein, R. G. (1999). *The Human Career: Human Biological and Cultural Origins. Second Edition.* Chicago: University of Chicago Press.

Tattersall, I. & Schwartz, J. H. (2000). *Extinct Humans.* Boulder, CO: A Peter N. Nevraumont Book/Westview Press.

Chapter 1
Dawn at Twilight Cave

Ambrose, S. H. (1998). Chronology of the Later Stone Age and food production in East Africa. *Journal of Archaeological Science* 25, 377-392.

Deacon, H. J. & Deacon, J. (1999). *Human Beginnings in South Africa: Uncovering the Secrets of the Stone Age.* Cape Town: David Philip.

Eldredge, N. & Gould, S. J. (1972). Punctuated equilibrium: an alternative to phyletic gradualism. In (T. Schopf, Ed.) *Models in Paleobiology.* W. H. Freeman: San Francisco, pp. 82-115.

Eldredge, N., Gould, S. J., Coyne, J. A. & Charlesworth, B. (1997). On punctuated equilibria. *Science* 276, 338-342.

Singer, R. & Wymer, J. J. (1982). *The Middle Stone Age at Klasies River Mouth in South Africa.* Chicago: University of Chicago Press.

Chapter 2
Bipedal Apes

Brain, C. K. (1981). *The Hunters or the Hunted? An Introduction to African Cave Taphonomy.* Chicago: University of Chicago Press.

Dart, R. A. & Craig, D. (1959). *Adventures with the Missing Link.* New York: The Viking Press.

Haile-Selassie, Y. (2001). Late Miocene hominids from the Middle Awash, Ethiopia. *Nature* 412, 178-181.

Johanson, D. C. & Edey, M. E. (1981). *Lucy: the Beginnings of Humankind.* New York: Simon and Schuster.

Leakey, M. D. (1979). *Olduvai Gorge: My Search for Early Man.* London: William Collins Sons & Co.

Leakey, M. G. (1995). The dawn of humans: the farthest horizon. *National Geographic* 190 (9), 38-51.

Leakey, M. G., Feibel, C. S., McDougall, I., Ward, C. & Walker, A. (1998). New specimens and confirmation of an early age for *Australopithecus anamensis. Nature* 393, 62-66.

Leakey, M. G., Spoor, F., Brown, F. H., Gathogo, P. N., Klarle, C., Leakey, L. N. & McDougall, I. (2001). New hominin genus from eastern Africa shows diverse middle Pliocene lineages. *Nature* 410, 433-440.

McHenry, H. M. & Coffing, K. (2000). *Australopithecus* to *Homo*: Transformations in body and mind. *Annual Review of Anthropology* 29, 125-146.

Tobias, P. V. (1984). *Dart, Taung and the Missing Link.* Johannesburg: Witwatersrand University Press.

White, T. D., Suwa, G. & Asfaw, B. (1994). *Australopithecus ramidus*, a new species of early hominid from Aramis, Ethiopia. *Nature* 371, 306-312.

CHAPTER 3
THE WORLD'S OLDEST WHODUNIT

Backwell, L. & d'Errico, F. (2001). Evidence of termite foraging by Swartkrans early hominids. *Proceedings of the National Academy of Sciences* 98, 1-6.

Kimbel, W. H., Walter, R. C., Johanson, D. C., Reed, K. E., Aronson, J. L., Assefa, Z., Marean, C. W., Eck, G. G., Bobe, R., Hovers, E., Rak, Y., Vondra, C., Yemane, T., York, D., Chen, Y., Evensen, N. M. & Smith, P. E. (1996). Late Pliocene *Homo* and Oldowan tools from the Hadar Formation (Kada Hadar Member), Ethiopia. *Journal of Human Evolution* 31, 549-561.

Leakey, L. S. B., Evernden, J. F. & Curtis, G. H. (1961). Age of Bed 1, Olduvai Gorge, Tanganyika. *Nature* 191, 478.

Leakey, L. S. B., Tobias, P. V. & Napier, J. R. (1964). A new species of the genus *Homo* from Olduvai Gorge, Tanzania. *Nature* 202, 308-312.

Leakey, M. D. (1979). *Olduvai Gorge: My Search for Early Man.* London: William Collins Sons & Co.

Lee-Thorp, J. A., Thackeray, J. F. & van der Merwe, N. (2000). The hunters and the hunted revisited. *Journal of Human Evolution* 39, 565-576.

Semaw, S. (2000). The world's oldest stone arte-facts from Gona, Ethiopia: their implications for understanding stone technology and pat-terns of human evolution between 2.6-1.5 million years ago. *Journal of Archaeological Science* 27, 1197-1214.

Susman, R. L. (1991). Who made the Oldowan tools? Fossil evidence for tool behavior in Plio-Pleistocene hominids. *Journal of Anthropological Research* 47, 129-151.

Toth, N. (1985). The Oldowan reassessed: a close look at early stone artifacts. *Journal of Archaeological Science* 12, 101-120.

Toth, N., Schick, K. D., Savage-Rumbaugh, E. S., Sevick, R. A. & Rumbaugh, D. M. (1993). *Pan* the tool-maker: investigations into the stone tool-making and tool-using capabili-ties of a bonobo (*Pan paniscus*). *Journal of Archaeological Science* 20, 81-91.

Walker, A. C. & Leakey, R. E. F. (1978). The hominids of East Turkana. *Scientific American* 239(2), 54-66.

Wood, B. A. (1993). Early *Homo*: how many species? In (W. H. Kimbel & L. B. Martin, Eds.) *Species, species concepts, and primate evolution.* Alan R. Liss: New York, pp. 485-522.

CHAPTER 4
THE FIRST TRUE HUMANS

Delson, E., Harvati, K., Reddy, D., Marcus, L. F., Mowbray, K. M., Sawyer, G. J., Jacob, T. & Márquez, S. (2001). the Sambungmacan 3 *Homo erectus* calvaria: a comparative mor-phometric and morphological analysis. *The Anatomical Record* 262, 380-397.

Gabunia, L. & Vekua, A. (1995). A Plio-Pleistocene hominid from Dmanisi, east Georgia, Caucasus. *Nature* 373, 509-512.

Gabunia, L., Vekua, A., Lordkipanidze, D., Swisher, C. C., Ferring, R., Justus, A., Nioradze, M., Tvalchrelidze, M., Antón, S. C., Bosinksi, G., Jöris, O., De Lumley, M. A., Majsuradze, G. & Mouskhelishivili, A. (2000). Earliest Pleistocene hominid cranial remains from Dmanisi, Republic of Georgia: taxonomy, geological setting, and age. *Science* 288, 1019-1025.

Goren-Inbar, N. (1994). The Lower Paleolithic of Israel. In (T. E. Levy, Ed.) *The Archaeology of Society in the Holy Land.* Leicester University Press: London, pp. 93-109.

Isaac, G. L. (1977). *Olorgesailie.* Chicago: University of Chicago Press.

Kohn, M. & Mithen, S. (1999). Handaxes: prod-ucts of sexual selection? *Antiquity* 73, 518-526.

Leakey, R. E. F. & Walker, A. (1985). A fossil skeleton 1,600,000 years old: *Homo erectus* unearthed. *National Geographic* 168, 625-629.

Oakley, K. P. (1964). The problem of man's antiquity: an historical survey. *Bulletin of the British Museum (Natural History) Geology* 9, 86-155.

Rightmire, G. P. (1990). *The Evolution of Homo erectus: Comparative Anatomical Studies of an Extinct Human Species.* Cambridge: Cambridge University Press.

Ruff, C. B. (1993). Climatic adaptation and hominid evolution: the thermoregulatory imperative. *Evolutionary Anthropology* 2, 53-60.

Santa Luca, A. P. (1980). The Ngandong fossil hominids. *Yale University Publications in Anthropology* 78, 1-175.

Schick, K. D. & Dong, Z. (1993). Early Paleolithic of China and Eastern Asia. *Evolutionary Anthropology* 2, 22-35.

Schick, K. D., Toth, N., Garufi, G., Savage-Rumbaugh, E. S., Rumbaugh, D. & Sevcik, R. (1999). Continuing investigations into the stone tool-making and tool-using capabilities of a bonobo (*Pan paniscus*). *Journal of Archaeological Science* 26, 821-823.

Swisher, C. C., Curtis, G. H., Jacob, T., Getty, A. G., Suprijo, A. & Widiasmoro. (1994). Age of the earliest known hominids in Java, Indonesia. *Science* 263, 1118-1121.

Swisher, C. C., Rink, W. J., Antón, S. C., Schwarcz, H. P., Curtis, G. H., Suprijo, A. & Widiasmoro. (1996). Latest *Homo erectus* of Java: potential contemporaneity with *Homo sapiens* in southeast Asia. *Science* 274, 1870-1874.

Chapter 5
Humanity Branches Out

Arsuaga, J. L., Martínez, I., Gracia, A., Carretero, J. M., Lorenzo, C., García, N. & Ortega, A. I. (1997). Sima de los Huesos (Sierra de Atapuerca, Spain). The site. *Journal of Human Evolution* 33, 109-127.

Bermúdez de Castro, J. M. (1998). Hominids at Atapuerca: the first human occupation in Europe. In (E. Carbonell, J. Bermudéz de Castro, J. L. Arsuaga & X. P. Rodriguez, Eds.) *The First Europeans: Recent Discoveries and Current Debate*. Aldecoa: Burgos, pp. 45-66.

Churchill, S. E. (1993). Weapon technology, prey-size selection and hunting methods in modern hunter-gatherers: implications for hunting in the Palaeolithic and Mesolithic. In (G. L. Peterkin, H. M. Bricker & P. A. Mellars, Eds.) *Hunting and Animal Exploitation in the Later Palaeolithic and Mesolithic of Eurasia*. American Anthropological Association: Washington, D. C., pp. 11-24.

Clarke, R. J. (2000). A corrected reconstruction and interpretation of the *Homo erectus* calvaria from Ceprano, Italy. *Journal of Human Evolution* 39, 433-442.d'Errico, F. & Nowell, A. (2000). A new look at the Berekhat Ram figurine: implications for the origins of symbolism. *Cambridge Archaeological Journal* 10, 123-167.

Goren-Inbar, N. (1986). A figurine from the Acheulian site of Berekhat Ram. *M'tekufat Ha'even* 19, 71-12.

Jerison, H. J. (2001). Adaptation and preadaptation in hominid evolution. In (P. V. Tobias, M. A. Raath, J. Moggi-Cecchi & G. A. Doyle, Eds.) *Humanity from African Naissance to Coming Millennia*. Witwatersrand University Press: Johannesburg, pp. 373-378.

Rightmire, G. P. (1998). Human evolution in the Middle Pleistocene: the role of *Homo heidelbergensis*. *Evolutionary Anthropology* 6, 218-227.

Roebroeks, W. & van Kolfschoten, T. (1994). The earliest occupation of Europe: a short chronology. *Antiquity* 68, 489-503.

Ronen, A. (1998). Domestic fire as evidence for language. In (T. Akazawa, K. Aoki & O. Bar-Yosef, Eds.) *Neandertals and Modern Humans in Western Asia*. Plenum Press: New York, pp. 439-447.

Ruff, C. B., Trinkaus, E. & Holliday, T. W. (1997). Body mass and encephalization in Pleistocene *Homo*. *Nature* 387, 173-176.

Thieme, H. (1997). Lower Palaeolithic hunting spears from Germany. *Nature* 385, 807-810.

Wynn, T. (1991). Tools, grammar and the archaeology of cognition. *Cambridge Archaeological Journal* 1, 191-206.

Wynn, T. (1995). Handaxe enigmas. *World Archaeology* 27, 10-24.

Chapter 6
Neanderthals Out on a Limb

Bahn, P. (1998). Archaeology: Neanderthals emancipated. *Nature* 394, 719-721.

Berger, T. D. & Trinkaus, E. (1995). Patterns of trauma among the Neandertals. *Journal of Archaeological Science* 22, 841-852.

Bocherens, H., Billiou, D., Mariotti, A., Toussaint, M., Patou-Mathis, M., Bonjean, D. & Otte, M. (2001). New isotopic evidence for dietary habits of Neandertals from Belgium. *Journal of Human Evolution* 40, 497-505.

Boëda, E., Geneste, J. M., Griggo, C., Mercier, N., Muhesen, S., Reyss, J. L., Taha, A. & Valladas, H. (1999). A Levallois point embedded in the vertebra of a wild ass (*Equus africanus*): hafting, projectiles and Mousterian hunting weapons. *Antiquity* 73, 394-402.

Cann, R. L., Stoneking, M. & Wilson, A. C. (1987). Mitochondrial DNA and human evolution. *Nature* 329, 111-112.

d'Errico, F., Villa, P., Pinto Llona, A. C. & Ruiz Idarraga, R. (1998a). A Middle Palaeolithic origin of music? Using cave-bear bone accumulations to assess the Divje Babe I bone 'flute'. *Antiquity* 72, 65-79.

d'Errico, F., Zilhão, J., Julien, M., Baffier, D. & Pelegrin, J. (1998b). Neanderthal acculturation in Western Europe? A critical review of the evidence and its interpretation. *Current Anthropology* 39, S1-S44.

Defleur, A., White, T., Valensi, P., Slimak, L. & Crégut-Bonnoure, É. (1999). Neanderthal cannibalism at Moula-Guercy, Ardèche, France. *Science* 286, 128-131.

Dibble, H. L. (1987). The interpretation of Middle Paleolithic scraper morphology. *American Antiquity* 52, 109-117.

Duarte, C., Maurício, J., Pettitt, P. B., Souto, P., Trinkaus, E., van der Plicht, H. & Zilhão, J. (1999). The early Upper Paleolithic human skeleton from the Abrigo do Lagar Velho (Portugal) and modern human emergence in Iberia. *Proceedings of the National Academy of Sciences* 96, 7604-7609.

Hoffecker, J. F. (2001). *Desolate Landscapes: Ice-Age Settlement in Eastern Europe.* New Brunswick, NJ: Rutgers University Press.

Ingman, M., Kaessmann, H., Pääbo, S. & Gyllensten, U. (2000). Mitochondrial genome variation and the origin of modern humans. *Nature* 408, 708-713.

Krings, M., Capelli, C., Tschentscher, F., Geisert, H., Meyer, S., von Haeseler, A., Grossschmidt, K., Possnert, G., Paunovic, M. & Pääbo, S. (2000). A view of Neanderthal genetic diversity. *Nature Genetics* 26, 144-146.

Krings, M., Stone, A., Schmitz, R. W., Krainitzki, H., Stoneking, M. & Pääbo, S. (1997). Neanderthal DNA sequences and the origin of modern humans. *Cell* 90, 19-30.

Mellars, P. A. (1996). *The Neanderthal Legacy: An Archaeological Perspective from Western Europe.* Princeton: Princeton University Press.

Ovchinnikov, I. V., Götherström, A., Romanova, G. P., Kharitonov, V. M., Lidén, K. & Goodwin, W. (2000). Molecular analysis of Neanderthal DNA from the northern Caucasus. *Nature* 404, 490-493.

Pearson, O. M. (2000). Postcranial remains and the origin of modern humans. *Evolutionary Anthropology* 9, 229-247.

Richards, M. P., Pettitt, P. B., Trinkaus, E., Smith, F. H., Paunovic, M. & Karanovic, I. (2000). Neanderthal diet at Vindija and Neanderthal predation: the evidence from stable isotopes. *Proceedings of the National Academy of Sciences* 97, 7663-7666.

Ruff, C. B., Trinkaus, E. & Holliday, T. W. (1997). Body mass and encephalization in Pleistocene *Homo. Nature* 387, 173-176.

Santa Luca, A. P. (1978). A re-examination of presumed Neanderthal fossils. *Journal of Human Evolution* 7, 619-636.

Shea, J., Davis, Z. & Brown, K. S. (2001). Experimental tests of Middle Palaeolithic spear points using a calibrated crossbow. *Journal of Archaeological Science* 28, 807-816.

Solecki, R. S. (1975). Shanidar IV, a Neanderthal flower burial in northern Iraq. *Science* 190, 880-881.

Sommer, J. D. (1999). The Shanidar IV "Flower Burial": a re-evaluation of Neanderthal burial ritual. *Cambridge Archaeological Journal* 9, 127-129.

Tattersall, I. (1999) *The Last Neanderthal: The Rise, Success, and Mysterious Extinction. Revised Edition.* Boulder, CO: A Peter N. Nevraumont Book/Westview Press.

Tattersall, I. & Schwartz, J. H. (1999). Hominids and hybrids: the place of Neanderthals in human evolution. *Proceedings of the National Academy of Sciences* 96, 7117-7119.

Trinkaus, E. & Shipman, P. (1993). Neandertals: images of ourselves. *Evolutionary Anthropology* 1, 194-201.

Turk, I., Dirjec, J. & Kavur, B. (1995). The oldest musical instrument in Europe discovered in Slovenia? *Razprave IV. Razreda SAZU* 36, 287-293.

White, T. D. (2001). Once were cannibals. *Scientific American* 265, 48-55.

Zilhão, J. & d'Errico, F. (1999). The chronology and taphonomy of the earliest Aurignacian and its implications for the understanding of Neandertal extinction. *Journal of World Prehistory* 13, 1-68.

CHAPTER 7
BODY BEFORE BEHAVIOR

Adcock, G. J., Dennis, E. S., Easteal, S., Huttley, G. A., Jermlin, L. S., Peacock, W. J. & Thorne, A. (2001). Mitochondrial DNA sequences in ancient Australians: implications for modern human origins. *Proceedings of the National Academy of Sciences* 98, 537-542.

Ambrose, S. H. (1998). Chronology of the Later Stone Age and food production in East Africa. *Journal of Archaeological Science* 25, 377-392.

Bowler, J. M. & Magee, J. W. (2000). Redating Australia's oldest human remains: a sceptic's view. *Journal of Human Evolution* 38, 719-726.

Bowler, J. M. & Thorne, A. G. (1976). Human remains from Lake Mungo: discovery and excavation of Lake Mungo III. In (R. L. Kirk & A. G. Thorne, Eds.) *The Origin of the Australians*. Australian Institute of Aboriginal Studies: Canberra, pp. 95-112.

Deacon, H. J. (2001). Modern human emergence: an African archaeological perspective. In (P. V. Tobias, M. A. Raath, J. Moggi-Cecchi & G. A. Doyle, Eds.) *Humanity from African Naissance to Coming Millennia*. Witwatersrand University Press: Johannesburg, pp. 213-222.

Dolukhanov, P., Sokoloff, D. & Shukurov, A. (2001). Radiocarbon chronology of Upper Palaeolithic sites in Eastern Europe at improved resolution. *Journal of Archaeological Science* 28, 699-712.

Gillespie, R. & Roberts, R. G. (2000). On the reliability of age estimates for human remains at Lake Mungo. *Journal of Human Evolution* 38, 727-732.

Grayson, D. K. (2001). The archaeological record of human impacts on animal populations. *Journal of World Prehistory* 15, 1-68.

Henshilwood, C. S., Sealy, J. C., Yates, R. J., Cruz-Uribe, K., Goldberg, P., Grine, F. E., Klein, R. G., Poggenpoel, C., Van Niekerk, K. L. & Watts, I. (2001). Blombos Cave, southern Cape, South Africa: Preliminary report on the 1992 – 1999 excavations of the Middle Stone Age levels. *Journal of Archaeological Science* 28, 421-448.

Ke, Y., Su, B., Song, X., Lu, D., Chen, L., Li, H., Qi, C., Marzuki, S., Deka, R., Underhill, P. A., Xiao, C., Shriver, M., Lell, J., Wallace, D., Wells, R. S., Seielstad, M. T., Oefner, P. J., Zhu, D., Jin, J., Huang, W., Chakraborty, R., Chen, Z. & Jin, L. (2001). African origin of modern humans in east Asia: a tale of 12,000 Y chromosomes. *Science* 292, 1151-1153.

Klein, R. G. (1994). Southern Africa before the Iron Age. In (R. S. Corruccini & R. L. Ciochon, Eds.) *Integrative Paths to the Past: Paleoanthropological Advances in Honor of F. Clark Howell*. Prentice-Hall: Englewood Cliffs, New Jersey, pp. 471-519.

Kuhn, S. L., Stiner, M. C., Reese, D. S. & Güleç, E. (2001). Ornaments of the earliest Upper Paleolithic: new insights from the Levant. *Proceedings of the National Academy of Sciences* 98, 7641-7646.

Martin, P. S. (1984). Prehistoric overkill: the global model. In (P. S. Martin & R. G. Klein, Eds.) *Quaternary Extinctions: A Prehistoric Revolution*. University of Arizona Press: Tucson, pp. 354-403.

McBrearty, S. & Brooks, A. S. (2000). The revolution that wasn't: a new interpretation of the origin of modern human behavior. *Journal of Human Evolution* 39, 453-563.

O'Connell, J. F. & Allen, J. (1998). When did humans first arrive in Greater Australia, and why is it important to know? *Evolutionary Anthropology* 6, 132-146.

Parkington, J. E. (2001). Milestones: the impact of the systematic exploitation of marine foods on human evolution. In (P. V. Tobias, M. A. Raath, J. Moggi-Cecchi & G. A. Doyle, Eds.) *Humanity from African Naissance to Coming Millennia*. Witwatersrand University Press: Johannesburg, pp. 327-336.

Rightmire, G. P. (2001). Patterns of hominid evolution and dispersal in the Middle Pleistocene. *Quaternary International* 75, 77-84.

Roberts, R. G., Flannery, T. F., Ayliffe, L. K., Yoshida, H., Olley, J. M., Frideaux, G. J., Laslett, G. M., Baynes, A., Smith, M. A., Jones, R. & Smith, B. L. (2001). New ages for the last Australian megafauna: continent wide-extinction about 46,000 years ago. *Science* 292, 1888-1892.

Roberts, R. G. & Jones, R. (2001). Chronologies of carbon and of silica: evidence concerning the dating of the earliest human presence in Northern Australia. In (P. V. Tobias, M. A. Raath, J. Moggi-Cecchi & G. A. Doyle, Eds.) *Humanity from African Naissance to Coming Millennia*. Witwatersrand University Press: Johannesburg, pp. 238-248.

Schwarcz, H. P. (2001). Dating bones and teeth: the beautiful and the dangerous. In (P. V. Tobias, M. A. Raath, J. Moggi-Cecchi & G. A. Doyle, Eds.) *Humanity from African Naissance to Coming Millennia*. Witwatersrand University Press: Johannesburg, pp. 249-256.

Tchernov, E. (1998). The faunal sequence of the Southwest Asian Middle Paleolithic in relation to hominid dispersal events. In (T. Akazawa, K. Aoki & O. Bar-Yosef, Eds.) *Neandertals and Modern Humans in Western Asia*. Plenum Press: New York, pp. 77-90.

Thorne, A., Grün, R., Spooner, N. A., Simpson, J. J., McCulloch, M., Taylor, L. & Curnoe, D. (1999). Australia's oldest human remains: age of the Lake Mungo 3 skeleton. *Journal of Human Evolution* 36, 591-612.

Wolpoff, M. H. & Caspari, R. (1996). *Race and Human Evolution: A Fatal Attraction*. New York: Simon and Schuster.

Woodward, A. S. (1921). A new cave man from Rhodesia, South Africa. *Nature* 108, 371-372.

Chapter 8. Nature or Nurture Before the Dawn?

Ambrose, S. H. (1998). Late Pleistocene human population bottlenecks, volcanic winter, and differentiation of modern humans. *Journal of Human Evolution* 34, 623-651.

Bar-Yosef, O. (1998). On the nature of transitions: the Middle to Upper Palaeolithic and the Neolithic Revolution. *Cambridge Archaeological Journal* 8, 141-163.

Chauvet, J.-M., Brunel Deschamps, É. & Hillaire, C. (1995). *Dawn of Art: The Chauvet Cave* (P. G. Bahn, Trans.). New York: Harry N. Abrams.

Clottes, J. (1996). Thematic changes in Upper Palaeolithic art: a view from the Grotte Chauvet. *Antiquity* 70, 276-288.

Knight, A., Batzer, M. A., Stoneking, M., Tiwari, H. K., Scheer, W. D., Herrera, R. J. & Deininger, P. L. (1996). DNA sequences of Alu elements indicate a recent replacement of the human autosomal genetic complement. *Proceedings of the National Academy of Sciences* 93, 4360-4364.

Lai, C. S. L., Fisher, S. E., Hurst, J. A., Vargha-Khadem, F. & Monaco, A. P. (2001). A fork-head-domain gene is mutated in a severe speech and language disorder. *Nature* 413, 519-523.

White, R. (1992). Beyond art: toward an understanding of the origins of material representation in Europe. *Annual Review of Anthropology* 21, 537-564.

White, R. (1993). The dawn of adornment. *Natural History* 102, 61-67.

Appendix. Placing Ancient Sites in Time

Cooke, H. B. S. (1984). Horses, elephants and pigs as clues in the African later Cenozoic. In (J. C. Vogel, Ed.) *Late Cainozoic Palaeoclimates of the Southern Hemisphere*. A. A. Balkema: Rotterdam, pp. 473-482.

Deino, A. L., Renne, P. R. & Swisher, C. C. I. (1998). $^{40}Ar/^{39}Ar$ dating in paleoanthropology and archaeology. *Evolutionary Anthropology* 6, 63-75.

Feathers, J. K. (1996). Luminescence dating and modern human origins. *Evolutionary Anthropology* 5, 25-36.

Schwarcz, H. P. (1992). Uranium series dating in paleoanthropology. *Evolutionary Anthropology* 1, 56-62.

Schwarcz, H. P. (1997). Problems and limitations of absolute dating in regard to the appearance of modern humans in southwestern Europe. In (G. A. Clark & C. M. Willermet, Eds.) *Conceptual Issues in Modern Human Origins Research*. Aldine de Gruyter: New York, pp. 89-106.

Taylor, R. E. (1996). Radiocarbon dating: the continuing revolution. *Evolutionary Anthropology* 4, 169-181.

INDEX